ALSO BY SALLY V. KEIL

Those Wonderful Women In Their Flying Machines:
The Unknown Heroines of World War II

TO LIVE IN THE WORLD AS OURSELVES:

SELF DISCOVERY AND BETTER RELATIONSHIPS

THROUGH JUNG'S TYPOLOGY

Sally V. Keil

FOUR DIRECTIONS PRESS
RHINEBECK NEW YORK

Published in the United States by Four Directions Press,
P. O. Box 417, Rhinebeck, New York, 12572.
www.fourdirectionspress.com

ISBN 978-0-9981144-1-5

LIBRARY OF CONGRESS CONTROL NUMBER 2013934616

Printed by CreateSpace, an Amazon.com Company

Published July 2017
SECOND EDITION

Available from Amazon.com and other book stores

Book and cover design by Sean McCarthy

For Robert

The priviledge of a lifetime is to become who you truly are.
— Carl Gustav Jung (1875-1961)

CONTENTS

Introduction

THIS BOOK PRESENTS one of the most important discoveries from the earliest days of the psychological age for today's psychologically aware readers. Simple and accessible, yet profound in its implications, it describes how our psychology creates our own personal experience of life, our style of relating and the way we come to understand the world around us. From the very first pages are insights that are easy to understand and apply to your life, so you can live with mindfulness of who you are and do things and relate to others in *your own way*, the way in which you are at your best and that will be most personally fulfilling. Knowing this information has been invaluable to me for over twenty-five years. I use it every day wherever I am and in all my encounters with people, as well as in making decisions for how best to live my own life.

A century ago, pioneering psychologist Carl Jung saw the need for individual self-awareness when he described human nature as featuring both fundamental commonalities and differences. In his years as a doctor, he noticed that people orient themselves toward their circumstances in different but perceptible ways. These innate commonalities and differences were found among peasants and laborers, as well as among the educated and aristocracy, among both men and woman and among children as well as adults. Jung described natural human dispositions, gave them names and wrote about them as "typology," which he used in all his relationships, speaking in the language suited to each person's individual nature.

Jung published his discoveries in *Psychological Types* in 1921, which remains one of the pillars of Jungian psychology. But going far beyond merely an exercise in categorizing people or affixing a personality "type" label, Jung envisioned nothing less than a clear description of the inner workings of every human being—you, me and everyone we know or might meet. These on-going dynamics—an "inner technology" if you will—are fundamental to human nature and consciousness. This book will help you use typology to its full advantage—as practical but powerful psychological knowledge to live with, and live by, in your daily life.

Understanding our commonalities and differences today has taken on new meaning and urgency. More than ever before, we need to know such psychological fundamentals, as we face unprecedented challenges in our personal and work lives. Today we must relate to people of many cultures, backgrounds, points of view and generations, all the while trying to be true to ourselves amid fast-changing events. Wherever our lives take us, whatever our relationships and work may present to us, we need practical psychological knowledge that we can rely on—tools for our psychological toolkits, as it were—to guide us any time, anywhere, in any situation.

Jung identified the orientations of extraversion and introversion that, thanks to Susan Cain's best-selling book *Quiet,* are familiar to many, who now realize how these orientations are crucial to our wellbeing and relationships. But Jung went much further to reveal the different ways in which people actually perceive and process the events of their lives. These basic differences explained why so many couples Jung worked with were struggling to make sense of their different interests and responses to life. Jung identified four inherent capabilities—he called them functions—within human consciousness and named them Thinking, Feeling, Sensation and Intuition. These four functions guide everyone's interests and choices; they direct what we notice around us and how we come to understand our circumstances. Every person possesses all four functions to draw on to accomplish all the psychological tasks vital to a full human life. But—and this is an important "but"—individuals, as part of their very nature, use different functions to interact with their environment. These differences cause many common misunderstandings and interpersonal struggles—"type clash"—that as we will see can easily be avoided or resolved once such differences are recognized and understood.

Knowing Ourselves

It is not easy to know yourself well enough to make choices and decisions consistently that are right for you—for you specifically. The aim of this book is to give you some real clarity about who you are and how you need to live in order to thrive, and on a practical level. It is very stressful to try to live, work or relate when we go against our natural psychological make-up, especially when faced with the mystery of another person. The chapters ahead will provide descriptions and real-life examples that help you recognize yourself on a deep level, so you can do what expresses who you are and say "no, thank you" to what does not. Your expectations of yourself and others become grounded in psychological reality, thus opening exciting new possibilities for yourself and for more creative, harmonious and mutually beneficial relationships. With self-knowledge and self-acceptance, you can more easily guide others in relating to you. Moreover, when you let others express themselves in their way, using their four functions as they are made to do, even tough, long-time relationship struggles can be transformed.

Practicing Typology

In this book, I have gone back to Jung's original ideas to present typology as I have come to know it and benefit from it every day. From personal experience, I have found that learning about typology is an on-going revelation, as well as a fascinating life practice. No training or expertise is needed, yet readers with a background in psychology or in other fields and traditions will find how well these ideas interrelate.

Typology opens up a whole new world of understanding, but also offers countless practical applications in the here and now. Every situation or relationship has typological aspects that can be observed and worked with — or around — creatively. As it is part of being human, typology and its influence are in evidence in ourselves and in others wherever we are, even in cultural and world events. You will be able to draw on this knowledge any time you meet a new person, face a challenging situation, need to make an informed decision or are just feeling in need of inner guidance.

In the chapters devoted to each of each of the four psychological functions — Sensation, Intuition, Thinking, Feeling — we enter the whole realm of life that the function covers. You will come to recognize when you are using each function and to identify the functions you use most often and with the most ease — your typological gifts. You may notice how other people predominantly use a certain function and spend considerable time engaged in its vital activities, so you can understand and relate to them better. Further, guidance is offered to people of each typology for living skillfully, as well as for relating to them with understanding and appreciation.

An enjoyable and fruitful method as you read is to take each aspect that "strikes" you and observe how that aspect resonates throughout your daily life. Typology is going on everywhere within and around you, so examples won't be hard to find. Typology may shed a new light on many aspects of your life. As you make this knowledge your own, important mysteries may be solved, such as why you are attracted so some people and find others difficult to relate to or fathom; why you gravitate toward certain activities yet want to avoid others; why a certain relationship isn't working and how it can. You may notice ways in which you are different from some of the norms operating in your family, work or social environment, and even in your culture. This is very useful information to know and work with mindfully.

Exploring and being true to our typology throughout our life is part of the vital psychological activity of becoming ourselves. Personal psychological priorities may differ, but we are all wondrously four-functional and have the essential capabilities of extraversion and introversion, Thinking, Feeling, Sensation and Intuition within us. Endowed with our four functions and with the skill to extravert and introvert in our own way, each of us is made to live a full and successful life. Indeed, as we come to know each of these powerful inner capabilities and the tailored ways we are made to use them, we grow in consciousness, psychological versatility and compassionate understanding of ourselves and others. Understanding the richness of our own nature, and in fact of human nature, we also become open to the common ground that we share with others, whoever they may be, so that we can live, share and contribute in the world as our true selves, which our world needs now more than ever.

You and the World:

Extraverts and Introverts

NEW YORKERS Jennifer and Tom left the city for a much-needed vacation at the seashore. By mid-afternoon, after a long drive, they arrived at the beach house they had rented. After unpacking the car and carrying everything inside, Tom stood in the middle of the living room rubbing his hands together with excitement. "I'm going out to take a look at the boardwalk and to ask people where to get fresh seafood for dinner."

Jennifer looked at Tom in amazement. "How can you go rushing off? We just got here! I want to get stuff put away, check out the kitchen, maybe in a little while go walk on the beach..." Tom stood in the doorway holding his windbreaker and looking uncertain.

On a Friday night, two friends Emily and Sarah arrived at a party they had looked forward to all week. A dozen people were already there. The music was loud and the mood was celebratory. Emily spotted the host across the room and called to him, "Hey, Jay!

Where's the Rolling Rock?" as she put her hands in the air and made dancing movements to the music. Somebody whistled. Beside her, Sarah stood clutching her purse and smiling slightly, her eyes darting around the room to see who was there.

When Jim came home from work, his wife Jeanette had already arrived, having picked up their two children. As Jim was taking off his coat, he was greeted boisterously. "Daddy! Daddy! I got 100 on my spelling test!" "Wanna see my new baseball glove?" "How was your day? I can't wait to tell you what happened on the Bolton account!"

Jim hung up his coat and made his way past them mumbling, "Yeah," "Oh, great, sweetheart, good for you," "Later, okay, hon?" and went straight to the bedroom, flopped down on the bed and picked up a book.

In these scenes, we find Extraverts and Introverts responding to each other in everyday situations. While the two orientations may seem self-evident, the differences in point of view are significant and many-layered. Extraverts and Introverts live in landscapes as different as Times Square and an enclosed garden. Each of these two worlds is equally stimulating, fruitful, varied and fulfilling to those who feel at home there and who, in fact, prefer to spend most of their time there. While we may be able to recognize almost immediately if someone is extraverted or introverted, we may not realize how profoundly these two fundamental, yet contrasting orientations influence our choices, our relationships, our work and all our social interactions. This chapter describes some recognizable characteristics of an Extravert and an Introvert, as well as some ways to live as one, and to relate to one, successfully.

Extravert and Introvert, extraversion and introversion, extraverted and introverted, extraverting and introverting—these words themselves, as nouns, adjectives and verbs, describe the wide-ranging dimensions of our subject. A person is an *Extravert* or an *Introvert*. He or she is acting in an *extraverted* or *introverted* way. Meanwhile, everyone *extraverts* or *introverts* at certain times of the day or week and during certain phases of a project or even whole periods in life. *Extraversion* and *introversion* describe two essential human psychological capabilities that we all have, two locations, so to speak, for our attention and psychological activity. *Extraverting* and *introverting* are behaviors that can be included in just the right way for each of us. As we examine the psychological roles that extraversion and introversion play—and play out—in our daily lives, we will see ourselves and the world around us in a new way. We can be true to our own orientation, while also relating with sensitivity to the people around us.

Living in Two Worlds

How do you think of the world? Is it "right here," with you in the midst of it? Does the world seem to be "out there" with you observing it as if from afar? Psychologically we are made to live in both the world without and the one within, but most of us prefer to be in one more than in the other. In his many years of pioneering psychological observation, Carl Jung noted that people relate to the world in two distinctive ways. Some of us seem to live much of our lives out in the world, constantly exchanging information and energy with others. Others of us take events inside ourselves, feeling little need to interact with others in order to understand what is happening in and around us. Jung called outward-oriented people *Extraverts* (literally outward-turning) and more inward-turning people *Introverts*.

According to Jung, extraversion and introversion are like two halves of the whole of human experience, like breathing out and breathing in. Both are natural ways in which different human beings approach and apprehend their on-going life. They are like opposite poles—without or within—and we are most often drawn toward one of them. For every John Lennon or Paul McCartney, there is a "quiet Beatle" like George Harrison or Ringo Starr. No one is 100% extraverted or introverted, though we have a natural tendency toward one orientation or the other, making us "extraverted" or "introverted" overall. Extraversion and introversion form a continuum, from extreme extraversion at one end—Will Smith, Jim Carrey or Madonna may serve as examples—to extreme introversion at the other end, such as Marlon Brando, Jacqueline Kennedy, or poet Emily Dickinson. Everyone fits comfortably somewhere along this continuum between the two poles.

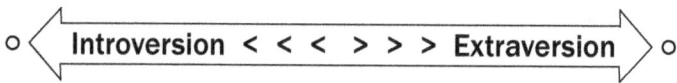

o ⟨ **Introversion < < < > > > Extraversion** ⟩ o

Among the people at a social or business gathering, Extraverts are the ones with the open personalities and faces. They walk into a room and easily initiate conversation. A distinguishing characteristic of Extraverts is often a "chin-up" posture, while the Introverts can be spotted standing back, chins down, looking quietly "out their eyes" and responding in polite monosyllables. Extraverts like to sit in the front or middle of a restaurant; Introverts prefer a quiet table near the back.

Extraverts get energy from being with people and Introverts get energy from being alone. While an Extravert seizes every excuse to go "out" and does so with ease and delight, an Introvert on some visceral level braces for such forays into what may feel like edgy, hostile territory. Extraverts are like air breathers enjoying exchanges with the lively and varied world above. Meanwhile, there is a whole universe below the surface and introverted beings made to live happily there. Like a scuba diver, an Extravert can come to appreciate the underwater world. However, his or her oxygen tank gets used up, and he or she has to come back to the outside air and breathe freely. By contrast, Introverts, after exploring vast dry land of the outer world, must take their psychic gills back down into the deep where they thrive.

Our balance point along the extraversion-introversion continuum can move, at least temporarily. An extraverted art professor getting her PhD, for instance, took a sabbatical and introverted for six months to go deep into her research and writing. A book tour took an introverted writer out into the crowds in an intense period of extraversion. Recovery from a sports injury forced an extraverted architect to be introverted; he worked on his laptop and got caught up on his reading.

Normally, however, with the exception of a versatile few who are in the middle—"ambiverts," so to speak—our first responses will usually carry us outward or inward. As individuals, we prefer either engaging with people or observing them. Whether it is out in the midst of everything or within the container of ourselves, extraversion or introversion is where we feel most at home psychologically, where we want to process what is happening to us and where we go to recharge mentally and emotionally.

If we find we want to avoid certain kinds of activities, this may well be a wise and healthy choice according to our psychological makeup. We are made to specialize psychologically; it is in our nature. In every Extravert facing a weekend retreat or even a Saturday night alone, there can be a little voice that says, "I don't really want to do it," or "I'm not very good at that." Similarly in every Introvert, when facing certain prospects, the inner voice also arises that says, "I don't want to" or "I'm not good at...," say, holding a dinner for 12, running for political office or working the crowd at a big trade show.

There are times in which everyone "extraverts" and other times in which we "introvert" and become more introspective. Extraverts can enjoy their privacy; Introverts can have a great time at a party. But day-to-day, following our inherent mode of operating psychologically, we fit somewhere on this natural continuum between public and private.

Nature and Nurture

On a fundamental level, Extraverts live according to humanity's survival need for interdependence, for connecting, cooperating and working together. Introverts, meanwhile, are more conscious of a certain wariness of others felt by nearly all creatures in nature, a creaturely desire for the freedom and safety of independence to go about their business. Human nature includes both of these instinctive directives and imperatives, and we all experience their attractions at various times.

According to Jung, an inclination toward introversion or extraversion can be influenced by outer circumstances. Warm sunny climates such as California or Italy encourage extraversion; human beings living in indoor-oriented regions of the world such as England or Scandinavia tend toward introversion. An extraverted American corporate manager named Kristin, who recently moved to Denmark, found herself fearing the corner grocer. "At first, I thought she was gruff and stand-offish," Kristin said, "Then I realized she was just shy." In other words, the corner grocer was an Introvert. An extraverted American businessman returning from London commented on "the language problem," not concerning the mother tongue of English per se, but introverted British English. "People never look at you when they speak to you," he said. "They look down and swallow entire phrases. It is done in deference, but I kept worrying if I was missing something important."

Different eras can have extraverted or introverted styles. Consider the gilded angels who seem to leap off the ceilings and altarpieces of Italian Baroque churches as compared with the simple painted wood interiors created by the Quakers in early America. Some holidays encourage extraversion, while others call for introspection. Even the cycles of nature reflect this outward-inward polarity, with summer encouraging extraverted activities and winter introverted ones. Family, education, culture and environment can all encourage the expression of who we are typologically, or they might cause us to try to act "against type," resulting in subtle discomfort or even deep inner conflict and struggle.

The general tendency in a personality is evidenced very young, as psychological researchers are finding. A Harvard study of 400 children found that, while the majority of children tested somewhere in the middle, the number of children they called "consistently inhibited" was the same as the number who were "consistently uninhibited."[1] A "temperamental bias" toward "inhibited" tendencies has been found in infants as young as two months, with consistency in "inhibited" responses thereafter. Another study reported that 15-20% of babies are "shy and anxious by nature" and "behaviorally inhibited." A confident and sensitive "parenting style" was then recommended to help "shy" little ones "grow out of" their early "awkwardness" or "stranger anxiety," "coax them out of their shells" and "learn to take emotional risks." Or are these little ones simply introverted?

Outside the research lab, parents need only live with their children to observe the Extraverts and Introverts. When a parent comes home from work, a child may jump up into Mommy's or Daddy's arms jabbering away. Another child will be just as alert to a parent's arrival but hold back, anticipating a closer reunion when things quiet down. If his or her name is called out in the midst of the clamor as a signal that he or she is seen, the little Introvert will be pleased deep inside.

When they get together, one lively, extraversion-oriented Massachusetts family is like an orchestra warming up, with family members talking and laughing, all at once, full-voice. The youngest son, whose name is Sean, could be seen standing on the perimeter of the gathering listening to snatches of conversation. From time to time, Sean would go outside, walk around the yard and come back in to re-engage. Family members learned to break away from the group to go and talk with him one-on-one, though there was some concern about his emotional adjustment. Then Sean learned from a relative about extraversion and introversion. "I'm an Introvert!" he announced one day with exasperation and pride. From then on, his way was accepted and honored, and everyone was happy.

Discerning between Extraverts and Introverts became a valuable lifetime skill for this young Introvert in a lively extraverted family; he became a successful sales representative and later a company executive. Early on, he caught the attention of his boss at a meeting. "You really listen when someone talks," his boss told him, "and you respond in their same tone." Sean explained: "I speak gently, quietly with an Introvert, and with a lot of force with an Extravert. It works."

Tips on Recognizing an Extravert:

Here are some likely indicators of a person's extraverted orientation:

Chin up
Open face, eyes wide, often a full smile

Immediately engaging with you verbally, perhaps physical
    contact, such as hand on your shoulder, elbow or back
Steps toward you in approach or greeting
Direct eye contact (with chin up)
Leans into conversations, whether they're standing or sitting
Expansive gestures, arms and hands entering the space
    between you
Stands or sits in the middle of social interaction
Constant flow of communication, verbal and physical

Tips on Recognizing an Introvert:

Chin down
Often downward gaze, perhaps brief glancing around
Direct eye contact (chin down) revealing inner processing
Expectant facial expression, or enigmatic "Mona Lisa" smile
Physical movements contained in a prescribed space
Stands or sits on the periphery of the action
Is mostly listening to others
Seems to be an observer of the scene, or
Quietly doing his or her task, even surrounded by lively activity
    and interaction

The Spark of Opposites

Introverts and Extraverts often fall in love, as if nature wants a balance of labor between outgoing exchanges with the world and inward perception and contemplation. In fact, it was Jung's work with so many couples in distress during the early 1900s that first alerted him to the existence of inherent extraversion and introversion in different human beings. He noticed how frequently these opposites bonded together and how many relationship issues resulted unless this dynamic was understood.

In a great many couples and partnerships, there is an Extravert and an Introvert. The American President is often Extravert-in-Chief, while the First Spouse is frequently more introverted. Even in literature and film, art imitates life in famous couples such as Scarlet O'Hara (Extravert) and Rhett Butler (Introvert), Cathy (Extravert) and Heathcliff (Introvert), Elizabeth Bennet (Extravert) and Mr. Darcy (Introvert), along with film couple Katharine Hepburn (Introvert) and Spencer Tracy (Extravert).

We often have a weakness for our typological opposites. Whatever orientation or functions we don't see in ourselves often attract our admiration in others. An Extravert may fall in love with someone with mysterious and enigmatic qualities that seem hidden and alluring, or may see a monastic sage as a saint because of the transcendent wisdom and understanding resulting from a life of solitude and contemplation. An Introvert may gaze admiringly from the sidelines as a dynamic and articulate extravert mesmerizes the crowd or commands a great meeting or is the life of the party. This attraction to our typological opposite is a living dynamic that brings energy to our lives and spurs our growth.

Not only couples, but many friendships and work partnerships feature one who is more out-going and socially engaged and one who is more inward and reflective, making for a complementary relationship. In social situations, Extraverts easily do the talking or presenting, providing a foil or protecting the Introvert from over-eager social approaches. Introverts, while not at ease coming up with small talk, often help Extraverts talk things out one-on-one. While the Extravert brings in vital information about the world, the Introvert often provides perspective and meaning, not to mention a good audience.

Even if both people are the same, either extraverted or introverted, one becomes more so than the other, so that the different psychological tasks are taken care of in their life together. In a couple of two Introverted writers, the woman became the one who interacted with people at social events, while her boyfriend stood silently, gratefully by her side. Accommodations are made. In a marriage of two very attractive and dynamic publishing executives, both Extraverts, the husband was overheard at a small dinner party saying in affectionate exasperation, "Please, Emily, you have talked for long enough, it's my turn!"

When opposites attract, however, they find themselves living with a person who is quite different from them. One leaps out of bed in the morning loquacious and full of energy, while the other needs to make a gradual transition from the inner to the outer world. One likes to go out several nights a week, while the other likes to order in food and spend evenings at home watching a movie. One afternoon, a couple named Aaron and Sarah on a family outing found themselves around the corner from their friends Jane and Dave and gave them a call. "We're in the neighborhood with the kids," they said. "Can we stop in?" "Terrific! Come on over!" exclaimed Jane, an Extravert, and hung up. "What!?" her introverted husband Dave said. "People are coming over?" He was thinking to himself, "Where can I hide?"

While unplanned guests may sound an alarm for an Introvert, for an Extravert, they are the blessed news of the day. Through acknowledging each person's reactions and needs, a couple can come up with workable compromises. Jane and Dave can agree, for instance, to permit a spontaneous visit, but Jane will go to the door and welcome their friends and lead the interaction for the first ten minutes, while Dave gets dressed and collects himself before joining them. They might agree to limit the visit to one hour, allowing the visit to occur but reassuring the Introvert and honoring his comfort level. Given an Introvert's natural slow-building pace of engagement, at the end of the hour, he might be just warming up and want everyone to stay.

With understanding and cooperation, opposites together create a life-enhancing division of labor. After all, the social butterfly keeps the invitations coming, allowing the Introvert to be in wider circulation and in greater touch with the world. The Introvert, meanwhile, keeps the ground firm under their relationship, home or business with his or her quiet observation and considered reflection. Introverts are grateful to Extraverts for their natural inclusiveness and for so cheerfully carrying the burden of making introductions and keeping the conversation going. Extraverts appreciate Introverts as good listeners and find an Introvert's quiet depth intriguing. One warm and engaging Extravert named Linda says she has always been drawn to Introverts because she finds them calming.

By relating with sensitivity to our partners and joining them from time to time where they live so comfortably, we come to know and explore a less familiar opposite realm within ourselves. This self-knowledge in turn does wonders for our capacity for relationship.

Extraverts and Introverts at Work

Most jobs have both extraverted and introverted aspects and Extraverts and Introverts often work together. An extraverted librarian in Scottsdale, Arizona, for instance, organizes library activities programs for the city's children, while her introverted colleagues order books and other materials, manage special collections and keep the library's information systems current. There are extraverted and introverted teachers, attorneys, physicians, engineers, chefs, writers, administrators and managers. Many jobs and organizational cultures are malleable enough so that, with consciousness and creativity, one can perform at work in one's own style, whether extraverted or introverted, and keep activities requiring one's opposite to a comfortable minimum. A successful introverted ad sales representative for an on-line company made more than fifty phone calls a day—Introverts often feel more comfortable and effective on-line or on the phone—and was able to limit personal meetings to pleasant lunches with customers he liked. An extraverted attorney creates balance in her days by doing introverted tasks like legal research or completing forms and also serving on the local school board and organizing fund-raisers for school teams and trips.

Organizations, companies, schools and other workplaces have their own cultural norms that encourage extraverted or introverted activities and behavior. It is worth being alert to the overall culture of a place, keeping in mind one's own personal needs as an Extravert or an Introvert. Are there a lot of meetings and presentations? How much of a job is done in a team and how much sitting alone at a computer screen? How much interpersonal communication is going on and how much would you ideally want to participate in? Is the boss extraverted or introverted, and how does that fact shape the behavior of his or her staff or team? With awareness, adjustments can perhaps be made in one's modus operandi, though not too many. When job hunting, a look around can give one a good idea of how well and how comfortably one might fit in and make one's best contribution.

Knowing that a certain phase of a project will require introverting, an Extravert can make sure lunches are lively and sociable. If an Introvert faces a week of making presentations or working a trade show, he or she can bring along inspiring reading, music or a yoga mat for restorative alone-time. An introverted frequent business traveler chooses hotels by the quality of their room-service meals, so she can dine alone. An introverted writer who is a frequent lecturer says, simply, "I go to my room and close the door."

Psychological fact: Having to work in our opposite mode for too long can take its toll on our overall attitude toward life, even on our health. If the demands of a job require too much extraversion or introversion for comfort, we may need to survey our options more diligently. An introverted promotion manager at a large publishing house found her workdays so full of meetings with management, sales reps and design staff that every free lunchtime she found herself retreating to the quiet of a local church. Because she paid out all her limited extraversion at the office, her social life dwindled. Sunday nights were anguished. When she developed crippling back trouble, she decided to make a change.

Type Clash Between Extraverts and Introverts

While opposites can view one another with appreciation and fascination, some significant type clashes are ignited when Extraverts and Introverts misunderstand one another's needs and ways of responding. The opposite orientation, being different from the "norm" of oneself, can be seen as maladapted or willfully contrary, neither of which may be the case.

Living as if in two different worlds, Extraverts and Introverts may literally not know where the other is coming from. An extraverted theater producer says, "I walk into a room full of people and it's, like, '*Ready, set, go!*' I feel confident that there will be someone there worth meeting, and that I will get into interesting conversations." An Introvert, on the other hand, might take a deep breath, brace himself, then enter the room a few steps at a time. While an Extravert is loving being in the center of things, an introverted companion, though socially adept and poised, may be focusing on avoiding attention. By then, the Extravert is in the middle of a lively group, but looking around, wondering, "Hey, where did he go?" Both are feeling confused, even slightly abandoned.

Naturally advancing towards or retreating from external events, Extraverts and Introverts often misread one another's psychological signals or take them personally. An Extravert can misinterpret an Introvert's natural and necessary withdrawal for a while as a personal rejection. Meanwhile, an Introvert may misunderstand an Extravert's need to go out into the world as dissatisfaction or boredom in the relationship. As a psychological imperative, Extraverts must express themselves and interact with others, while Introverts must withdraw inward in order to process the many stimuli from the sights, sounds and human interactions in their lives. "The Introvert," Jung writes, "defends himself against all demands from outside, to conserve energy." [2]

Personal styles can easily elicit type clash. To Extraverts, an Introvert might be seen as uncommunicative, closed, inhibited or secretive. "He's not an easy guy to get close to, as far as I can tell," columnist Dave Barry wrote about *A Prairie Home Companion* host Garrison Keillor. "He truly is the shy person he has always claimed to be. He always seems to be keeping a major part of himself hidden, somewhere inside his big shaggy head." [3]

Meanwhile, to an Introvert, an Extravert's enthusiastic sociability might seem overwhelming, overbearing, domineering, "in your face" or "coming on too strong." Extraverts can offend by overstepping Introverts' boundaries or seeming to grab all the attention. On the other hand, Extraverts can be exasperated with an Introvert's hesitant communication and suspicious or annoyed when an Introvert doesn't come right out and say what he or she is thinking of feeling. An Extravert might issue sanctions when denied an Introvert's attentive companionship. Meanwhile, an Introvert issues sanctions when an Extravert overwhelms him or her with exuberance or too much activity or information.

While an Extravert is processing life out in the world of people, situations and events, an Introvert is experiencing an equally rich interior world of thoughts, feelings and perceptions. An Extravert will call several of her friends to talk over a dilemma; an Introvert may go to his or her journal, computer or gardening shed or go for a walk and share very little.

It's hard to believe that the outside world or inside world could be as rewarding as the one we know and love. An Extravert thinks an Introvert who is not going out must be experiencing a painful vacuum. Meanwhile, an Introvert assumes an Extravert who has spent a day shopping at ten different stores plus meeting friends for lunch has to be "escaping" or on "overload" and exhausted when she comes home. She's not. She's refreshed and happy.

A good rule is to assume that the person next to you might not be not like you. He or she is experiencing the same immediate situation you are, but in his or her own way. Their way of experiencing is just as personally involving and complex as yours. There are many creative and respectful ways of allowing others to be who they are, while expressing our own nature. The Extravert in a couple learns the art of being a delightful social butterfly who nonetheless remembers to touch base regularly with an Introvert partner, so he or she will not feel abandoned. Introverts can develop the delicate art of saying, "Hi, give me a minute, I'll be with you shortly," without hurting their Extravert's feelings or making them feel dismissed.

Recognizing and respecting both orientations goes a long way toward fine-tuning our personal interactions. Indeed, becoming aware of another person's extraverted or introverted nature or current state of mind is a relationship skill of great sensitivity. As the young introvert named Sean, now a successful sales executive, observed,

"Extraverts talk in order to think; Introverts think in order to talk." This typological truism, simple and self-evident, can open many doors.

On Extraverts and Extraverting

Extraversion is in evidence in so many environments that it is easy to take for granted, but it is worthwhile recognizing the unique characteristics—and value—psychologically of extraversion, extraverting and Extraverts themselves. Naturally friendly, out-going people like Tom, Emily and Jeanette in the examples at the start of the chapter constantly give others the gift of themselves. They are made to interact with others and get things said and done out in the world. In a social or business situation, the first voices one hears are usually the Extraverts. Encountering someone, they make direct, immediate contact, often with a ready smile. "To walk into a room full of people, many of whom I don't know — the opportunity to see and interact with all these souls — is fantastic," an extraverted entrepreneur named James exclaims. "What is comfortable and comforting for me is to cook dinner for 20 people," he adds, while his introverted wife, hearing this, pulls her head in like a turtle.

"Extraversion is characterized by interest in the external object, responsiveness, and a ready acceptance of external happenings," Jung wrote, "a desire to influence and be influenced by events, a need to join in and get 'with it,' the capacity to endure bustle and noise of every kind and actually find them enjoyable, constant attention to the surrounding world, the cultivation of friends and acquaintances, with a strong streak of altruism." [4]

Extraverts process and work through what they think or how they feel through exchanging with others. Former New York City

Mayor Ed Koch was famous for striding the city streets and asking everyone he saw, "How'm I doing?" Typical of an Extravert, he was finding out about himself by consulting and interacting with people around him. Extraverted actress Meryl Streep says, "I don't think I exist until I am with someone." An Extravert's "whole consciousness looks outward, because the essential and decisive determination always comes from outside," Jung writes. [5] Admitting all the journals she began and abandoned, extraverted actress Helen Mirren observed, "I have more interest in living the life than recording it." [6]

Meeting Extraverts for the first time, they will likely introduce themselves and give you all the pertinent information you need to communicate well. You will find out who they are, perhaps where they come from, whom they work for, what is happening in their lives, what their spouse does, details about their children and their opinion about the current situation you share. As facts or feelings pour out openly, you have the immediate comfort of knowing who is before you and what is going on from their point of view.

For an Extravert, so much that happens in a day is on the outside. Highly verbal, Extraverts get information and work out problems personal and professional from talking things out and bouncing ideas off others. They process in constant resonance with people. Some Extraverts seem even to wake up talking. "I love Company, Chat, a Laugh, a Glass, and even a Song, as well as ever," wrote American Founding Extravert Benjamin Franklin. Extraverts often express a running account of their thoughts, as if to announce them to the world for its response. An extraverted sister gets ribbed by her siblings for announcing to the family a play-by-play of whatever she is doing: "I am going to the refrigerator," she says. "I'm going upstairs to get a sweater." "I'm getting the mail, I'll be right back." It is as if she is saying, "Hello, I'm here, is anyone out there?" in a perpetual game of

Marco-Polo. Such out-in-the-open self-presentation is refreshing and endearing, and also inspires trust.

Unselfconscious, naturally gregarious, Extraverts seem to throw their whole selves into the space between them and others. One other person is instantaneously a party, and the arrival of three or more is even better. Extraverts provide a social spark. "I walk into a group and think, ''This is dull,' and go up to the first person and introduce myself," says an extraverted former teacher named Catherine living in a retirement community. "I introduce them to someone else and things get going."

Making the World Go 'Round

Extraverts are the world's great communicators and networkers. They make new arrivals feel welcome, organize people to get things done, keep schools and communities running smoothly and effectively and raise funds for causes and organizations. They give receptions and offer to hold meetings. They greet people at front desks and seat them in restaurants. With ease and gusto, they verbalize for themselves, for a group or for a nation.

While some skills in extraverting are almost a necessity for success in most workplaces, professions do exist that might be less hospitable to Extraverts, such as medical research, computer code writing or perhaps playing in an orchestra. "We're four Extraverts that in a lot of instances have felt like sore thumbs," says violist Ralph Ferris, founding member of Ethel, a successful string quartet modeling themselves after a rock band, "and we found three other thumbs to go along." [7]

Modern life creates frequent opportunities to be at one's extraverted best, from staff meetings, community activities and book groups, to just walking down the street. A free-market economy encourages people to leave home, exchange information and shop in stores small and huge. Democracy itself requires and encourages public debate and participation in running schools, towns, counties, states and the nation itself. Working in teams is often encouraged in companies and classrooms. Team sports abound. Indeed, innate extraversion is advantageous, both to an individual and to his or her environment, particularly in a society that welcomes friendly self-assertiveness in social interaction.

Once an Extravert, furthermore, always an Extravert. A 97-year-old grandmother goes to church every morning, her health permitting, for the communion not only with the Divine, but also with other people. Other people, she says, are her lifeline.

Lonely Too Long

Extraversion may seem easy, but an Extravert must truly make sure he or she is getting enough contact with other people. They need to, psychologically; it is their sustenance. Social media are energized by Extraverts, but ultimately relating on line is no substitute for the real stimulation and nourishment of live interaction. Even when in a close relationship with an Introvert, an Extravert needs to go out and participate, perhaps helping organize community, school or family events or becoming active in local politics.

Contemporary life, while normally extraversion-friendly, can also threaten us with isolation. Those who work on a computer in a cubicle in a silent office or make a long solitary commute often have the challenge of making sure they get enough interaction with people at lunch time, in the evenings or on weekends. If an Extravert does not have enough exchange with the world, he or she withers psychologically. Extraverted writers like to write in cafés. After a long stint in the library, an Extravert needs time in the student center. Being stuck at home is an Extravert's nightmare. "Thank God for the telephone!" an Extravert exclaimed to a friend during a snowstorm. She had such cabin fever, she reported, she found herself running out to flag down a passing snowplow and shouting, "Some snowstorm, eh?" just to get some human contact. An extraverted high school teacher, confined to her home for a semester to nurse her pregnancy, kept herself entertained counting the weeks and envisioning all the activities, visits and social events ahead after her child was born. "This is surreal," she admitted. "I'm used to interacting with a hundred children a day, plus my colleagues!"

While a natural extraversion is often an asset, truly successful Extraverts may have to go through a sometimes-painful education process to discern necessary boundaries. Parents may need to tame a little Extravert's natural openness for the sake of protection out in the community. Extraverted children's outgoing and generous impulses become refined with rules of politeness, manners and wise self-control. Even older Extraverts often must learn to read the signs in other people that signal "too much, too fast." Skillful Extraverts come to see on people's faces when they have lost their listener's friendly receptivity, so that they do not waste their extraversion's valuable contribution.

An Extravert in the Inner World

The opposite of our natural way of responding exists within our psychology, though it may get scant attention. Our opposite realm is often avoided, not because we may not like or value it, but because when we are there or faced with it, it can be too intense, even overwhelming. For an Extravert, the realm of introversion is excessively potent with inner energies that fairly quickly threaten to overload his or her psychological circuits, so that he or she reaches for the phone or grabs a coat and leaves the house for the familiar haven of the outside world. In the same way, an Introvert, faced with a room full of people, can become overwhelmed by all the talk and interaction and want to retreat to safety by the door or in the back row.

The Extravert, Jung commented, "is far more influenced by his [or her] psychic inner world than he suspects. He cannot see it himself, but the people around him, if observant, will always detect the personal purpose in his striving. Hence his golden rule should always be to ask himself: 'What am I really after? What is my secret intention?'" [8]

For Extraverts, introverting voluntarily, even for a short while, puts them in touch with their most important personal issues and needs. Attending a workshop, art class or religious service or visiting a mediation center offers an opportunity to gather with others while getting an experience of their inner world. Just a period of introversion in silence every day reading, gardening, writing in a journal, doing carpentry or yoga, knitting, practicing a musical instrument, taking a run or just sitting in reflection, brings surprising new focus to an Extravert's sense of self, as well as insights to take back out into the world.

Modern life for everyone often produces signals that "all circuits are busy." If we go from one activity to the next for too long without conscious direction from within, our extraversion "crashes." Even brilliant Extraverts burn out when their talents (or handlers) thrust them too long in the public spotlight, as the annals of politics, Hollywood and the music business attest. In an extraverted culture like America, it is more often introversion that must call for our attention, extraverts and introverts alike, at times forcefully. We get an illness or an injury that lands us at home in bed for some reflection time.

For each of us, there is a right balance between extraversion and introversion that best serves our overall wellbeing. Wherever our lives take us, we can attend to this balance. A program director for a large international Non-Governmental Organization (NGO) named Nicole is extraverted enough to make arduous two-week trips to Africa and Asia. Not wanting to waste a minute with her usually far-flung colleagues once there, Nicole pre-arranges conferences, presentations to government officials and visits to her NGO's projects in remote areas. When she gets back home, she says, it takes a week of an eased-up schedule to rest up physically, but she also finds that she is reluctant to call her friends that first week back. Nicole felt guilty about this until she realized that, just as her body needed a quiet week to recover her physical energy, her psyche needed a period of introversion to recover her inner footing on home ground and absorb all her experiences while away. She also began to take an hour to herself here and there, even an entire evening, during her demanding trips.

Some Tips on Relating to Extraverts

Relating to Extraverts may seem easy, as they themselves relate so readily. But some refinements can help facilitate your encounter.

Listen. Give Extraverts the gift of really listening. For them, "introspection" may require that they talk to someone and work things out. They don't necessarily need advice. They will figure out their own solutions. Your attention is the resonance they need. Acknowledged or not, attention from the important people in their lives means the most.

Chin up. When approaching an Extravert, you can assume you are welcome. To encourage an Extravert's trust, put your own chin up in a body-language pose of openness and social confidence. Look them in the eye and, if appropriate, smile.

Speak up. Extraverts thrive on exchange and communication. Even an argument is better than no exchange at all. In everyday situations with an Extravert, it is a gift of relationship to say *something*. Rather than just to get up and leave the room, for instance, offer something as simple as, "I'll be right back" of "I'll see you later." That's what they do.

Let them extravert. Don't take an Extravert's need to be "out and about" as a personal rejection of your company. He or she must have enough social stimulation to feel alive and fulfilled. Enough introverting together is good for relationship, but Extraverts will resist too many evenings in a row at home "alone." An "extraversion night" out with friends can refresh an Extravert for a week. Let him or her take you out and show you one of their discoveries.

On Introverts and Introverting

A popular introverted department head was being promoted to an executive-level job. His last day with his department, while he spent an hour meeting with the company president, his staff ordered in food, chilled bottles of champagne, and tied helium balloons on chairs all around the department. When his administrative assistant announced he was on his way back, everyone gathered in the center of the department. As he walked through the door, they popped champagne corks and erupted in applause and cheers. He stood stunned, turned around and ran back into the corridor.

When Greta Garbo said, "I want to be alone," she was merely expressing in her sultry way that she was an Introvert. She needed time to think things over, and she couldn't do that with all those people around. Existentialist philosopher Jean-Paul Sartre once said, less gracefully, "Hell is other people." Spoken as a true Introvert.

The beginning of the classic film *Around the World in 80 Days* takes place in a venerable London men's club in which members traditionally do not ever speak to one another. They sit in their leather armchairs and read *The Times* to the sound of clocks ticking. Extraverts in this environment would find themselves knocking over the tea service just to get some response. But Introverts need the equivalent of such a club somewhere, a quiet and inviolable place and time to be free to be and enjoy their own selves, even if it is a cubicle or corner of a bedroom.

An American art dealer realized that he was an Introvert while on an art buying trip to London. He felt surprisingly relaxed there because he knew that his privacy would be transgressed only in the most polite manner. English social norms, the art dealer noticed, put palpable space between people. He and an American colleague, an Extravert, stopped to have mid-afternoon tea before calling on an artist. Uncertain of the artist's address, his colleague approached a woman at a nearby table having her tea alone and asked her a question about the neighborhood. Sitting happily, her tea things spread out around her, she visibly started, then smiled and asked most politely what she could do for him.

The two Americans in London learned to approach Introverts in gradual steps. First, one aggressed with, "I beg your pardon." When that got a response, one could approach again, gingerly, with, "I wonder if you might tell me..." the time or where the nearest tube station was. Walking down a street, the art dealer caught Londoners stealing quick peeks at him, as if giving themselves instantaneous takes on the human-scape without intruding. A nod was sufficient greeting, with no requirement to go further in terms of human interaction. Politeness was developed into a high art to protect introversion, while respecting the necessity of social life.

Extraverts find it hard to believe, but Introverts are happy sitting and reading a book or spending the evening under the car or down in the basement at their workbench doing carpentry or repairing a lamp. Just as Extraverts thrive on socializing, Introverts find solitude refreshing and restorative, like a dip in a peaceful lagoon. A busy introverted investment banker living in New England calls being housebound by a snowstorm "the Introverts' Ball."

"[T]he psychic life of this type is played out wholly within," Jung wrote. "For him [or her] self-communings are a pleasure. His own world is a safe harbour, a carefully tended and walled-in garden, closed to the public and hidden from prying eyes. His own company is best. He feels at home in his world, where the only changes are made by himself." [9]

An Introvert is processing everything internally and then, after much reflection, may come out with monosyllables. Introverts ration their external communications. They might take a couple of days to return a phone call. Once in intimate conversation with an understanding listener, however, they may suddenly wax eloquent, downloading results from dozens of concepts or feelings that they have been processing in their minds all along.

The World Is Too Much With Us

It's not that Introverts aren't interested in other people and the world; on the contrary, they find interaction with them so stimulating that they need to protect themselves by imposing certain limits. An introverted governor of Massachusetts had ropes put up across the corridor to his chambers and the elevator buttons deactivated to limit access to his office floor. A little bit of the world goes a long way with Introverts, and when they learn to live their lives with just enough, they thrive.

In contrast to Extraverts, who process life's experiences while in the midst of them, Introverts follow a pattern of engagement and disengagement. They need to withdraw regularly from social interaction in order to process and assimilate what has happened to them and consult their rich inner life. "There is always the temptation for me to go inside myself," introverted actor Benicio Del Toro, once told *Parade*.

In extraverted Hollywood, introversion has long been romanticized as an aspect of manliness, making the enigmatic and soulful inarticulateness of the "strong silent type" into classic masculine portrayals such as Clint Eastwood's *Dirty Harry*, John Wayne's *The Quiet Man* and James Dean's *Rebel Without a Cause*. Actor Paul Newman once described his longtime friendship with fellow actor and Introvert Robert Redford, who played the Sundance Kid to Newman's Butch Cassidy in their 1969 film classic. "We are both private people," Newman said. "He is even more private than I am. There are a lot of silences, both of us looking up at the ceiling."

An All-American Introvert: The Cowboy

Though America encourages extraversion overall, one of the most American of characters, the cowboy, is a classic Introvert, a taciturn, romantic loner, a man of few words. A magazine writer in New York City named Sabine described spending an evening with a boyfriend of hers from West Texas and his tall tan football coach father. When the father arrived at her apartment to join them, the two men shook hands vigorously and nodded, then sat down, propped their long legs up on her coffee table, folded their arms across their broad chests and sat. And sat. "How's Mom?" her boyfriend asked, at length. "Oh, she's fine," the father said. More silence. "Like your job?" the father asked. "Yep." Silence. Over an hour went by.

At first, Sabine felt uncomfortable, as she searched her mind, unsuccessfully, for subjects of conversation. She soon realized how comfortable the two men were in their quiet encounter, how truly glad they were to see each other and to be together. Talking wasn't their way. She relaxed.

Her boyfriend's father was around another couple of days, and they all sat a lot more. When the older man was leaving, they all stood out on the street in farewell. To Sabine's amazement, she was suddenly engulfed in a big Texas-size bear hug. "Sure was nice to meet you, Sabine," the father said, and he meant it. "Those two men taught me something," Sabine later recalled. "I'm an Introvert. It turned out I was just as happy to sit and be quiet for three days as they were."

Seeing Unseen

Introverts feel a certain natural self-consciousness in public. They don't much like to have their pictures taken (they often look noticeably uncomfortable in a group photograph), or to be in the spot-light. "I like being invisible," says Terry Gross, introverted host of the public radio interview show *Fresh Air*. "I like that the show isn't like prom night and I don't have to worry about my hair and clothes."[10] Introverts are often more comfortable when they have a concrete barrier or object between them and others, such as an interviewer's notepad, a camera, a grill, a table, a microphone, a dais. An Introvert often called on to give lectures to large audiences claims, "One of the safest places in the world is behind a podium." He adds, "I also wear a tie. For protection."

A talented Introvert may become a public person, but he or she usually works out a clever ploy to avoid admiring crowds, such as keeping in constant motion. An introverted college president, who conducts two orchestras and is a dynamic fund-raiser, is legendary for never standing still except to focus his considerable talent or per-suasive charm. Even when called to stardom, Introverts often dis-like attention. Introverted actress Jessica Lange doesn't even want an assistant on the set. "The few times I've been on a movie and they've given me an assistant, I can't get away from them quick enough," she told *More*. "I'm hiding out in my trailer so my assistant can't find me." Scheduled to be honored by the Film Society of Lincoln Center at a major event, actress Jennifer Jason Leigh had performance anx-iety. "It would be such a great thing," she said, "especially if I didn't actually have to go." [11]

Going Out on a Mission

Anyone can be an Extravert on a Saturday night out with friends. Normally, though, purpose is the key word. An Introvert who is extraverting at the right time, for the right purpose, can be quite comfortable doing so. An Introvert tends to go out into the world on a mission. Amelia Earhart was an Introvert. Introverts must have an intent in order to leave the house, studio or cubicle, even if it is just to go out for coffee or a breath of fresh air. Inevitably, essential activities like work, shopping, social life and vacations, take Introverts out into civilization, but going out has to have a reason. "I find it much easier to socialize if I have a purpose," says Tamara, an introverted consultant for an education publishing house. "Like a specific subject I need to talk with someone about who is going to be there. If I'm just going into a room of people without knowing what I'm doing there, I feel much more uncomfortable."

If socializing goes on too long with its continuous demands on their attention, Introverts can even panic. When an Introvert named Ron became a new parent, he was eager for friends to see his tiny son. After a day of steady visitors, more good friends arrived bringing dinner for the busy new parents. Suddenly, Ron got up and asked them to leave. He had emails to answer, he said, bills to pay, phone calls he had to return. Seeing their friend obviously in a state of intense distress, Rob's friends left the food on the kitchen counter for reheating and collected their coats, assuring the new parents they understood. Immediately relieved at the prospect of solitude, Ron regretted his abrupt inhospitableness with good friends. He had been carried too far out on the limb of extraversion to protect himself politely, and he called his friends the next day to apologize.

The Art of Introverting

Even with the increasing awareness about introversion, many Introverts still don't fully realize how their limited capacity for constant socializing or their reluctance to "reach out" is due merely to being an Introvert. For anyone with an introverted psychology, the stimulation of the "outside world" is naturally an amplified experience. Wanting to retreat after a bout of social interaction, to go inward to process and get back to themselves, is for them normal, healthy and, in fact, necessary.

When an introverted writer has guests staying at his house, he socializes for an hour or two, then gently announces, "I'm going to go hermit now." He goes to his room, lies down on his bed and reads or puts on earphones and listens to a talking book. Withdrawing as artfully as he can is ultimately an act of kindness to the people he cares about. "I'd alienate them from me in one way or another, and usually less gracefully," he says.

Introversion can take planning and ingenuity — and daring— to be honest with oneself and others. An introverted director of a large city government agency says she periodically has to excuse herself, go and sit in the ladies room for ten minutes to get her psychological bearings. Introverts must become particularly skilled, and at times forceful, at knowing and protecting their boundaries. But once in their room or private office or alone in nature, magic occurs. Ideas and insights come; creativity flourishes. Writing can be a refuge for Introverts. For introverted novelist Rick Moody, writing became "a release from the vertiginous anxiety of speaking." Novelist Jonathan Franzen wrote his best-selling novel *The Correction* wearing earplugs, earmuffs and a blindfold, his fingers oriented to the keyboard by the small raised bumps on the keys. Determined to deprive himself of outside stimuli, his inner world came alive.

Introverts need not retreat to a forest ranger's cabin as did introverted novelist Jack Kerouac or move themselves and their operations to an iron platform on concrete pilings in the middle of the North Sea, as did introverted "off-shore data haven" entrepreneur

Sean Hastings. Introverts can be observed to cook, use the computer, play music with earphones, play an instrument, paint furniture, surf, garden, hike, repair engines, play golf, sew, create pottery, even do housework in self-contained contentment. An introverted investment banker says that when he gets home from work, he loves to vacuum, which encloses him in a protective wall of sound.

"Mornings are important to us Introverts," an Internet marketing manager says. Introverts appreciate having time to themselves to organize their day or get their thoughts together. Immediately calling a meeting is not their way, nor is attending one first thing, unless it is remotely.

Introverts have been handed great boons with the Internet, smartphones and other personal communication devices. Texting, blogs and chat rooms provide the intimacy of pure communication without the intimidating intensity of actual physical proximity. Technology in general is an Introvert-friendly industry, and not only because of Microsoft's famously introverted founder Bill Gates. According to *USA Today*, more CEOs today than ever are introverted, which challenges the presumption that sociability and outgoing charisma are necessary for success. While many CEOs rise from marketing and other extraverted areas of business, they are now just as likely to come from finance or information technology sectors.

When an art dealer named Basil needed information from an artist whose paintings he was selling, he called the artist several times and left messages, but the artist did not return the calls. Then it occurred to Basil that the artist might be an Introvert, and that he should try texting or emailing him. He decided to send his queries in an email, and the artist responded within the hour with a return email containing all the requested information.

Introverts in an Extraverted Culture

A special word of encouragement is in order for Introverts trying to make their way in America or any extraverted culture or environment. According to an introverted financial manager in a moment of honesty, "I feel I have to beat back the world that always seems to 'come at' me, wanting my attention." Like a kind of minority, Introverts often have to struggle to be their true selves against social expectations and the patterns of behavior that encourage extraversion.

As a cultural barometer of societal sentiment, language is quite revealing. While Extraverts are seen as outgoing, sociable, gregarious, friendly, charismatic, good with people, able to "work a crowd," Introverts are at best described as private, pensive, reserved or quiet loners, but are often accused of being shy, antisocial, unfriendly, aloof, stand-offish, uncommunicative, inaccessible, inhibited, remote, secretive, awkward, stiff, distant, reticent, withdrawn, rude, bashful, tongue-tied, unresponsive or reclusive, even depressed. "I was known as an 'ice queen' in high school," an Introvert remembers. Most Introverts have to admit it: these epithets hurt.

It is easy for Introverts in an extraverted culture like the U.S. to suspect there is something wrong with them and to question their inward natures as perhaps "shutting themselves off" or "shutting others out." Loneliness can arise from comparing themselves to prevailing interpersonal norms. Generations of Introverts have headed straight for the bar for assistance at social functions. Now they are being targeted by pharmaceutical marketers with medications that might help them fit in better with an activity-intense extraverted culture. Parents worry about a "shy" child. In fact, just being an Introvert may be seen in some quarters as pathology. The Diagnostic and

Statistical Manual, the Bible of the psychology profession, includes a diagnosis of "social anxiety disorder," and there is the Social Phobia Inventory (SPIN) self-test ("I am bothered by blushing in front of people." "I am afraid of doing things when people might be watching me.")

Fortunately, some experts disagree. "There are Introverts who are exuberant in their own way with their passion for reading, for example, or sculpting or collecting," Johns Hopkins psychiatry professor and author Kay Redfield Jamison told an interviewer. "If everyone were openly effervescent, the world would be an exhausting and chaotic place. We're well served by our diversity of temperaments."

American culture itself may be making a correction, as evidenced by a surge in awareness of the importance of boundaries and the appearance of websites and books exploring the phenomenon of introversion, spearheaded by Susan Cain's *Quiet: The Power of Introverts in a World That Can't Stop Talking*, which has topped best-seller lists. According to Margot Talbot in an article in *The New York Times Magazine*, the percentage of Americans claiming to be shy jumped from 40 to nearly 50 percent between the 1970s and the 1990s alone. "Maybe more people feel shy in a culture in which the omnipresent media is so full of the aggressively unshy," Talbot suggests. "Maybe we'll find ourselves sorely missing the meek and the mild, the stoic and the taciturn among us. Is somebody out there inventing the drug to treat excessive perkiness?" [12]

An Introvert Speaks Up

Savvy cultural adaptation is achieved by alert Introverts, including one who benefited from some "assertiveness training," though indirectly. An introverted manager named Carole who worked in a large international banking organization was stressed in her job. While she felt confident and did well in one-on-one sessions with her boss and colleagues, there were numerous larger meetings she had to attend. Her extraverted colleagues enjoyed expressing themselves and being the focus of attention. Uncomfortable with such an assertive style, Carole found she could never get to contribute what she knew. She left meetings feeling frustrated, ineffective and defeated, and "not aggressive enough."

At an off-site management seminar on teamwork, Carole was put in groups with people who worked in other parts of the organization, freeing her to be herself. "I discovered something about Extraverts," she said. "One can interrupt them. They interrupt one another all the time!" From observing, she saw how to do so, without hurting anyone's feelings or earning their disapproval. "Wait a moment, Harry," she learned to say, "I need to interject something here..." This simple technique changed Carole's work life. Once she learned how to interrupt, politely but firmly, she found she was able to make her views heard.

Skillful Extraverting for Introverts

Busy processing inside themselves, Introverts are by nature selective about what they engage with on the exterior, as well as when and how. Yet when an Introvert really wants to do something or go somewhere, he or she can muster the energy and charge forth with excitement, commitment and a rewarding sense of rightness. "Sometimes I just have to get out and be with people," says an introverted commercial real estate appraiser named Jeremy, who spends many hours alone researching in town records and on the Internet. "I don't necessarily interact with anyone. It mainly stems from a need to feel as if I am alive in a populated world, and that I am part of that world."

Social expectations may dictate responding in an extraverted way, but Introverts rarely feel totally genuine greeting people with a big smile (though the smile is often there inside). Jung called adapting with an unnatural degree of friendliness, exuberance or assertiveness "inferior extraversion," and the Introvert knows when he or she is "imitating" extraversion in this way. Caught up in "inferior extraversion" due to socializing too long or at the wrong time, an Introvert can lose touch with himself or herself—as well as with the person he or she came with.

Since extraversion is just not their natural rhythm of interpersonal engagement, Introverts must go out into the world *as Introverts*. To do things their way can take ingenuity. A writers group in New York, for instance, meets once a month by conference call. "No need for babysitters, no burning fossil fuel, no worries about the weather—it's ideal!" the introverted group leader says.

Rules of politeness are a great boon to Introverts. Good manners are society's "extraversion training" and create easy fallback phrases and behaviors that serve Introverts in many social situations. Introverts often learn how to ask just the right questions to get someone else going on a long discourse. Star reporters often start out simply as skillful Introverts.

In general, though, it takes a certain bravery in America to stay faithful to one's introversion without doubting oneself or secretly yearning for others' ability to socialize with ease. In a lively extraverted culture, Introverts can easily feel awkward if they can't find anything to say. If they retreat, as they need to, they might fear they will miss out, be forgotten, get left behind. The social swarm may seem delightful and enticing, yet require a great effort to leap into its midst.

Fortunately, Introverts are often brave on the inside. Far from being banished socially by Extraverts, Introverts are often right *next* to the life of the party and making a contribution that is ineffable. "An Introvert...can spread a glow of life and make life in his surroundings into a symbolic festival, better than any Extravert! " Marie-Louise von Franz writes in *Jung's Typology*. "[I]f an Introvert can come out with his extraversion in the right way, he can create an atmosphere where outside things become symbolic: drinking a glass of wine with a friend becomes something like a communion." [13]

When Introverts do express themselves, it is often written, painted, sung, played on an instrument, acted, designed as a garden or conveyed in intimacy over a cup of tea, as they provide a thoughtful overview and perspective. In these ways, Introverts mount significant accomplishments while the world isn't looking, and even while it is. "You have to accept whatever comes and the only important thing is that you meet it with courage and with the best you can give," wrote famously introverted Eleanor Roosevelt in *This I Believe*. Italian opera star Andrea Bocelli, blind since early adolescence, admits he has stage fright. "I try to do my best always," he told an interviewer, "but this (constant attention) makes me nervous. But that is my destiny. This is my work." [14]

Some Tips on Relating to Introverts

When someone first said, "A penny for your thoughts," he or she was probably addressing an Introvert. Introverts have an innate sense of privacy and personal boundaries, and the wrong approach can trigger a psychological fight-or-flight response. An Introvert's apparent social awkwardness can be disconcerting on first acquaintance, and intimate relationships offer all too many of opportunities for misunderstandings or erroneous assumptions. To ease communication and avoid *faux pas* with the Introverts in one's life, keep in mind the following:

Stop and get quiet before approaching an Introvert.

Keep some physical distance between you and the Introvert. When you see that a person is an Introvert, take a step back, either literally or in your mind.

Chin down. Lowering your head is body language that helps convey that you respect them and their introversion.

Knock before entering. Preliminaries and lead-ins are appreciated by Introverts, who may not engage comfortably. Offer an invitation to relate, such as, "Do you mind if I ask you a question?" or halt outside their door, asking, "May I come in?" or "Is this a good time?"

Taper in and taper out. When meeting or greeting someone who is introverted, try not launching into conversation right away. Rather, offer tea, show the person around or some other socially relaxing activity. As a guest of an introverted host, tapering into relating helps. After relating has been going on for a while, do not take your leave abruptly. Winding down respects what has occurred between you.

Watch the eyes. "Know that Introverts avoid eye contact, and Extraverts want it," social worker June Azoulay told a group of real estate brokers with high-powered New York clients. "Introverts need to get to know you. Give them space. Don't invade it."

Allow buffer time. Introverts will defend and protect their space, gruffly if necessary. An Introvert may first need some "buffer time" to adjust to new social or intimate demands. When they are ready, they often reward you with surprising warmth. In an interview, introverted actor Sean Penn answered monosyllabically until the reporter stopped firing questions and sat back quietly. On his own, Penn then started to talk.

Don't assume you know what is in an Introvert's mind or how he or she is feeling. Don't put thoughts or feelings in his or her mind, as tempting as it may be to fill a seeming void. Introversion is an inner pacing and is not intended as a personal affront to anyone. The best invitation for an Introvert to express himself or herself to you is a respectful and open-minded attitude.

Ask. Introverts often wait for a cue, internal or external, to begin speaking. They can wait, comfortably or uncomfortably, for a very long time. If you want to know what an introvert thinks or feels, provide them with an invitation, a sign; ask him or her to weigh in, or some equivalent of "a penny for your thoughts."

You call them. It may be necessary for you to initiate contact. Introverts may not reach out to you, even if they want to, or call or write you right back. They do not mean to be rude. It is simply part of their natural reticence vis à vis the "outside world." Feel free to contact them. Many Introverts like being "found."

A Lifetime Trend Towards Introversion

As people mature, there is a natural psychological movement from extraversion toward introversion. The years from adolescence through the thirties are a naturally extraverted time of life when people, extraverts and introverts alike, are full of social and physical energy and naturally seek one another and their place in the world.

They test and prove themselves professionally, find the right partner, have and rear families and interact in their communities. Towards the middle of life and beyond, as activity and energy levels wane and philosophical or metaphysical issues attract them, even Extraverts are drawn to spending more time on inner pursuits.

Later in life, Introverts feel more at home than ever as their contemporaries value turning inward. They may even lead the way for Extraverts discovering a new world within. Meanwhile, Extraverts remain Extraverts. At every age, they must seek family, friends, church, political or community activities that provide the extraverted milieu in which to thrive as their true selves. Even at 101, an extraverted great-grandmother spends her time happily talking with relatives and friends on the phone, receiving visitors, sitting at her window watching neighbors walk down the street and work in their yards, and feeling a part of the great human world that is her natural domain.

2

The Four Functions

HUMAN BEINGS ARE admirably complete psychologically. Not only do we have access to the continuum of extraversion and introversion, we also have four psychological functions to help us interact intelligently with all the different realms of life. We are able to apprehend the physical aspects of our life with our Sensation function. We can see possibilities, plan and discern the meaning and implications of events with our Intuition function. We can organize information mentally and analyze and make sense of it logically with our Thinking function. We can relate to people, understand our instinctual responses and value ourselves, others and life itself with our Feeling function.

To understand these four functions is to master one of the most important fundamentals of psychology. As we will describe more fully in the next chapter, two of these functions, Sensation and Intuition, are *perceiving* functions that take in information about our life situation. Two functions, Thinking and Feeling, are *processing* functions that help us make sense of this information and make decisions. Each function can be used in an extraverted way, that is, focused outward toward what is happening "outside" ourselves, or turned inward and used in an introverted way focused on our inner thoughts and feelings.

In the chapters ahead, we will explore each of the four functions in depth in the chapters ahead—how it works, what it does in us and how we relate to its realm, as well as how it shapes the personalities of people who are made to use this function often and well. To get us started, however, here are brief introductions to the Sensation, Intuition, Thinking and Feeling functions and to their vital roles in human nature.

Minding Matter: The Sensation Function

We are all physical beings living in a physical world, in bodies with senses and an overall physical awareness. Psychologically, we apprehend this sensory information with our Sensation function. Through the Sensation function, we perceive what our bodies pick up every moment — temperatures, colors, shapes, textures, noises, smells, and all the other physical stimuli provided by the conditions, people, objects and places around us. Through our Sensation function, we perceive our muscles in movement or relaxed, our comfort or pain and all kinds of physical states, responses and reactions that provide essential information as we move through the world.

Allowing us to perceive and communicate directly with the material aspects of our environment—with matter—and orienting us in our physical surroundings, our Sensation function makes us "down-to-earth," hands-on and aware of our body's signals and needs. With our Sensation function we pay attention to attire and decor. We use our Sensation function when we take care of ourselves and others physically, provide good-tasting food, protective and sensuously pleasing clothing and safe, comfortable and esthetically appealing living and work environments. Our Sensation function wants a roof without leaks, a solid foundation under our feet, a healthy body and tools and appliances that work well. Sensation gives us a material sense of reality, as to what is literally, concretely *real.*

Without the Sensation function, there would be no good restaurants, orchestras, opera and dance companies, art or art galleries, gyms, spas, hospitals, sports teams, military operations, fashion collections, gardens, farmers markets or golf courses. A prominent or high-ranking Sensation function in someone's psychological hierarchy brings with it natural good taste, but also physical energy, strength, and ability. People who use Sensation as their First Function — Sensation "types" — perceive the physical world in great detail. Tactile, practical, focused on concrete results, they observe, annotate, shape and create a lot of what we see around us.

With its inherent attentiveness and abilities in the physical realm, Sensation is used in many workplaces. The list is long of professional areas where the Sensation function thrives and makes its contribution, from health care to horticulture, from sports to engineering. Scientists, with their ability to count fruit flies, discern the stripes on bird's wings or record details of chemical reactions, usually have prominent Sensation functions. While financial speculation requires Intuition perception, the Sensation function covers the realm of money as cash, income, bottom-line facts and figures. Acumen in business matters often comes with a high-ranking Sensation function.

With its deliberate and graceful tempo, natural and not machine-like, the Sensation function attends to all the physical details of measuring, stirring, painting, stacking, polishing, counting, prodding, holding, moving, and all the other operations one does in caring for the material world. As the Sensation function becomes intimately involved in all manner of physical experience, the position of Sensation in our hierarchy profoundly affects our approach to health, appearance and our environment.

The Visionary: The Intuition Function

Intuition is our capacity to see past the appearance of things to apprehend meanings, connections and possibilities and to perceive influences underlying what is seemingly obvious, solid and material. Our Intuition function gives us an inner knowing that comes in a flash of insight or perhaps a quiet suspicion or hunch. It scans our environment looking for significance and clues. It surveys the news for trends and the market for opportunities. It penetrates a person's conversation for meaning and behavior for motives.

While Sensation looking at an object sees its color, placement, texture or shape, Intuition sees its past, future, possible use or why someone put it there. Surveying an idea, Intuition tries to go to its source, explore its possible meaning and relate it to similar ideas in other fields. We use our Intuition function in order to see possible options, future implications and consequences. Intuition anticipates, warns us of danger and makes "intuitive leaps" to what seems likely to happen. Our Intuition function connects the dots, always pioneering toward the unknown.

Though it is generally less than trusted today in a modern world that tends to value and reward tangible proof and concrete results, this "sixth sense" was once vital to human survival, and still is. Not everyone is inclined to peer deeply into the future or the nature of reality, but some people are psychologically configured do so and to convey to the rest of humanity what they see. These are Intuitive "types." But we all have this remarkable faculty of perception within us that seeks to incorporate a sense of direction, meaning and purpose into our lives.

The Great Organizer: The Thinking Function

Our Thinking function allows us to accomplish the process of rational, objective, consciously directed thought. The Thinking function takes perceptions, facts, ideas, concepts, information and experiences, breaks them down into their component parts and organizes them, thus making them comprehensible to our intellect.

The Thinking function clarifies, orders, categorizes, compares, delineates and defines. In school and at work, Thinking structures and outlines papers, articles and memos and creates logical, orderly presentations. Our Thinking function works hard to *know*, formulating ideas and concepts and getting the facts, quotes, examples and rationales to support them. The Who-What-When-Where-How format of news article writing and the expository form of thesis-antithesis-synthesis of academic writing are natural to people who process information with their Thinking functions.

Thinking makes lists and organizes what we know. In its quest for intellectual clarity, the Thinking function is methodical and deliberate. It uses procedures, formulas, recipes and directions. Thoughts follow one after another in a sequence of logical connections and step-by-step progressions. How would a Thinking type fix a paragraph, a bit of binary code, a faucet? Would a Thinking type like some more lasagna? "Let me think about it..." is the response. In the Thinking process, no step is skipped; otherwise the chain of logic is broken and the Thinking function loses its way causing disorientation and distress.

The human Thinking function created the notion of time and is our timekeeper. Tuned in to the clock and the calendar, Thinking orders our day, schedules our week and takes command of our year. The Thinking function remembers and builds on what has worked in the past and lays out a time-line for the future.

Modern civilization would crumble into chaos without the Thinking function. The Thinking function is responsible for laws and courts, production and transportation schedules, computer code, instructions, all kinds of organizations and most of our educational system. The contributions of people with highly placed Thinking functions are considerable, as are their responsibilities. They abound among the "experts" of the modern world. They often rule and govern their countries, their cities, their communities, their businesses and organizations, and their families, too. Whether a Thinking type knows best may be subject to debate, but when it comes to debates, guess who will win?

The Thinking function works with perceptions provided by our Sensation and Intuition functions. When Thinking processes the information gleaned by the Sensation function, Jung called it "practical thinking." Combined with Intuition's insights, Thinking accomplishes visionary and "speculative thinking," by which we conjecture about what may lie ahead.

The Great Connector: The Feeling Function

With our Feeling function, we enter the realm of human values and relationships, the realm of the heart. While the Thinking function processes our life experience objectively and intellectually, the Feeling function responds personally, in a subjective way, to who or what appears before us. It brings us the intelligence of our instincts and affinities—our EQ. In our Feeling function, we come to understand the language of our entire organism, as it is tells us about our life and the people in it. Just as our Thinking function strives for logic and rationality, our Feeling function guides us toward our well-being, toward "feeling good" and away from what feels "bad."

With our Feeling function, we like or dislike something; we care about it or it "leaves us cold." Something may feel important or trivial. In any moment, we may be feeling uneasy or content, sad or uplifted. These and many other feeling states guide Feeling "types" particularly through their daily lives, but they are going on regularly in everyone.

The Feeling function is not to be confused with the physical experience of emotion. In fact, emotions are often the result of one's Feeling function being ignored, overridden or discounted. When Feeling processing is recognized and developed, it is as subtle, refined and informative as the finest rational thought.

In our Feeling function, we experience a visceral connection; we can feel the very nature of the people and situations we encounter. In the process of relating, much vital information is processed. Feeling processing is needed in relationships and inherently thrives there. In situations in which objectivity or efficiency is paramount, the Feeling function tends to remain unacknowledged or banished and the quality of relationships often deteriorates.

Valuing is a primary activity of the Feeling function. Our Feeling function allows us to feel how much we value and care about whoever and whatever is in our lives, including ourselves. Feeling lets us know who and what are really important to us. Gazing on a person, a pet, our home, even a favorite tree or mountain, the very feeling of valuing nourishes us to our very depths.

Our Feeling function allows us to tap into the accumulated intelligence of thousands of years of human experience, a vast store of wisdom for life aimed at our overall wellbeing. For many people today, understanding the Feeling function can bring a new frontier of awareness and experience to be found right within our own natures.

Our Four-Function Hierarchy

Our individual psychology chooses certain functions to specialize in; we develop them and use them naturally and often. Each of us has an inner psychological hierarchy of functions that shapes our personalities, interests and choices. As we explore further in Chapter Four, where each function is placed, first through fourth in order, greatly influences how we interact with its realm. Our First and Second functions are the ones in which we enjoy the most natural facility, and our success and happiness are greatly enhanced when we understand which functions provide this natural endowment. But we all have the four functions within us, giving us the necessary psychological breadth to live and thrive as our "fully-functional" unique selves in our world.

— 3 —

The Psychological Basics:
Perceiving and Processing

ANNA WENT TO see a massage therapist named Jill. As Anna sat in the waiting room, a magazine article on the coffee table caught her attention. Just as she was picking it up, Jill came out and greeted her. "So, what do you think of my flowers?" Jill said, as she ushered Anna into the treatment room.

"Flowers..." said Anna.

"Yes! Didn't you see my flowers in the waiting room?" Jill asked.

"Actually, no, I didn't, but I will certainly look when I go back out," Anna said guiltily.

"How could you miss them? And I spent all that money!" said Jill, teasing her client with a hint of annoyance.

After the massage, Anna emerged from the treatment room and sure enough, a magnificent vase of flowers sat prominently on the coffee table, right next to the magazine that had caught her eye.

People see the world in very different ways, as well as different things in the world. As we gather information about what is happening around us, we notice different aspects of our environment. We come to understand this information and make choices and decisions in different ways, as well. By becoming aware of extraversion and introversion, we are already "practicing" typology. Often the next aspect we can identify is what a person is noticing, or how he or she is processing a situation to relate to it and understand it.

The first two functions in our personal psychological hierarchy do precisely these two tasks. One function is a *perceiving* function that notices information that is pertinent to us. Another function is a *processing* function that helps us comprehend our perceptions and make decisions and choices.

In this chapter, we broaden our psychological expertise by learning to determine which function we (and others) use to *perceive* the world and which function we use to *process* our perceptions. Each of the four functions of Sensation, Intuition, Thinking and Feeling is a powerhouse of psychological capability. We will get to know them in the context of the vital psychological roles they perform—either to *perceive* what is happening within and around us or to *process* and make sense of this vital information.

A perceiving function may come first in our function-order hierarchy, or a processing function may be our first and primary psychological activity. Either way, each of us has both abilities contained in our first two functions. This potent combination of processing and perceiving defines our psychological "type," but more importantly it shapes how we see and come to understand the world. Every person we encounter is perceiving and processing, and so are we. When people do these tasks using different functions, misunderstandings can easily result, but awareness opens countless opportunities for understanding and cooperation.

Perceiving and Processing Our Lives

The functions of Sensation and Intuition are *perceiving functions*. They guide our awareness of the world and ourselves in it. The functions of Thinking and Feeling are *processing functions*, which help us assess and make sense of our experience. According to Jung, "When we think, it is in order to judge or to reach a conclusion, and when we feel it is in order to attach a proper value to something. Sensation and Intuition, on the other hand, are perceptive functions—they make us aware of what is happening, but do not interpret or evaluate it. [They] are simply receptive to what happens." [1]

We all have both perceiving functions and both processing functions within us to use when we need them. But according to our innate psychological makeup, we naturally prefer a particular perceiving function and a processing function to do these crucial psychological tasks for us. These first two functions in our hierarchy work together in a remarkable synergy to help us experience and interact with life according to our own nature.

Because they do the same psychological tasks in very different ways, the two *perceiving* functions and the two *processing* functions are considered psychological opposites.

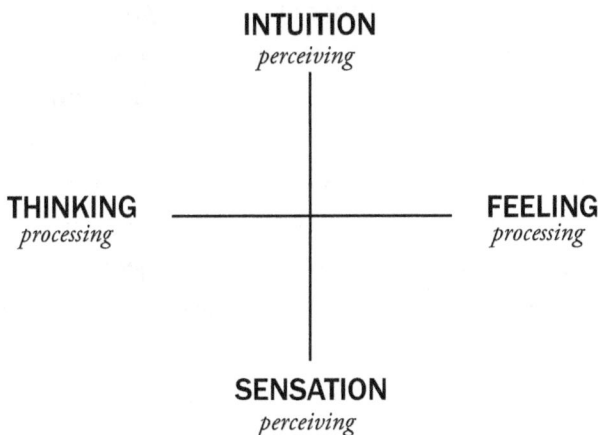

INTUITION
perceiving

THINKING ———————————— **FEELING**
processing   *processing*

SENSATION
perceiving

Whenever we are using a certain function to perceive or to process, its opposite must be "switched off" from our psychological awareness, so that we can do the task efficiently. The functions we use naturally to perceive and process reveal volumes about how we approach and interact with the world.

Our perceiving function of Sensation or Intuition guides our attention and interests. At any given moment, each of us is apprehending aspects of our environment either in terms of physical detail via our senses or intuitively by what significance something may hold. Typologically one is, so to speak, a *Sensation perceiver* or an *Intuition perceiver*. Do we notice the flowers on the table in the waiting room? We are perceiving with our Sensation function, our senses. Do we spot an interesting article on a magazine cover? We are noticing with our Intuition function, which signals that it is meaningful to us in some way. When we meet a woman, do we immediately see the color of her dress or try to interpret the expression on her face? In the first instance, we are using Sensation to perceive, in the second, Intuition sees meaning in her furrowed eyebrows or the down-turned corner of her mouth.

To come to understand our outer and inner perceptions, we most often use either our Thinking function or our Feeling function. We are primarily a *Thinking processor* or a *Feeling processor*. Do we want to define a problem, ascertain the facts and consult expert opinion in order to make a decision? We are using our Thinking function to get clarity on the problem. Do we look at the situation and get a "gut feel" about it in order to know what is happening? We are consulting our Feeling function. When we are listening to a person speaking, are we objectively taking in the facts of the subject, organizing them and comparing them with what we have learned in the past? We are processing with our Thinking function. As we are listening to the person, are we aware of liking or disliking him or her or what he or she is saying? Our Feeling function is processing the conversation.

Our first two functions represent our "type." Working together to perceive and process our lives, they make up the strong core of our personality. But more importantly, they are what we *do* psychologically much of the time. Typology helps make inner psychological activity observable. Intuitive-Thinking types and Thinking-Intuitive types, for instance, can be observed perceiving with Intuition's insightful scanning for significance and processing these perceptions with Thinking's ability to organize, define and analyze logically. Sensation-Feeling and Feeling-Sensation types can be seen using their senses to perceive and collect information and processing this information using gut-level Feeling responses.

Some people *perceive* as their first psychological priority; they attend to the information in their surroundings in great detail, either its characteristics or its significance. Other people *process* as their first priority, responding and trying to understand in considerable depth each perception. This is often quite evident. Intuitive-Thinking types, for instance, spend more time intuiting and pursuing possibilities in their minds; Thinking-Intuitives, on the other hand, spend more time thinking about and analyzing an idea or topic. Thinking-Sensation types spend more time thinking, and Sensation-Thinking types spent more attention energy looking at the material aspects of their environment.

There are eight different typological combinations of perceiving and processing functions:

First Function	Second Function
SENSATION	THINKING
SENSATION	FEELING
INTUITION	THINKING
INTUITION	FEELING
THINKING	SENSATION
THINKING	INTUITION
FEELING	SENSATION
FEELING	INTUITION

**The Eight Combinations of First and Second Functions
for Perceiving and Processing**

"Practicing" Function Recognition

We can already start observing perceiving and processing functions in action. After all, everyone is almost always taking in information pertinent to them and processing their experiences for understanding. These are precisely the jobs of the first two functions in the forefront of everyone's psychology. When we recognize the functions we ourselves use most naturally to perceive and process, our inner workings become much clearer. When we recognize the functions being used by the people around us, our expectations and our communication are transformed.

How often are you conscious of your body's sensations during the day or of the colors, textures and furniture arrangement in the rooms you enter? Whenever you are, you are using your Sensation function to perceive. How often do you envision the consequences of something that happens, or seek out a person's motivations? When you do, you are using your Intuition function for perception. In a given situation, are you "thinking your way" through it logically, or "feeling your way" along, responding to what happens next? Focusing on the facts and logical presentation of a subject in a conversation is using your Thinking function to process it. If you are more interested in relating well to the person you are with, you are using your Feeling function in the situation.

Someone who walks up to us and immediately feels the fabric of our jacket is using his or her Sensation function and is probably a Sensation perceiver. Someone who immediately starts wondering "what if" and imagining possibilities is using Intuition and is likely to be an Intuition perceiver. If someone lists the four reasons why he or she wants to go somewhere or do something, he or she is likely a Thinking processor, who makes decisions with the help of specific reasons. If a person asks with genuine sympathy how we are feeling after a stressful day, he or she is probably a Feeling processor, who is attuned to your state of wellbeing.

If we are observant, we can come to recognize when a particular function is being used to perceive or to process. At a postmortem on a party, a Sensation perceiver will likely remember what everyone was wearing and what the apartment looked like. An Intuition perceiver will tell you what the party meant to the people who were there and what might come out of the event. After the same party, a Thinking processor will recall what subjects he discussed with people and the sequence of what happened when. A Feeling processor may mention the people he or she liked best, who was not getting along with whom or who connected up with whom by the end of the night. While the

Sensation perceiver noticed the shoes and tie a man was wearing, an Intuition perceiver noted a certain look in his eye. A Thinking processor was considering the man's job title, the college he went to, the factual details of their conversation, while a Feeling type was feeling an inner "relaxation response" that said, "He's a good man, I can relate to him directly."

Type Clash: Different Perceivers and Processors

Our first two functions feature prominently in our relationships, as we will see in Chapter 10. Two Sensation perceivers may have a great time together shopping, cooking or on the golf course or ski slopes. Two Thinking processors may launch immediately into a lively discussion of books, politics or sports. Two Intuition perceivers can talk for hours about trends they see in a business or global situation or what might be going on in their lives or with a colleague or in a relationship. Two Feeling processors can be together in complete comfort and mutual support, sharing a Feeling connection that all is right in their world.

Inevitably, however, we encounter people who use different perceiving or processing functions from the ones we use, those that are "normal" and familiar to us. In our families and in our love lives, at work or school or in our communities, people can appear frustratingly incomprehensible to one another. Knowing how people naturally perceive and process reality— literally what is likely to be on their minds at any given moment — can help avoid confusion, misunderstanding and many pitfalls in our relationships and in all areas of our personal lives.

On any ordinary day, we can witness the results: typology-based challenges—or "type clash." A Sensation perceiver might find an

Intuition perceiver to be flighty, vague, lazy, insubstantial or too "all-over-the-place," because she was not as aware of the concrete details of their environment. Meanwhile, an Intuition perceiver may judge a Sensation perceiver of being too "superficial" and materialistic because he paid so much attention to his wardrobe and the look of his home.

Because our psychologies work differently, people experience discomfort or even conflict when others are merely using another function. Until they understand this, different perceivers can run into a type clash situation by not noticing what the other sees as totally obvious. Different processors can experience type clash causing stress ranging from daily annoyances to life-long hostilities. A Thinking processor may find a Feeling processor to be volatile or self-absorbed. A Feeling processor might judge a Thinking processor as "flat" "cold," arbitrary and insensitive. A Thinking processor might feel out of his or her element and vulnerable when the interpersonal terrain of a relationship gets too murky, overheated and disorderly—too Feeling-intense—and withdraw from the relationship. Meanwhile, a Feeling processor, feeling alienated or disinterested when a discussion turns overly intellectual and abstract, may depart, seeking company that feels more companionable. Type clash can almost always be addressed and alleviated with an understanding of the different functions being used.

The Perceiving Functions: Sensation and Intuition

We have both Sensation and Intuition functions within us, but one perceiving function most often directs our awareness and serves as our initial perceptual interface with the world. The two "functions of perception" give "welcome assistance to thought or feeling," Jung wrote [2]. They also profoundly affect our experience. Even if Thinking or Feeling comes first in our psychological hierarchy, it is our preferred perceiving function, whether Sensation or Intuition, that notices and selects what we pay the most attention to. We come to rely on its messages to orient ourselves in our various circumstances.

Surveying our current situation and picking up information, both Sensation and Intuition see attributes, similarities, dissimilarities, and connections, what "goes" with what, yet they do so in totally opposite ways, one seeing the concrete and physical, the other getting flashes of meaning and significance. Sensation and Intuition will notice different aspects of the same scene. An Intuitive real estate broker, for instance, saw an old barn with potential but needing painting, while a Sensation-type broker saw an antique barn that had "attained a beautiful patina." Whether we use Sensation or Intuition, we are all "seers," though of quite different things.

When we use our Sensation function, we register what is being revealed to us by our bodies and by our five senses of sight, hearing, touch, smell and taste. Working in real-time, Sensation picks up sensory signals and physical details, such as, colors, shapes, scents, movements, spatial arrangements, noises, temperatures, the yellow of a lemon and green of a pine bough, the tactile softness of fur, the hot spice of chili, the position of one's fingers on a basketball, bodily pleasures and pains. All these stimuli are taken in psychologically via our Sensation function.

While Sensation perceives what exists physically, Intuition sees "into" things. Intuition perceives the world by *in-sight*. It is the human ability to be visionary, to glimpse around the corner, as it were. It takes a particular selection from our surroundings and sees meaning, perhaps something about its past or its present characteristics, that implies "something else." Intuition sees psychological implications of an expression or gesture. It envisions the meaning of a poetry metaphor.

Just as Sensation informs us where furniture is so we can walk safely across the room, the Intuition function establishes a mental context for where we are. It scans forwards and backwards in time and across cultures. Sensation sees that a cup is yellow with red flowers; Intuition sees that it is an antique, possibly French, maybe inherited from a wealthy or at least tasteful grandparent — a *clue!*

A Sensation perceiver sees the physical attributes or qualities of a piece of pottery, its colors, what it is made of, what kind of glaze the potter used, how its shape compares with a piece of pottery on the next shelf. Intuition perceivers are primarily interested not so much in how a piece of pottery looks, but in whom it belonged to before, its "provenance," how it might have been used, what the painted pattern meant in Chinese or Minoan or Native American cosmology or expressed the state of mind of its creator.

Sensation perceivers see what goes well with what, such as paint chips and fabric swatches, items of furniture in a room or plants in a garden store or a landscape. When they look out a window, they see that the color of the leaves matches the color in the grass or that the arch of a tree branch echoes the shape of a garden trellis. An Intuition perceiver looking out a window may be seeing a green blur, while he or she is actually seeing something from a conversation an hour ago: "Oh, that's what he meant!"

A Sensation Perceiver and an Intuition Perceiver Look at a Painting

If we could step inside the mind of a Sensation perceiver looking at a painting on a nautical theme, we might see a sailboat with white sails edged with yellow sunlight and a forest-green hull plying dark blue water flecked with whitecaps. As an Intuition perceiver gazing at the same picture, we might see a sailboat sailing in a stiff wind (extrapolated from the whitecaps) possibly off New England, (judging from the look of the water and sky that reminds us of our cousin's place on Cape Cod); the boat reminds us of our cousin's, then of that great day we had sailing last summer.

In both cases, we are "observant," but the Sensation perceiver sees *what* is there, while the Intuition perceiver sees *why* it is there. A Sensation perceiver sees the visual facts of the painting, the colors, shapes and composition; an Intuition perceiver sees a detail and immediately speculates and extrapolates to create a composite mental image made up of ideas and images that span styles or periods of time. While the Sensation perceiver sees a boat and deep-blue water, an Intuition perceiver "sees" a stream of consciousness inspired by or "around" the boat and sailing. If many artists are Sensation perceivers, art critics are often Intuition perceivers, whose inspired musings go far beyond what a painting actually looks like.

Reality Check

Everything that exists in our world has both physical characteristics and a meaning or significance. Our Sensation function perceives its physical aspects; our Intuition function sees their meaning, like the apple and honey eaten at Rosh Hashanah to symbolize a sweet new year.

Sensation gives us a sense of concrete reality, of what is right there in front of us, and of ourselves in our body, right here and now. With Sensation perception, we take whatever is in our environment just as it is, in its concrete aspects and details. For this reasons, Sensation perceivers seem very embodied, competent and at home with what is around them.

Intuition perceivers, by comparison, can seem quite ethereal, "not all there." Their attention is scanning for items of interest or value, not just in what lies before them, but also in what is being said and done and in what "comes to mind" in their own imaginations. What is real to them is what has significance, what intrigues them.

Sensation seems to be the predominant function that defines "reality" in our pragmatic Western culture, which is often concerned with counting, measuring and exploring the material aspects of our world. Meanwhile, Intuition is valued for it's ability to strategize for the future, read the signs and see trends and other dimensions of reality that exist hidden from the Sensation-perceived world.

More about Sensation Perceivers

Sensation perceivers orient themselves according to their physical sensations. As their Sensation functions register sights, sounds, tastes, odors, temperatures, surface textures, their whole bodies are sources of data to tell them where they are and what is going on around them. People who perceive with their Sensation functions relate to what exists right in front of them *in the moment*, noting what people are wearing, the taste of cumin in the marinade, a chair moved to a new position or a door newly painted.

Naturally seeing physical details, Sensation perceivers pay attention to, and therefore take good care of, their clothes, their hair, their children's clothes, their physical health, their animals, their yards, the decor and arrangement of their houses, apartments and offices. Their appearance is a creative personal expression. They shop with relative ease and keep their vehicles well maintained. Cooking or at least good eating is usually a priority. They have a natural facility for examining, manipulating and enhancing the physical, material world.

A Sensation perceiver's eyes may glaze over when an Intuition perceiver starts speculating about where they might go on next year's vacation or wondering why their friend may have broken a dinner engagement; these are abstractions far from the Sensation perceiver's physical experience in the present. "I don't care what the painting means," a Sensation-perceiver art history student said. "I'm looking at the brush strokes."

Sensation perceivers are responsible for a lot of the physical beauty and prowess in the world, in homes and gardens, on fashion runways, dance, theater and concert stages, in art museums and also on courts and playing fields. Renowned Sensation-endowed individuals like Marilyn Monroe, Picasso, Elvis Presley, Pelé or Madonna are merely iconic examples of the Sensation function in all of us whenever we cook a meal, decorate for the holidays, take a run or a shower, face our closets in the morning, style our hair, surround ourselves with music or make love.

For Sensation perceivers, the relationship between money and the material aspects of life is concrete and tangible. Many relate to financial matters as a natural fact of life. One Sensation perceiver balances her checkbook to relax. Hands-on and practical, Sensation perceivers gravitate toward "real-world" professional fields such as business, medicine, the culinary arts, engineering, natural science, retailing, building, agriculture, painting and sculpture, fashion and home decor, skilled trades, dancing or playing in a city orchestra. What they can't actually see, touch or experience concretely may appear only dimly on their radar screens; what isn't right in front of them gets less of their psychological attention than the immediate physical aspects of their life.

More about Intuition Perceivers

Intuition perceivers too see what is around them, but in their own unique way. There is nothing physically wrong with their eyes, ears, nose, or other senses, but Intuition perceivers can be completely unaware of their bodies' signals or of many of the details of their physical environment. An Intuition perceiver's hands are doing one thing and their eyes are looking elsewhere. They are looking for "what's going on here?"

Intuition is an inward perception, our ability to see significance, possibilities, what might be or "appears" to be real or true. Rather than noting many sensory stimuli, Intuition selects a meaningful few and from them envisions the possible whole. Intuition perceivers scan the environment with an invisible eye which registers, often without their awareness, key details — a scent, the set of a jaw, a look in the eye, a photograph on a piano, a chair out of place. From these they extrapolate, elaborate and come up with a viable "take" on the situation. Intuition perceivers look for a hint of a direction or a way in which things are connected or working. A Sensation perceiver sees his wife's gray running shoes on the floor. An Intuition perceiver sees that his wife's running shoes are there, so she must be back home from her run, and, "That was quick, she must have been really pushing!"

Intuition perceivers may not be fascinated by how a toaster works or how to match drapes with a new armchair, but they "connect the dots" among facts and ideas to create a mental picture with meaning and significance. From its standpoint in the present, Intuition "sees" across eras and cultures, putting together an imaginable collage, an intuitive art form. Intuition sees patterns in what to others is random chaos. It also sees signs of the future in the present, implications of what is evolving. The subject of a phone call relates to something they were reading. Three people in one day have mentioned moving out of the city — "Aha, perhaps a trend!"

The connections Intuition makes can be very funny. Intuition perceivers are often quick to laugh. Comedians are often Intuition perceivers.

Intuition perceivers are prominent among the world's visionaries, inventors and innovators, such as mathematicians and physicists Albert Einstein and Stephen Hawking, entrepreneurs Steve Jobs and Bill Gates, psychologists Carl Jung, William James and Abraham Maslow. Many filmmakers are Intuition perceivers, like Steven Spielberg and Wim Wenders. Strategic planners, investment managers, think-tank members, editors, journalists and news and cultural commentators are usually Intuition perceivers, as are visionary artists like William Blake and Wassily Kandinsky, poets like Samuel Taylor Coleridge, Mary Oliver and Rainer Maria Rilke and perceptive novelists exploring human nature.

Intuitive perceivers seem always to be seeking a better, easier way to live or to do things. They like to experiment, at least in their imaginations, but Intuition perceivers do not have the Sensation perceiver's automatic ease and comfort with hands-on practical tasks. In fact, too many physical steps in a process and they get flustered or are reluctant to approach the task at all.

Typology Alert! – Blind Spots

We all have psychological blind spots in our opposite perceiving function, the one we normally "switch off." This is useful to know, so we can be aware of what we might not otherwise notice. Walking along a city street with a friend, an Intuition perceiver was listening to her so intently that she walked right into a signpost. A Sensation perceiver, who is a theater set designer, was so absorbed in building a stage model on his desk that he didn't show up for a producers meeting and got bumped from the project. "Where were you?!" exclaimed an exasperated colleague. "How could you not see how important it was to go to that meeting?"

Depending on which perceiving function predominates, some aspects of reality are automatically "more real" or more important than others. It is useful to remember the existence of the "other world," the one we perceive less frequently or in less detail until it hits us in the face, so to speak. Sensation perceivers may normally monitor the concrete, material world perceptible by the physical senses, and Intuition perceivers may ordinarily attend to the invisible world of underlying significance, importance, meaning and direction, but purposefully turning to the other perceiving function within them helps them keep in touch with that other dimension of reality.

An acknowledgment of both realms helps us not only in our own lives, but also in our relationships with those who perceive differently. When we can recognize and appreciate that others are expressing what they see naturally, everyone benefits.

Type Clash! Trouble on the Home Front

"What is so difficult about replacing the hall light?" a Sensation perceiver named Hank asked his Intuition-perceiver son, Hank Jr. "Here's $5. Just go to the store, get a package of light bulbs, put up the ladder, take out the old bulb, screw in the new one and put the ladder away!" Hank Jr. glared at his father. His Intuition was imagining all the physical aspects of the task, which seemed to him daunting and even slightly scary.

As typological opposites, Sensation and Intuition perceivers living or working together can experience subtle annoyances and strains. The Sensation perceiver becomes frustrated because the Intuition perceiver resists doing a simple household task or doesn't seem to care where they might put a new chair. Meanwhile, an Intuition perceiver explaining why their child might be having trouble in school, may feel offended and angry because a Sensation perceiver has obviously stopped listening, as if to say, "You figure it out." Awareness of people's main perception functions can help clear up relationship "issues" that elicit confrontations, minor and major.

We tend to avoid the opposite function and its realm in our lives, as if we just don't want to "go there." Psychologically, it is challenging to switch back and forth between opposite perceptual modes. Sensation perceivers can let the "intuitive" side of their lives go, losing sight of distant plans or being reluctant to examine their own or another person's motives. Meanwhile, Intuition perceivers can ignore the Sensation aspects of their environment until they can't find anything on their desk or clean matching socks. With psychological awareness, we can "go there" enough so that we can experience that "other" realm and take adequate care of ourselves in it.

Indeed Sensation and Intuition perceivers living or working together can enjoy a mutually advantageous and appreciative partnership and division of labor, as each sees what the other does not. An Intuition perceiver can be very grateful to a Sensation perceiver, who offers to clean the living room before their guests arrive. The Intuition perceiver may feel less comfortable washing the wedding crystal than the Sensation perceiver, who might shy away from doing the dinner-party seating chart with all its psychological implications. While the Sensation perceiver makes sure the car is working well, the refrigerator is stocked and there are clean bath towels for their weekend guests, the Intuition perceiver can help the Sensation perceiver strategize about how and when to ask for a raise or how to approach a difficult team member or customer. Encouraging everyone to see and do what they do naturally, all aspects of life will be well taken care of, and often enjoyably.

The Processing Functions: Thinking and Feeling

A kitchenware catalog company moved into a newly renovated loft building. Soon a candle factory moved in next door, and hundreds of candles were burning to test different chemical compositions. Every time the candle factory door opened, the fumes entered the hallway and crept beneath the front door of the catalog company. When some of the catalog staff began to experience difficulty breathing, they met with the company president about what to do.

"Let's get someone in here to test this air to see if it is safe," proposed a staff member.

"But we already know this air is toxic, we're all sick!" argued another staff member.

The company president honored both approaches. He ordered a chemical test of the air to show proof if necessary, but he also went to the landlord and was promptly offered better office space for the same rent in another part of the building.

Confronted with reality's complexities, we have to be able to understand what is going on around us and to decide what to do.

Working with information provided by our Sensation function or orienting flashes of significance provided by Intuition, we make sense of them psychologically by using one of the processing functions—Thinking or Feeling. With the Thinking function, we organize our perceptions and thoughts intellectually. We make distinctions, define, differentiate, compare and categorize them. The Feeling function helps us relate to people and events subjectively and feel how much we value them. Psychologically, we process our reality primarily by utilizing logic, organization and analysis or by evaluating people and situations through our feeling responses, our visceral intelligence and "gut instincts." We are, so to speak, *Thinking processors* and *Feeling processors*.

The Thinking processor at the catalog office filled with candle fumes wanted to do tests of the air to see if the candle factory was a polluter. For the Feeling processor, her personally distressing responses were proof positive that the fumes were toxic. Neither way of processing was "wrong," in fact, both were psychologically right depending on the person's processing function.

The Thinking and Feeling functions work in very different, indeed opposite ways. According to Jung, "thinking organizes the contents of consciousness under concepts, feeling arranges them according to their value." [3] Thinking processes with our intellect and tells us what is logical and makes sense rationally. Feeling processes the intricate signals of our instincts and body chemistry telling us what we like or dislike, what feels good or right or bad or wrong. The Thinking function works toward the clarity of what is reasonable. Feeling aims toward affinity and harmony within ourselves, with others and with our surroundings. Thinking analyzes facts received on good authority; Feeling consults our organism for its personal, heart-felt truth.

Head and Heart

Both Thinking and Feeling are powerhouse psychological functions. The Thinking function, as our rational intellect, processes the objective, factual world through organizing and analyzing information, solving problems and making decisions logically. The Feeling function is our personal, subjective processing of our experience, especially our relationships and interactions with others, our ability to value and care and to know by feeling it what is good and life-enhancing for us and make choices accordingly.

We have both Thinking and Feeling functions built into our psychology, giving us tremendous psychological breadth, capacity and protection. We have both of these vital aspects of life covered, as it were. Our Thinking function relates us to the order and form that structure reality. Our Feeling function relates us to life's constantly changing human landscape, inner and outer, and to the cycles and processes of nature of which we are a part.

As each realm is highly complex and very different in character, however, our psychology naturally selects one way of approaching and processing experience. We develop it and turn to it most often for understanding and direction. We are hard-wired, as it were, to approach the demands of life by thinking them through or responding to them personally, viscerally. All Thinking processors have Feeling functions and all Feeling processors have Thinking functions, and we all have access to both. But as we try to comprehend our life and our world day to day, we feel most competent, reliable and at home when we are using our main processing function of either Thinking or Feeling.

Doing It Our Way: Thinking and Feeling Processors

An editor of a publishing house named Simon walked into a restaurant with his lunch guest, an author named Eric. While continuing their discussion, Simon checked his watch to make sure they were on time for his reservations. Looking around the restaurant, he noted there were almost no empty tables, confirming the restaurant's popularity reported in the restaurant reviews. He knew he was going to try the strip steak that was consistently recommended. Simon was processing the scene using his Thinking function.

Eric, Simon's author and lunch guest, was a Feeling processor. Looking around the restaurant, he immediately liked the place and felt comfortable there. The people were enjoying themselves and the food looked really good. The wait staff seemed happy and were serving people in a professional yet personal way. He glanced around to see if anyone he knew was there. This restaurant was definitely better than the last one his editor had taken him to, and he was grateful and happy to be there. Eric was processing with his Feeling function.

IQ and EQ

Our processing functions are the rod-and-piston workings of our psychological intelligence. Thinking distinguishes whether what we see is consistent or inconsistent with a set of facts. It defines, categorizes, compares, diagnoses a problem and logically, step by step, builds an explanation, a solution or a decision. Feeling relates to people and situations "with one's whole person." It is the working of instinct that responds in personal, visceral evaluations and judgments that convey that something or someone is good or bad for us, pleasurable or displeasing, frightening or safe, harmonious or out of sync.

Intelligence is frequently equated with processing by the Thinking function and IQ is assumed to relate to someone's ability to learn, organize and present facts and information in a clear, logical, efficient way. Many people, however, process experience first and foremost with their Feeling functions. In his pioneering book *Emotional Intelligence*, psychologist Daniel Goleman called this way of processing "EQ." Goleman points out that success in life often comes from the ability to respond and relate sympathetically in the personal and interpersonal realms.

We can readily distinguish between Thinking and Feeling in ourselves and in others simply by watching and listening. Thinking processors tend toward a reasoned, considered approach to life situations, while Feeling processors tend to experience life viscerally and emotionally "all the way," as Feeling processor Frank Sinatra famously sang. The Thinking function aims for clarity, objectivity, order and logical consistency. On the other hand, when processing using Feeling, one "feels strongly about" someone or something, perhaps without an identifiable reason.

Feeling processors value, love and appreciate, as well as reject and find worthless, at times passionately. A Feeling processor discriminates by liking and disliking and ranking as to "better" or "worse," "more important" "less important" according to a hierarchy of values. Feeling processors particularly value quality and also what is "real." "Authentic" and "genuine" are good, "false" or "inauthentic" is suspect. When their Feeling function rejects, Feeling processors experience a physical feeling of aversion.

Meanwhile, Thinking processors are "thinking about it." Examining the facts from their reading, experience, training, study, tradition, the "tried and true," they are working out in their minds what is reasonable, logical and valid for them. They often hold to a philosophical or ethical "honor code" of rules to live by, which they consult intellectually in making decisions and taking action. In this world-view, concepts such as fairness and justice are more than abstract intellectual ideas, they are living principles in their minds that guide and motivate them.

Book Smarts and Street Smarts

How was the book or the film? A Thinking processor and a Feeling processor will give very different answers. A Thinking processor wants an ingenious, logical plot with no loose ends and on an interesting subject. In contrast, a Feeling processor wants the characters to be real, the story to be true to life and the director to be knowing.

How was the trip to France? The Thinking processor might describe it in terms not of "how" it was, but rather "what" it was: "We got to all the places on our list," the Thinking processor might say. "The first day, we did the Louvre. That night we went to the Left Bank for dinner at a restaurant with a Michelin rating of two stars. The second day, we did the Musée d'Orsay in the morning and the Rodin Museum in the afternoon. Our second night, we took a dinner cruise on the Seine..." For the Feeling processor, *how* means *how good* or *how bad*. "It was just *great*," he might say, beaming. "We had a *fabulous* time. Jet lag was not fun. But we loved Paris. The food was wonderful. Everyone was really nice and helpful to us..."

Thinking and Feeling processors make decisions and choices in their own distinctive ways that work for them. Thinking processors tend to seek facts and specifications to factor in about a product; Feeling processors may like to read the user comments. Thinking processors consult or create a template in their minds. They determine the next step to take and come to a conclusion based on logical consideration of the facts and information. In contrast, Feeling processors proceed on the basis of personal preference and value judgments; they can, often quickly, evaluate everything in their world by feeling its relative importance, genuineness and worth—a Feeling processor's gut-logic.

In finding solutions or setting priorities, Thinking solves, Feeling resolves. Thinking processors seek the known facts and figure out each next step. Feeling processors consult their own inner truth and seek to resolve any conflicting feelings. Thinking processors like to argue to help themselves refine their intellectual discriminations. They are open to discussing and arguing ideas, even strongly, then breaking for a friendly lunch. A Feeling processor would get indigestion. For Feeling processors, arguing may feel too much like disharmony. When a Feeling processor says something, it comes from his or her most personal core. Though they register protest when they feel something is wrong, there can be no arguing about feelings.

Thinking or Feeling Processor?

From people with Thinking as their main processing function, you can expect step-by-step proposals, detailed plans and analyses, well-reasoned, factual presentations and clear explanations. Meanwhile, Feeling processors reveal themselves in enthusiastic or emotional self-expression, in conveying interpersonal empathy, in the ability (in the extraverts) to "work a crowd" and easily make an intimate connection or otherwise relate in a personal way to people.

To help distinguish between a Thinking and a Feeling processor, we may observe communication styles. Consistent with where they are processing experience, people generally literally use their heads or their whole bodies. Thinking processors string more words together and cite more factual details on a subject, for instance, than Feeling processors, whose body language is often eloquent. Feeling processors will communicate expressively with non-verbal sounds, facial expressions, hand and arm gestures, and other forms of body language, often as much as words. Note how their gestures indicate feeling responses, such as clutching their throats, holding their hearts or stomachs, stretching out their arms as if to embrace the whole world or dancing in place.

Managing Complexity and Leading Change

Natural abilities in the realms of Thinking and Feeling processing have caught the attention of keen observers of organizational behavior. Harvard Business School professor John Kotter distinguishes between management, the realm of the Thinking processor, and leadership, where the Feeling processor can thrive. According to Kotter, both management and leadership serve a vital purpose in a complex and volatile business environment. "Management is about coping with the complexity of a large organization," he wrote in the *Harvard Business Review*. [4] "Without good management, complex enterprises tend to become chaotic in ways that threaten their very existence. Good management brings a degree of order and consistency to key dimensions like the quality and profitability of products… Complexity is managed by planning, analyzing and budgeting; organizing and staffing; and controlling, monitoring and problem-solving." In short, by Thinking processing. No surprise that Thinking processors excel in management.

"Leadership, by contrast," Kotter continues, "is about coping with change...Major changes are more and more necessary to survive and compete effectively in this new environment. More change always demands more leadership." Change is led in large part "by aligning people to create coalitions committed to accomplishing the vision; and motivating and inspiring these people to persevere, despite obstacles, by appealing to basic but often untapped human needs, values and emotions." These are talents that come naturally to many Feeling processors. It is clear to Kotter, however, that, for a number of reasons, "Most U.S. corporations today are over-managed and under-led." [5]

More About Thinking Processors

Jung called our intellect "directed thinking." Thinking processors direct their thinking toward order, structure and organization, which is how the intellect works. While everyone has a Thinking function, Thinking processors use it as their psychological workhorse. "I think in outline form," a Thinking-processor teacher says. Thinking processors' minds are objective, methodical and logical. They sift through factual information and organize it. They make lists. They keep careful calendars — one Thinking processor maintains two, one for her children's schedule and one for her own. They seek the next step in a process, and they follow up to make sure the next step is taking place.

In general, Thinking processors are recognizable for their logical clarity of mind and orderly "thinking things through." They often have a gift for words and an interest in discussion. Thinking function gives them a certain objectivity, an ability to compartmentalize, a tendency to "stand back" from feelings and analyze situations rationally.

Having a high-ranking Thinking function is a great boon in school, as well as in innumerable professions. Education hones and encourages intellectual abilities. The Thinking function helps organize research papers and, later, articles and memos and create logically persuasive, substantive presentations. There is an abundance of satisfying work that requires a logical, analytical, efficient mind. Thinking processors enjoy success in business management and finance, the law, publishing, journalism, engineering, banking, academia and education at all levels, advertising, medicine, science, computer technology, banking, insurance, accounting, all of which require significant amounts of Thinking processing every day.

While a Feeling processor can give the timely rousing speech to rally the troops, the person who discourses fluently and substantively on a subject is usually a Thinking processor. The man or woman doing the daily crossword puzzle is likely to be a Thinking processor (or a Feeling processor purposefully exercising his or her Thinking function).

Using their strong Thinking functions, Thinking processors have *interests*. They read books and newspapers, keep many specialty magazines in business and pore over the Internet researching subjects from purchases and medical decisions to genealogy. Many jazz lovers are Thinking processors, who appreciate its "cool" sound and underlying musical structure. Thinking processors are frequently found around bridge tables and scrabble boards. Baseball statisticians are likely to be Thinking processors.

"And What Do You Do?"

In social interaction, a Thinking processor often connects with people through facts. For the sake of clarity and order, Thinking processors think of people according to helpful categories, such as their company affiliation, college class, home state or their place on the family tree. A person's title or field of expertise helps them identify the person. Entering a gathering, Thinking processors will think of pertinent subjects to discuss: "There's George, he will know about what happened at last night's Yankees game." "There's Emily, who has been doing research on solar energy technology." "Robert is on the town council, I can ask him about the rezoning initiative."

In their relationship style, they may make an effort to be reasonable and objective, but being a Thinking processor does not mean he or she does not feel. Indeed, Feeling is alive and well as the person's Third or Fourth function with a special role in their lives, as we shall see in Chapters 7 and 9. But for the most part, Thinking processors tend to keep at a neutral distance and to engage with the facts of the situation, as their intellects step up to the plate to make sense of what is happening. Not that they aren't warm and loving, not that they cannot hold impassioned views. But a Thinking processor's mind will usually shine through first and most consistently as he or she responds to other people and to the world.

More About Feeling Processors

The Feeling function works in the visceral realm of instinct, which is far more sophisticated than most people realize. The Feeling function is how our psychology processes the wisdom of eons of human evolution.

Everyone has emotions, but the Feeling function processes them psychologically as information and can do so in refined detail. Feeling processors use their feeling responses to evaluate and understand nearly everything and everyone in their lives in a flow of subjective evaluations. "I like that t-shirt." "I don't like abstract art." "I loved Thailand." "I hate that new color for cars." "I like that idea!" "I like him!"

Feeling processors attend to the language spoken by their biochemistry in response to people and situations. A Feeling processor feels happy, angry, upset, safe, content, disturbed and other feeling states, and *knows* it. Their bodies tell them when a person, situation, behavior or idea is right or wrong for them, real or fake, safe or dangerous. They get an often-instantaneous physical reaction — their stomachs jump, their hearts leap, their throats constrict, their jaws and fists clench, their cheeks heat up.

Feeling processors know what they know directly. Like the Feeling processor responding to candle fumes at the beginning of the chapter, Feeling processors don't need scientific studies to know with an instinctive certainty what is true and real for them, just as surely as a Thinking processor knows intellectually that a fact is factually correct if it's in the *Encyclopedia Britannica*.

Just as Thinking processors follow a train of thought, Feeling processors experience a "train of feelings"—comfort or alarm, attraction or aversion, being on-guard or relaxed and confident, often one after the other. Remembering and sharing a lot of precise factual details about a subject is not as important to them as the on-going process of feeling how they are responding to it, as well as to the person discussing it. A succession of feelings guides them through circumstances to their destination: resolution, harmony and feeling good about themselves, others or the situation. While Thinking processors assess circumstances with mental objectivity, Feeling processors take everything personally, indeed they must do so. The work of the Feeling function in all of us is to *relate* to our world and to discern how much we *value* the people and things in it—totally subjective tasks.

Feeling immediately understands Feeling, just as logic communicates automatically between Thinking types. Two Feeling processors enter a paradise of relatedness, without realizing how special this is.

Feeling is psychological processing beyond words, though poets often try. As for a Feeling processor in the flesh, we can recognize one responding with a natural warmth of enthusiasm, empathy and appreciation, or evident distress. Stanley Kowalsky's anguished cry for his wife, "Stella!" in Tennessee Williams' *A Streetcar Named Desire* is an eruption of pure Feeling, but the subtlety and range of the Feeling process are visible in many performances, for instance, by actors Sean Penn, Al Pacino or Meryl Streep or maybe by one of your own siblings, children, parents or friends. With Feeling processors, one knows what and whom they care about. To be valued by a Feeling processor, overtly or silently, is a life-enhancing experience.

Person to Person

The Feeling function is in its full glory in the realm of human relationships. Feeling is communicated as if through an energy field between people. Even the most introverted Feeling processor constantly "feels" the presence of others, and they feel him or her. Feeling processors attend both to how they are feeling and to how others are feeling—all-important information for them in any situation. How someone else might respond matters and affects their choices, as in, "Jennifer will feel annoyed if I call her back so soon to see if she got my memo," or "William will feel bad if I ask his friend Jason to the party and not him."

While schooling tends to train our Thinking function officially, the Feeling function is educated most often unofficially, outside of class. As students, however, Feeling processors learn best when they have a personal relationship with a teacher or professor, rather than being lectured to from afar about remote abstractions. All their lives, information comes to them through personal encounters. They even find it hard to write an article, paper or memo, paint a picture or work on a project or at a job they do not *like*.

Feeling on the Job

Feeling processors are valued for their "people skills," as well as their palpable engagement with life. As leaders and mentors, they can be effective, popular, even downright charismatic, motivating their staffs to excel and work together harmoniously. Feeling processors enjoy success in sales and marketing, human resources, organizational consulting, executive search, counseling and human services, and the world of hospitality, as well as in music, film and other creative fields.

For Feeling processors, though, success is often hard won. Indeed Feeling processors can feel at a disadvantage. Mastering academic work can be a struggle, as can navigating a culture which values and rewards logical reasoning, organizational skills, dispassionate analysis and efficiency. There is no question that in many contemporary environments, allowing the Feeling function to do its work presents challenges for anyone trying to honor Feeling values.

Type Clash: Thinking and Feeling Processors

We tend to expect others to understand circumstances and respond in the same way we do, that is, to use the same processing function. They may not. Recognizing the Thinking processors and

Feeling processors among our friends, spouses, siblings, lovers, parents, neighbors, colleagues, bosses, clients, customers, and anyone we encounter is extremely useful in relating with skill and tact, as well as in managing our expectations of others.

From a safe distance, at least, different processors do admire one another. A Feeling processor may look with awe at a Thinking processor's cool efficiency and clear analysis of a stack of information, while the Thinking processor gazes with amazement at the Feeling processor's passion, quick gut-level personal assessments and empathic connections with people. Thinking processors can gaze admiringly at a Feeling processor's ease and confidence "working a room," while Feeling processors are impressed as Thinking processors speak up with such assurance in meetings or in class and so readily "put their thoughts together."

With Thinking and Feeling processors, however, opposites do not always attract. With one person processing by reason and the other by visceral instinct, with one person following a train of thought and the other a flow of feelings, with one's point of view being naturally objective and fact-based and the other's being subjective and personal, Thinking and Feeling processors all too often find one another incomprehensible, annoying or frustrating—until they understand they are using different psychological processing functions.

Without realizing why, opposite types of processors can find themselves in a struggle. A Feeling processor who "lets it all hang out" may be carefully avoided by a Thinking processor or thought to lack boundaries or even intelligence. Meanwhile, a Feeling processor is left feeling frustrated, unmet, exasperated, rejected or cut off by a Thinking processor's attempts to be rational. Thinking processors have worked out their position step by step, getting supporting facts and expert opinion, so they are convinced they have a lock on reality. Meanwhile, Feeling processors believe they are right because they feel it so powerfully. "My sister always leaps to a strong feeling that for me is but an end point of a whole logical process," a Thinking processor laments. Meanwhile, the Feeling-processor sister is suffering great distress over their disagreement and is impatient for harmony to be restored. The Thinking processor wants clarity in expressing her position as an important step toward agreement; the Feeling processor doesn't want objective analysis, but rather mutual respect and valuing and the resumption of "good feelings" between them. The highest priority for one is the lowest for the other. With such different ways of processing, communicating and understanding situations, it is not surprising that the result too often is irritation, impatience, criticism, even long-standing anguish and conflict. It can take understanding, psychological sophistication and good will to bridge this typological gap.

Acknowledging the natural importance of Thinking and Feeling processing in different people's psychological life puts such struggles in a larger perspective. Thinking and Feeling may be different ways of processing, but both, when allowed to work as they are meant to do, arrive at truths in their distinctive and vital realms of logical clarity and interpersonal values. We all have access to both Thinking and Feeling processing at different times. Ideally, if both people allow one another to process as he or she must, the resolution can reflect a truth greater than they could know alone.

We are All "Right"

The purpose of psychological knowledge is to understand ourselves and one another, so we can make choices and decisions, express ourselves and act beneficially. We realize that, "I need to do it this way, and there is also another way." This "other" way often appears very different. But listening to one another, we can contribute the results both of what we perceive and of our own inner psychological process as information, as "intelligence," whether from the logic of intellect or from the certainty of feelings. This requires us to honor one another's psychological make-up, mystery that it may be. With this understanding attitude, conflicts can be defused, even avoided, and our own lives can be lived more fully and creatively.

When as Sensation and Intuition perceivers and Thinking and Feeling processors, we come to an understanding based on mutual acceptance and appreciation of our very different ways of experiencing life, it is a great and enriching achievement for us all.

— 4 —

Our Function Order

Hierarchy

IDENTIFYING OUR MAIN processing and perceiving functions hints at the importance of the underlying hierarchy of the four functions in each person's psychology. With our four functions, we have the ability to use our intellect (Thinking), evaluate and respond personally (Feeling), apprehend physical conditions and sensations (Sensation) and perceive possibilities and meaning (Intuition). However, our individual psychology orders these functions in a powerful personal hierarchy of priority that focuses our attention and directs our understanding and self-expression. We have a First Function, a Second Function, a Third Function and a Fourth Function, capitalized here because the position of each significantly shapes our experience with this function, as well as our relationship with the realm of life it covers.

The underlying factors that determine our First Function and the rest of our personal hierarchy have yet to be identified by science, but we can readily observe what our First, Second, Third and

Fourth Functions are, as well as the unique ways these particular functions work within us. There is an "economy of the psyche," Jung observed[1] With this awareness, we can encourage and enhance our own natural abilities. We can also learn to recognize in the people around us key aspects of their function order hierarchy, so we can relate to them with more sensitivity and understanding.

Our personal function order is not random; we already know that our first two functions include our main processing and perceiving functions. How all four functions are arranged in us has purpose and meaning for how our psychology works. Our First, Second, Third and Fourth functions, whether they may be Thinking, Feeling, Sensation, or Intuition, serve us in distinctive ways. They comprise an "inner technology" that goes on within us all the time. This inner technology tailors our abilities, guides our perceptions and shapes our personalities.

Knowledge of these inner dynamics helps us to live with greater awareness, skill and overall wellbeing, both within ourselves and in our relationships with others. As we get to know what each function does for us and how it works in us, we can identify that function in our own personal hierarchy. Furthermore, we can begin to discern who else seems to have the function prominently (or not) in their psychological hierarchy.

The Leader, the Partner/Mediator, the Standby and the Mysterious Fourth Function

Whether it is Thinking, Feeling, Sensation or Intuition, our First Function leads our psychological activities and responses. We begin to use our First Function very early and continue to refine, develop and rely on it throughout our life. We greet each new experience with it, and we tend to thrive in its realm. We often identify with it; it characterizes and describes "me," so much so that we may be barely aware that we are exceptionally "good" at it.

Our Second Function works right alongside our First Function as its able partner always ready to assist. As we saw in Chapter 3, if our First Function is a processing function, our Second Function is our main perceiving function. If our First Function is a perceiving function, our Second Function is our main processing function. As we shall see, our Second Function also acts as a mediator and go-between with our enigmatic and often troublesome Fourth Function.

Third in our hierarchy is our standby Third Function, a function waiting in the wings, which we can call on when it is needed. It is the other perceiving or processing function similar in psychological task to our Second Function.

Finally, situated last but definitely not least in our psychological hierarchy is our Fourth Function. This is the function "opposite" our First Function. In order to become an expert in the ways of our primary function, we most often keep its opposite switched off, though with significant consequences. Whatever function we use as our First Function, its opposite is positioned farthest away in our hierarchy as our Fourth Function. This descending order of psychological priority keeps opposite functions from interfering with one another, so we can access each one efficiently.

First		Fourth
Thinking		Feeling
Feeling	Its opposite is	Thinking
Sensation		Intuition
Intuition		Sensation

Our First Function and Fourth Function are the most important and influential set of inner opposites. While we rely on our First Function most often, we access our Fourth Function least frequently of all our functions. It remains the least familiar to us and, significantly, seems to be the least under our conscious control.

If our First Function is Intuition, for example, our Fourth Function is the opposite perceiving function of Sensation. In this case, the Second and Third Functions—Jung called them "auxiliary functions"—will be our two processing functions of Thinking and Feeling, with one being our main and preferred processing function, and the other being available to us but turned to less often. Here's how this hierarchy looks:

First	Second	Third	Fourth
Intuition	Thinking	Feeling	Sensation
or			
Intuition	Feeling	Thinking	Sensation

Similarly, if our First Function is Sensation, our Fourth Function is the opposite perceiving function of Intuition, with our two auxiliary functions of Feeling and Thinking as Second or Third.

First	Second	Third	Fourth
Sensation	Thinking	Feeling	Intuition
or			
Sensation	Feeling	Thinking	Intuition

If our First Function is Thinking, our Fourth Function will be Feeling. Our Second and Third Functions will be the two perceiving functions of Sensation and Intuition, with one as our main perceiving function.

First	Second	Third	Fourth
Thinking	Sensation	Intuition	Feeling
or			
Thinking	Intuition	Sensation	Feeling

If our First Function is Feeling, our Fourth Function is Thinking. Second and Third once again will be our two auxiliary perceiving functions.

First	Second	Third	Fourth
Feeling	Intuition	Sensation	Thinking
or			
Feeling	Sensation	Intuition	Thinking

The function order hierarchies shown here actually describe the various psychological "types." For example, an Intuitive-Thinking type has Intuition as his or her First Function, Thinking as his or her Second Function, the other processing function of Feeling as his or her Third Function, and Thinking's opposite function, Feeling, as his or her Fourth Function. This psychological hierarchy is Intuition-Thinking-Feeling-Sensation. In another example, a Sensation-Feeling "type" has a hierarchy of Sensation (First Function)-Feeling (Second Function)-Thinking (Third Function)-Intuition (Fourth

Function). Seen in this way, a person's typology offers an informative picture of how easily or often he or she uses each function and therefore experiences and interacts with the world.

Furthermore, every type can be extraverted or introverted, creating 16 possible combinations of function order hierarchies. Our inner technology here takes on a special refinement, in that if we tend to be extraverted, our First Function is extraverted, but as our hierarchy moves toward its opposite Fourth Function, it tends to become more introverted in orientation. If we are introverted, in our First Function we tend to be introverted, but our Fourth Function tends to be extraverted in its—that is, our—approach toward its realm.

Fine-tuning Our Psychological Knowledge

Situated in our function order hierarchy, the four functions of Thinking, Feeling, Sensation and Intuition work within us rather like four broadcast channels. One channel is on all the time — our First Function. It is the psychological activity we do first and most often, our most natural way of responding to what is going on around and inside us. A second channel is on in the background—our Second Function. We can tune it in and bring it to the fore whenever we want to use it.

The third channel, our Third Function, has a weaker signal, as if broadcasting from farther away in our awareness. We can tune it in, but it tends to fade in and out. The Third Function can be available when needed, but we tend to refer to it less often.

The fourth channel—our Fourth Function—is like a strong signal broadcasting from another city that comes in erratically, like a split signal on a radio. It is transmitting all the time, but we can't always pick it up at will. This remoteness is psychologically necessary, as the Fourth Function's broadcast would completely jam our First Function's operations. Under certain conditions, however, the Fourth Function suddenly breaks through and takes over our entire psychological circuitry. These Fourth-Function breakthroughs give us some of our most disconcerting experiences, including moments of annoyance or distress, but also of revelation and even genius.

That people are not operating on the same channel or frequency is often evident. Tuning into which functions are being used helps us better understand ourselves and relate more skillfully to the people around us.

Nature's Psychological Endowment

This inner hierarchy of functions reflects the natural order of our psychological preferences and affinities. We are naturally equipped to invest more time and energy doing certain things and to work in more limited ways in others. We have all four functions, but as we respond to the demands of each moment, a stream of psychological energy is distributed according to our typological hierarchy. As we know from experience, we pick and choose, psychologically. We do not have the same interest in every aspect of life at every moment; we respond, prioritize, engage and disengage. The ordering of our four functions plays a significant role in these priorities.

In our First Function, we have access to a lively and constant stream of psychological energy flowing to it; in our Second Function, we have a goodly amount of energy available; our Third has a limited but quite usable amount; and the Fourth Function receives but a trickle of psychic energy that can be used, but sparingly and with care. In our first two functions, we experience a natural ease and competence. In our Third and Fourth Function realms, we may experience more struggle and fatigue. In fact, we often instinctively turn to people who are more naturally inclined toward using our lower-positioned functions, just as others rely on us for our psychological specialties.

Like birth order in a family, the placement of each function—whether it comes First, Second, Third or Fourth—determines many aspects of our lives. Indeed, our function order hierarchy tells volumes about who we are and what we can expect and demand of ourselves. Where a function is placed also influences our experience with its realm. If we have Thinking First or Second, for example, we are likely to have a lively and confident relationship with our intellect and an ability and inclination to reason logically and analyze objectively. We are at ease in situations in which Thinking is needed, such as when outlining a presentation or paper, organizing a project or work-flow schedule, categorizing information, or making logical decisions. If we have Thinking in Third or Fourth place in our psychology, we may feel less confident and at home when called on to organize and present factual information or to participate in debates and discussions. We are able to do these things, even commendably when we need to, but we must give them time, special effort and concentration.

Our First and Second Functions together, being our main functions to process and perceive our life circumstances, give us our core psychological strength and endurance. They also encompass the vast terrain in life in which we can roam with the most success, enjoyment, skill and psychological comfort. Our main perceiving and processing functions are where we know, deep down, we are really at our best. Whether we might be a Thinking-Sensation type, a Feeling-Intuitive type, an Intuitive-Thinking type and so forth, our "type" reflects the importance to us of our first two functions; it offers a helpful shorthand for the natural way our psychology works. Whatever our type may be, our function order hierarchy reveals the powerful and dynamic inner workings underlying our experience as an intelligent and alive human being.

Our Fearless Leader: More About The First Function

Our First Function is our primary psychological function. Jung called it the "governing principle" of our personalities, the function that "predominates, in both strength and development" [2] and "the conscious function of which the individual makes principal use." [3] Whatever is happening in our lives, our First Function is our main, on-going response and psychological activity. Whether it is Sensation, Intuition, Thinking or Feeling, it is what we do automatically and most readily. In terms of typology, one is a Thinking type, an Intuitive type, a Feeling type or a Sensation type; what the terminology means is that this is the function you use the most. "It does no good to think of what 'matters' most when trying to discover one's type," psychologist Marie-Louise von Franz writes in *Jung's Typology*, "rather ask: "What do I habitually *do* most?" [4]

Not only is our First Function what we do most, it is usually what is most evident about us to other people. Jack is "always so well informed," (Thinking), Susan is "so insightful," (Intuition), Sean is "so great with people,"' (Feeling) Sara always dresses with such style (Sensation).

Our First Function may be a processing function or a perceiving function. We are, so to speak, First-Function processors or First-Function perceivers; that is to say, we tend to spend more of our time in the psychological activity of processing or of perceiving. If we have Thinking first, we are most often thinking, perhaps about an idea we have had, something we have read or witnessed or a fact we have learned. Our second-place perceiving function may provide some observations and perceptions, but our main activity and interest are in cogitating, organizing our thoughts, coming to conclusions, figuring out "what is the point?"—in other words, in *thinking*. If we have Feeling as our First Function, our main psychological experience is "feeling our way" through our day, responding to the people we meet and the situations we are in. We will take in perceptions, whether Sensation details or Intuitive "hits," but only secondarily. On the other hand, First-Function perceivers, people whose First Function is Intuition or Sensation, spend more time taking in the details of their environment or inner landscape; they process only when they have perceived enough and sufficiently to their satisfaction.

Our circumstances can encourage the use of certain functions—Thinking, for example, growing up in a family of philosophers or Sensation in a family of athletes or gourmet cooks. Individuals may try to adapt by developing a function that is particularly rewarded or required. If it is advantageous for us, we can overuse our Second Function or even our Third, creating what psychologists call a "distorted type." Rewarded or not, however, our First Function will always feel most like home to us psychologically, and we will want and need to use it more often than any other. Looking at our lives, we usually find that we gravitate toward environments, no matter how "unofficial," that encourage us to use and develop our First Function, that is, that allow us to be our true selves, whether it be the home of a relative or neighbor, a college, a workplace or a country halfway around the world.

The Perfect Partner: The Second Function

If the First Function is the ship that carries us though the variable waters of our life, the Second Function is the rudder. If our

First Function is a processing function, our Second is a perceiving function, which looks at the world outside or inside ourselves and feeds us information to be processed. If our First Function is a perceiving function, our Second Function helps us process and make sense of the information we take in. As Jung wrote, importantly, "Only those functions can appear as auxiliary whose nature is not opposed to the dominant function. The secondary function is always one whose nature is different from, though not antagonistic to, the primary function." [5]

If our First Function is "me," our Second Function is like our "best friend," close, familiar, loyal and always there for us. Our Second Function develops during early childhood to help enrich our capabilities and personalities. We can become very good at this auxiliary function in our personalities, so good in fact that it can be almost equal to our First. The Second Function feels like second nature to us and is a great gift, serving us with almost as much competency and ability as our First Function. We can develop, educate and train it. We can call it up and use it at a moment's notice. While our primary function rushes to the forefront of our consciousness, our Second Function is there one step behind to guide it, inform it, assist it, moderate it and set its style.

A Thinking-*Sensation* type, for example, enlarges his or her thought processes by accumulating physical and sensory experience. A Thinking-*Intuitive* type uses insights, perceived connections and imagined possibilities from Intuition in order to refine his or her Thinking process, to speculate and to "figure out" what is true.

While our First Function leads our psychological priorities, our Second Function is there to aid but not compete, looking up to our First, rather as a younger brother or sister might. We often admire people who have our Second Function as their First, as a younger sibling admires a more competent and confident older one.

Appearing slightly "smaller and weaker," the Second Function is experienced less clearly or distinctly than a First Function. Someone with Feeling second, for instance, is not as aware of what exactly he or she is feeling as someone with First-Function Feeling (that is, a Feeling type), whose Feeling process dominates more vividly. Someone with Sensation second would perceive their environment or physical sensations in less detail than someone with a First Function of Sensation (that is, a Sensation type).

As an auxiliary Second or Third Function, Thinking can be a special case. Given the constant demands on it, the Thinking function can often be overworked—it could be called the "over-function"—and may even come to dominate. As an auxiliary function, Thinking may override a First-Function Intuitive's visionary hunches, for instance, by too quickly demanding rational proof, corroboration by experts and authorities or legitimacy by conforming to conventional rules and opinion. Thinking may derail a Sensation type's creative experiments by doubting that they "make sense" or insisting on following what has been done before. These First-Function perceivers—Sensation and Intuition "types"— must make sure they are being true to their first psychological priority of scanning for new details, possibilities and directions, while using Thinking processing only enough to stay generally on track.

Our Standby: The Third Function

Our Third Function is the "other" perceiving or processing function opposite our Second Function. If our Second function is Thinking, our Third is Feeling, and vice versa. If our Second Function is

Sensation, our Third will be the other perceiving function of Intuition, and vice versa. This gives us fairly easy access to the "other" way of perceiving or processing when we need it.

The Third Function is like our psychology's ring finger. It can be trained and strengthened for use, as pianists do their ring fingers, and it can enrich and adorn our personalities similarly to the wearing of a ring, but it is not as sturdy and reliable as our first two psychological digits. A psychologist with Third-Function Sensation, for example, learned to do intricate wood inlay on harpsichords and to raise exotic aquatic flowers in a home-built pool, all with his "weaker" third-placed Sensation function. But for his day-to-day life, he chose to live in Intuition-friendly simplicity in a three-room apartment and eat simple vegetarian meals. A Thinking-Intuitive named Barbara, who has Third-Function Sensation, graduated from a top medical school, but she admits that what fascinates her most about practicing medicine is taking patients personal histories and doing diagnoses, both of which use her first two functions of Thinking and Intuition.

Like a planet with a more distant orbit, our Third Function is rather remote from our psychic center, and less of our psychic energy is available for its use. It takes more effort to do Third Function tasks. In our Third Function, we do not enjoy the same ease, confidence and sense of mastery that we experience with our first two functions. Its realm generally gets less of our attention, and because we use it less often, it remains less familiar.

Our Third Function may require that we make a special effort to turn our attention towards it. An Intuitive-Thinking type, whose Third Function was Feeling, for instance, was having a hard time not just conceptualizing, but actually experiencing what she was feeling. Asked about her weekend, after several moments of gentle concentration, she suddenly experienced a surge of feelings. "I had the BEST weekend with my parents and my sister and brother!" she said, as if landing upon a rare treasure. It took a little while to "call it up," but there was her Third-Function Feeling in all its richness and genuineness. She now knew her Feeling Function was very much there in her, as well as how and what it "feels like" to access it.

Our Third Function is not meant to be all-day-every-day function. After a while using our Third Function, we tend to become inattentive and we can tire easily. About her Third-Function Thinking, a writer said, "After an hour or so of thinking, I start wanting to cut corners." Our Third Function is stalwart, but its limits need to be acknowledged and respected. When we want to use our Third Function, it is helpful to give ourselves time, take breaks and be rested, as we have less attention energy for doing activities in its realm.

Whether Thinking, Feeling, Sensation or Intuition, however, our standby Third Function can be just as capable as anyone else's when we use it intelligently. When we make the effort, we can surprise ourselves, and others, with the quality of the results. We could pull up Third-Function Thinking to fill out a long form or organize and write an article or paper, though we would tire doing these tasks eight hours a day. Someone can call on Third-Function Intuition to offer insightful counsel, speculate on the significance of an event or to try to understand why someone made a hostile remark, but would unlikely be drawn to counseling as a profession. Someone can play an instrument or cook dinner for friends with Third-Function Sensation, without desiring to be a physical trainer or chef.

We may have less psychological strength in our Third Function, but we can certainly have a good relationship with it. This means getting to know it, its capabilities and limitations, and treating it and ourselves with respect and kindness when we must use it. This goes for someone else trying to use his or her Third Function, as well. If we observe the difficulty he or she may be having with a task or the special concentration being exerted, we can relate to him or her with sensitivity and encouragement, and perhaps offer to help if appropriate. Our Third and Fourth Functions provide many opportunities for practicing the Golden Rule of "doing unto others as you would have them do unto you."

The Mysterious Fourth Function

Because of its special position remote from our primary psychological activity, our Fourth Function has its own special nature, role and influence. Our Fourth Function and the realm of life it covers can present some of our most persistent personal challenges, as well as some of our greatest experiences of rapture and growth.

With the Fourth Function, we get into what Jung called "depth psychology." Whether it is Sensation, Intuition, Thinking or Feeling, our Fourth Function, from the deepest regions of our psychology, exerts a powerful influence on our lives and on our relationships. Every human being has a Fourth Function. This psychological fact of life is one of Jung's most significant insights, and acknowledging and understanding the Fourth Function, our own and other people's, can change one's life and one's relationships in profound ways.

How this mysterious function works, and how we can work with it, will be discussed in more detail in Chapter 9, and guides to each particular "type's" Fourth Function are included in upcoming chapters. For now, we will take a brief look at the Fourth Function and its "mysterious stranger" role in our psychological hierarchy.

Wild Card

Our Fourth Function represents a gap in the encompassing circle of our personality.

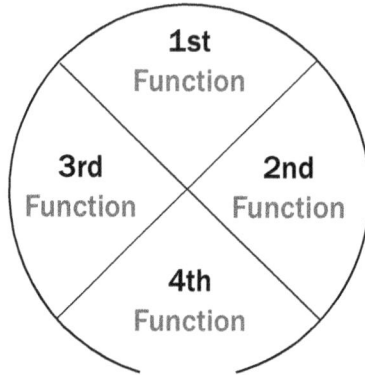

The Fourth Function is the area of our psychology most remote from our competent ego's reach. Our usual sense of authority, control and mastery do not readily extend to our Fourth Function and its domain. We often feel exposed, vulnerable and inadequate in our Fourth Function and lack the self-confidence built on the skill and success we have accumulated in our primary functions. We uncharacteristically resist or avoid Fourth Function tasks and activities. In our Fourth Function, we are just not "ourselves."

As we have said, our psychology must inhibit or switch off our Fourth Function, so that our First Function can do its job without confusion. Whether it is Thinking, Feeling, Sensation or Intuition, our Fourth Function often remains just out of sight as we live our normal daily lives. We do not "develop" our Fourth Function as we do our first three to varying degrees, nor do we access it easily, yet it is very much there in us and affects us, often to our consternation.

It can sometimes be easiest to identify a Fourth Function, our own or someone else's, as it tends to be the function that is quite obviously missing or causes a person exasperation and trouble. Examining our life to discern where we feel most stressed or at a loss may require some brave self-honesty, but recognizing our Fourth Function can be a revelation that can clear up considerable personal confusion.

From Ridiculous to Sublime and Back Again

A Thinking type watching a lover slam the door, a Feeling type being asked for an instant analysis of a change in company pricing policy, a Sensation type assigned to envision a five-year plan, an Intuitive standing in front of a big pile of laundry—each is face-to-face with his or her Fourth Function.

We often ignore or evade tasks in our Fourth Function realm, where we are not the competent sophisticate we normally experience ourselves to be. A Thinking type may avoid calling a friend going through a painful divorce, due to confusion in his or her responses in Fourth-Function Feeling. A Feeling type may procrastinate reading a legal agreement requiring Fourth-Function Thinking. An Intuitive may put off washing her car, which makes demands on her Fourth-Function Sensation. A Sensation type might take refuge in cleaning the kitchen to avoid participating in a soul-searching conversation going on in the living room in the immaterial realm of Intuition perception.

Little of our psychological energy seems to be available for accomplishing Fourth Function tasks and activities, which can frustrate, anger or exhaust us surprisingly quickly. Wherever we feel a persistent lack in our lives, wherever we find ourselves really struggling, our Fourth Function is often involved. We are uncharacteristically uncertain and vulnerable to fears and anxieties and easily influenced by the opinions of others. Jung said people are "touchy" in their Fourth Function. Most people feel a general oversensitivity to criticism in situations requiring their Fourth Function, and can get testy and defensive, even lash out. "I know when he in his Fourth Function," an observant wife says about her Thinking-type husband in the midst of a Feeling function crisis. "He never curses any other time." We must treat ourselves with care in our Fourth Function realm, and we must treat others with sensitivity and respectful caution when their Fourth Functions are activated.

The "Wow" Function

On the other hand, our Fourth Function can be the source of true creative inspiration "out of the blue." A notable example is Intuitive novelist Marcel Proust. A sudden experience of his Fourth Function of Sensation — the taste of a madeleine cookie — inspired him to write *In Search of Lost Time*, which transformed modern literature. Anyone can experience similarly powerful breakthroughs in his or her Fourth Function. In fact, Jung called the Fourth Function the "God function," because of the nature of the experiences that seem to come straight through to us in this realm.

People who have our Fourth Function as their First—our typological opposites—can dazzle us starry-eyed, or we may want to avoid them as incomprehensible, or both. Our Fourth Function is often activated when we fall madly in love, but also when we encounter a nemesis, someone who "drives us crazy." At times our Fourth Function seems infuriatingly, intractably, even perversely antagonistic. It seems to "act up." At other times it is magically alluring.

Though it may be difficult to use our Fourth Function, it seems to "use us" in remarkable ways. The Fourth Function provides the "je ne sais quoi" that is hard to identify. An introverted Intuitive professor created a meal for her suddenly ill husband from what was in their refrigerator that surpassed anything that a Sensation-type chef, her opposite, could create. A Feeling-type financial officer secluded himself for a week and wrote a memo distilling the essence of a complex agreement that had his Thinking-type colleagues shaking their heads in admiration. An extraverted Sensation type student experienced a life-changing flash of Fourth-Function Intuition, in which she envisioned her perfect career choice; with this goal, she found the right school, moved to a new city, made a group of life-long friends among her classmates, and on graduation (summa cum laude) found the perfect job. A Thinking-type food services manager, after receiving a special gift from a couple who had attended her wedding, wrote a thank-you note from out of her Fourth-Function Feeling that was so valuing of them that they broke down and wept when they read it.

We are not intended to become masters of this most remotely positioned function in our psychological hierarchy, but we can certainly develop a good working relationship with it and invoke its more magical qualities. It is best to treat activities and tasks involving our Fourth Function—and ourselves when faced with them—with understanding, respect, a sense of humor and a healthy dose of humility. Two general guidelines when having to use our Fourth Function (and our Third Function, as well): Ease into the task, and don't do it for very long.

To the Rescue: The Mediator Function

In one of its most crucial roles, our Second Function can serve as mediator with the remote realm of our Fourth Function, and in fact often does, without our realizing it. Our faraway Fourth Function can seem like a case of "I can't get there from here," like foreign and at times hostile terrain. Yet whatever our Fourth Function may be, it covers a significant aspect of our life and we must "go there" from time to time. Intuitive types must take adequate care of their bodies and physical environments, requiring Sensation. Meanwhile, Sensation types must find the meaning in important events and plan their life's direction, requiring their Fourth Function of Intuition. Feeling types must go to school, organize their bills and meet work and social schedules, all requiring their Fourth-Function Thinking. Thinking types must experience their deepest personal values and have rewarding intimate relationships with others, involving their Feeling function.

How do we "use" our Fourth Function as we must, when psychologically we can't seem to get to it directly? Via our Second or Mediator Function. As an auxiliary function, our Second Function is not functionally opposite our Fourth Function, so it can relate, even partner with it, as it does our First Function. Our Second Function is free to serve as the vital go-between, our emissary to the Fourth Function realm, easing the way, making the connection for us and providing a viable standpoint from which to approach essential Fourth Function activities. (Our auxiliary Third Function can also serve us as Mediator, if less readily.) For example:

*An Intuitive-*Thinking* type teacher and mother of three named Catherine must do considerable housework in the realm of her Fourth Function of Sensation. Using her Second-Function Mediator of Thinking, she keeps everything well organized, correcting early against the Fourth-Function chaos of clutter and organizes her week so that she cleans one room of her house a day.

*A Thinking-*Sensation* type named Rob uses his Mediator Function of Sensation in taking care of a beloved Labrador retriever.

Through his Mediator Sensation, Rob experiences the Fourth-Function Feeling depths of this precious relationship.

*A Sensation-*Feeling* type art student named Sandra had to write a paper on the meaning of an artist's paintings, a task requiring Fourth-Function Intuition. Using her Mediator function of Feeling, she picked an artist she loved and whose work moved her, thus helping her Fourth Function to get a glimpse into the artist's inspiration.

*A Sensation-*Thinking* type named Pamela, seeking insight into the ineffable realms of personal meaning and significance, approached her Fourth-Function Intuition via her Mediator Function of Thinking— by reading Karen Armstrong's erudite *The History of God*.

Our Mediator Function is invaluable in its ability to reach over and psychologically grasp hands with our Fourth Function. When we face an intense Fourth Function situation or know we need to do a Fourth Function task, we can turn to our Mediator to make the connection, at least for long enough to get the job done. We will discuss how the various Mediator Functions work in more detail in the chapters that follow.

Our Second Function takes on a new and important meaning for us when we understand this special role it plays. By approaching our Fourth Function via our Mediator Function, our attitude toward an often-troublesome realm of our life can change. Rather than dreading a Fourth Function task, we often find a pleasant surprise instead.

—— 5 ——

The Sensation Function

"The art of chocolate is the ultimate in self-expression. Like a work of art, each confection serves as a tiny canvas. Perfection is achieved when each flavor takes its rightful turn at the forefront, offering delightful combinations the way an artist depicts natural shades of color."

— Michael Recchiuti, San Francisco confectioner

SAN FRANCISCO, a feast for the eye and palate, is an ideal place to begin a discussion of the Sensation function. Known for its appealing and colorful architecture, breathtaking vistas, ocean beaches and parks and restaurants serving forth a renowned cuisine of fresh ingredients, the city resonates with that part of our psychology that apprehends the sensuous.

Our Sensation function connects us to what is around us via our five senses, as well as through our body's own awareness of what it is experiencing. Sensation is the most "natural" of the four functions in that it has the closest, most intimate relationship to the physical aspects of life, our bodies, nature and all that we see, hear, touch, smell and taste.

Through our Sensation function, we relate to ourselves as living, physical beings in a physical, material world. Thanks to Sensation's continuously stimulating and informative experiences, we are able to perceive our physical existence and communicate directly, respect-fully and confidently with *matter*.

Enjoying a Sensation moment, a Sensation type passes by a bunch of basil on a kitchen counter, dips her hands into the leaves and lifts her palms to her nose as she saunters on. Sensation types seem to bless the material world, as they touch every leaf, fabric, feather, chair, or take note of every sound or fragrance with the magic wand of their attention. Connoisseur-ship is not an affectation for Sensation types, but a birthright. They enjoy their Sensation function, refine it and contribute with it, as well as offer Sensation skills and pleasures to the rest of us.

Our Sensation function, wherever it may be in our psycholog-ical hierarchy, perceives the practical facts and characteristics of objects, bodies and other features of concrete reality. "Sensation is the psychological function that mediates the perception of a physical stimulus," Jung wrote in *Psychological Types* [1] With our Sensation function, sensory impressions are perceived, registered and accepted without judgment or analysis. Sensation simply notices what is there and often indicates something productive or beautiful to do with it.

When gaslight joined candlelight in Victorian homes, the Sen-sation function cut intricate patterns in glass dishes and bowls that sparkled on tables and in beveled-glass cabinets. Our Sensation functions continually allow us to make changes in our environment and to combine things in new ways to aid and please us and to get things done. It gives us a pleasing and viable environment in which to live, tools and machines that work smoothly and well. Our Sensation function takes care of our physical well-being and tends to nature's needs. Indeed, our Sensation function gives us a sense of "real life"— what is literally, concretely, three-dimensionally *real*.

A World of Sensation

The Sensation function is at work everywhere we look. It helps to create buildings, restaurants, orchestras, opera and ballet performances, art galleries, sports teams, fashion collections, cosmetics counters, clothing boutiques, gardens, farms, golf courses, gleaming and immaculate pick-up trucks and much of life in France, Italy and the state of California.

Our Sensation function allows each of us to be "down-to-earth," hands-on, matter-of-fact observers of What Is. A prominent Sensation function in a person not only perceives with special alertness, but also leads them to make a special effort to shape and report on our world. Scientists' Sensation functions help them count fruit flies, discern the stripes on bird's wings, observe cells or record details of chemical reactions. Their high-ranking Sensation functions help engineers, chefs, dancers, surgeons, designers, models, pro athletes, business executives and many musicians and artists, to name just a few Sensation-rich vocations, to do their work.

A Fruitful Partnership

The Sensation function helps us partner intelligently with the material aspects of life. Sensation perception tells us not only what something is, but what it realistically can and cannot do, as well as what it needs us to do with and for it. Throughout human history, the Sensation function has been indispensable in creating shelter, finding food and caring for ourselves, our children, our animals and our land. It has designed, used and maintained tools and machines. Sensation's perceptual skills once meant life and death to human beings when we lived in closer contact with nature. Though a high-tech modern life often requires us to ignore our Sensation functions for long periods, we enjoy ourselves more when Sensation perceiving is recognized and allowed.

The material world has its own language, properties, needs and laws. Our own senses can tell us about the matter in our surroundings. We feel the surface of an object with our fingertips; our eyes see its shape and coloration; our noses perceive its fragrance or odor; our ears hear the sound it makes when we tap it against a table and our muscles perceive its weight. Jung called the Sensation function the "perception of actualities." [2] A Sensation-type father knew when his soft-boiled egg was perfectly done by the look of the steam coming from it as he lifted it from the boiling water. He taught his son to see this, too.

Even folding laundry in Sensation mode becomes like a single-pointed meditation. Sensation types seem to be naturally "Zen." "Wash the dish. Totally," writes Gary Thorp, author of *Sweeping Changes: Discovering the Joy of Zen in Everyday Tasks*. "Hold nothing back. Feel the warmth of the water. Look at the reflection of the light on the surfaces of things. Let your fingers touch the sides of the knife blade, the flat of the spatula, the rim of the dishpan..." Sensation types do not have to read a book to have this experience many times a day.

Our Sensation function investigates: Will it stretch? How far? Is it loud or quiet? How will a dash of this sauce spice up the soup; how much is too much? We compare an object with other objects, finding out if it is bigger or smaller, heavier or lighter or bends or folds more easily. This kind of human activity is hardly news to Sensation types, who do such experimentation almost automatically.

Sensation permits us to apprehend the intricate marvels of nature, even if just for a moment. In Japan, a Sensation-rich culture, whole families go out of their homes to see what is going on in nature—a cherry tree in bloom, a particular flower at its peak, the sunset. So differentiated are their perceptions of the natural world that there are more than a hundred different words for rain in the Japanese language.

Exquisite Sensations

The Sensation function can be finely tuned, as in the Chinese chef in Hong Kong who extolled the delicacy of a couple of drops of rosewater added to steamed rice. Special Sensation sensitivities can be evident quite early in children. A Sensation-type investment banker recalls with gratitude how his parents, on family vacations on Cape Cod, would drive over an hour to a beach, which, unlike ones closer, had an outdoor shower, so he could wash the uncomfortably crusty layer of salt and sand off his skin after swimming. Another Sensation-type child, when a toddler, protested tearfully whenever his family went to the beach in Southern California. His mother realized that he hated the feel of sand under his feet, so she put on his sneakers and from then on he went happily.

Perceptions that go unnoticed by others can be profoundly disturbing for a Sensation type of any age. A Sensation type attending a meeting in the office of a colleague found the piles of papers and the haphazard furniture arrangement so jarring he could barely contribute anything to the meeting; it required all his attention energy to avoid looking at troubling aspects of his environment.

Our Bodies, Ourselves

The Sensation function perceives all kinds of bodily sensations—it is how we know we even have a body. It informs us what our body can do and what it needs, so we can take good care of it. Our Sensation function attends to the food we put in our mouths (preferably good-tasting and with "good mouth-feel"), protective clothing (preferably attractive), a solid roof over our heads, as well as furniture and tools for living that are useful and pleasing to the hand and eye.

Sensation conveys bodily changes and movements to our awareness; it's our kinesthetic sense. To see exceptional Sensation functions in action, merely witness a baseball game, a fashion runway, a dance performance, an ice skating championship or the Olympics. Such keen physical awareness provides a particularly good sense of balance, an innate sense of one's center of gravity, such as shared by dancer Gene Kelly, basketball player turned fashion mogul Michael Jordon, skateboard champion Tony Hawk and the entire Cirque du Soleil.

As the psychological ally of nature and our body that is part of it, the Sensation function likes physical movement, but not at cyber-speeds. Our Sensation function reminds us that we are not machines. Sensation's tempo is slow, deliberate and graceful, as we attend to all the details of measuring, stirring, slicing, hammering, painting, stacking, polishing, counting, prodding, moving left or right and all the other physical actions we do. Respectful of the physical world, our Sensation function prefers to do one thing at a time, rather than multi-task.

Making Sense of Sensations

Information coming in from our senses is processed by either our Thinking function or our Feeling function. When Sensation information is processed with the Thinking function, we order it in our minds, identify it intellectually, characterize it or give it a name or a classification. In noticing structures, forms and patterns, Sensation processed by Thinking can see a clear and lucid beauty in things. A Sensation-Thinking type financial marketer named Stan relies on making outlines. "An outline is a visual way of thinking out what I wish to say," he says. The Thinking function organizes material-world Sensation facts we have observed or learned and fits them into what we already know. It counts, annotates, compares and categorizes them, turns discernible patterns into laws and principles and finds consistencies and inconsistencies.

Processing with the Feeling function gives Sensation experience a "feeling-tone." We like it or don't like it or find that it feels nice or unpleasant. We select what gives us pleasure, what "appeals to our senses," what goes with what aesthetically, and we dispense with what does not "feel right" or good to us. Much aesthetic experience is Sensation processed with Feeling. Jung believed that there is no Sensation perception without a bit of Feeling evaluation attached. It allows us to *enjoy* our Sensation experiences. Sensation processed with Feeling is especially attracted to the natural, to colors, shapes and materials rooted in nature.

An Endangered Function

An Irish grandfather told a story about going to school in a one-room schoolhouse in County Cork. The schoolmaster, one Master O'Malley, was particularly hard on a certain young student who was having trouble with his lessons. After one school-masterly criticism too many, the young man finally shouted, "But, Master O'Malley, you can't make a chair! I can make a chair!"

With each generation, human beings have become further removed from the physical world that has been our home and workplace. Indeed, a modern world that increasingly tries to impose mind over matter is threatening to put Sensation on the "endangered functions" list. Yet physical effort and work are creative, enjoyable and enriching for the human Sensation function. Every year, the Irish grandfather from County Cork, by then a city dweller in America, went out to a relative's farm at harvest time to help bring in the hay, piling it with a pitchfork and tying it into neat bales by hand. Such tasks, traditionally shared by all, came almost as naturally as breathing for this Sensation type and kept him connected with the seasons and the earth.

Our Sensation function knows how to enjoy activity that puts our bodies and minds to work together in an on-going dialogue with the task before us. "Run-and-done" teams rarely get their jobs done well and enjoyably; having to do a task over again is alarmingly common when the Sensation function is left behind. Even our material possessions are too often demoted to mere "stuff" that we have to pay to store.

Today's disembodied on-line world, in which "hands-on" means texting, swiping, or using a mouse and keyboard, threatens to disenfranchise the Sensation function in all of us. "As a sculptor I believe that perception structures thought and that to see is to think and conversely to think is to see," Sensation-gifted artist Richard Serra recently told Williams College graduates. "The virtual reality of the media, be it television or the Internet, limits our perception and affects our sense of space....Don't let the rhetoric of simulation steal away the immediacy of your experience. Keep it real, keep it in the moment. No one perceives anything alike; we only perceive as we are and it is our individual reality that counts."

Modern life challenges all of us, and Sensation types especially, to find time to make chairs, as well as food, clothes, artwork or music, or to get out to the park, lake or mountain. We all need to relate physically with the world of the senses on Sensation's terms. A walk on a beautiful day is a feast for the Sensation function, with the warmth of the sun and cool of the shade on the skin, the sound of a woodpecker in our ears, the various shades of green in the leaves and grasses and the fresh smell of country air. And it's free.

Sensation Types

People with Sensation as their First Function are Sensation *types*. Sensation types live comfortably in their bodies and at ease in the material world around them. While others may get themselves from here to there preoccupied with their thoughts, Sensation types register what they are passing en route. They notice what they see, hear, or smell, or what their skin is feeling, as well as what their limbs are doing. Sensation types make each movement and gesture with what could be called Sensation love. They don't hop in and out of the shower, slap on lotion and makeup, throw on a shirt and pants or skirt, scuff their feet into their shoes and hurtle themselves out the door. They wash with attention and care. Every item of clothing is gazed at and caressed, perhaps tried in combination on the bed, carefully put on their body and adjusted in the mirror, not out of vanity, but as an artist looks at a work in progress. Every gesture is done with Sensation awareness.

Their home and work environments are usually eye-catching in terms of colors, shapes, textures and spatial arrangements, because, just naturally, they see and implement what looks right and works well physically. There is no bumping into furniture in their houses.

Sensation types together enjoy the material aspects of life in their own special way. A Sensation-type grandfather and his Sensation-type granddaughter, for instance, met in their own Sensation-rich world. Grandfather would sit silently smoking his pipe in his favorite chair, while his granddaughter would climb up on his knees and face outward, as he blew smoke rings all around her and she poked her fingers through the holes. They sat together for long periods, enjoying their Sensation functions and each other and creating life-long memories.

To process their Sensation perceptions, they have access to both Thinking and Feeling, while using one processing function more often.

SENSATION	THINKING	FEELING	INTUITION
First	Second	Third	Fourth

or

SENSATION	FEELING	THINKING	INTUITION
First	Second	Third	Fourth

Living in the Now

As the Sensation function desires in all of us, Sensation types do not like to get ahead of themselves; while doing something, they are not "thinking about the next thing." All the information they need is coming in through their senses right *now*.

Whatever they are doing instructs them as they go along. Sensation types don't just stir the soup, they attend to the patterns made by the different colors and textures of the vegetables and to the path of the spoon through the broth. Making a sautéed vegetable dish in a friend's kitchen, a Sensation-type chef and magazine editor named Michael chose a small paring knife for all his chopping, slicing and cubing, so he could make the exact sizes and shapes he wanted. In the hands of his Sensation function, like those of many chefs, *la technique* is more than a tradition of culinary practices, but a dance with the substances he is working with towards beautiful and tasty results.

Because they live in the here and now, Sensation types lack interest in looking ahead. "How are you going to make it in life if you can't plan?" asked a mother and father, deeply concerned for the well-being of their bright, attractive college-age daughter, an introverted Sensation type. To her worried parents, the young woman seemed withdrawn and inarticulate and seemed to be dodging their insistent questioning. But she was busy feeling her dog's ear, who had just come up for a patting, and had no inclination to discuss, much less decide then and there on a career path that seemed so far in the future.

Remarkably, Sensation types have a special genius for being in the right place at the right time, without long planning in advance. As Jungian psychoanalyst Robert A. Johnson has pointed out, "The big things in their life just land at their feet." [3] They live opportunistically, not worrying too much about what they might be missing. Their life is full, and everything that is supposed to happen somehow does.

The Sensation function is in its glory when presented with a problem on the spur of the moment. Whether it is animal needing care, a bookcase to assemble, a sail to hoist, a dish to cook or a burst water pipe, Sensation loves being called into action. When driving to work one morning, a school administrator named Julie heard a strange sound in the engine of her car. At work, she called for an appointment with her mechanic, but he was booked solid for the next week. She decided to drive to his repair shop on her lunch hour. Leaving her car running, she went in and saw her mechanic, a Sensation type. "Hi, Al, I'm hearing a funny sound, could you take a quick listen?" she asked. He came out and in a moment, her "fully booked" Sensation-type mechanic had the hood propped up and was checking various wiring connections and looking under the car. After ten minutes pursuing various hypotheses, he reassured her the car was safe to drive until she could make an appointment.

Made for Art

Sensation types use their sharp senses, not only as their special biological endowment, but for psychological reasons. Using their Sensation functions they feel most at home. "Decorating takes my worries away," Sensation-endowed actress Marilyn Monroe once said. As they meet the world, Sensation types lead with their eyes, ears, noses, fingertips, skin and taste buds to provide essential orientation. Their bodies tell them first and foremost what they need to know. Before identifying or categorizing anything with Thinking, before they have any positive or negative reactions with Feeling, they are busy registering details from their environment that other types overlook.

Sensation types are born to create, and many do so irrepressibly, without realizing they are exceptional in this regard. A birthday present from a Sensation type is so beautifully wrapped one almost doesn't want to open it. With so much attention-energy pouring into their Sensation functions, their imaginations work with exceptional inspiration using whatever materials are at hand. Out for dinner, a Sensation-type eight-year-old waiting for her hamburger even made art out of everyone's straw wrappers.

Acute awareness of material detail can also create vivid writing.

"What my grandfather did so well was interpret the mundane aspects of sitting and having a meal," Mariel Hemingway said of her Sensation-Thinking type grandfather Ernest Hemingway. [4]

Sensation-al

Sensation types are almost invariably blessed with good taste. Interior designers are often Sensation types, who make artful living spaces for their clients. A Sensation-type president of a jewelry company has decorated her house with over two dozen different wallpaper patterns, matching bold flower designs or stripes with contrasting draperies, which she made herself. Her house looks truly sensational, so much so that it was recruited as a movie set.

For many Sensation types, their most immediate art form is themselves. Sensation types all seem to have the French scarf gene. "Fashion is for the eye, not the intellect," designer Carolina Herrera once said. With their special awareness of materials and visual effect, Sensation types ignore conventional fashion rules, "do's" and "don'ts;" they set them. Jackie Kennedy was a Sensation type, who famously transformed fashion, as well as the interior decor of the White House.

Sensation types have an exceptional ability to adorn themselves and their environment in creative ways. However much or little money they spend, there will be an individual style to their look, the fit will be perfect, with a quirky detail or two that is just right. "I can't tell you how I achieve the looks I come up with," a Sensation-Feeling-type fabric designer named Kelly says, when complimented. "I just get dressed." The fabrics she wears and designs are not only beautiful to look at but also *feel* good.

A Sensation type is almost immediately identifiable by his or her haircut. A Sensation type's hair always appears to be freshly cut, and the hairstyle is perfect for them and maintained with ease and skill. They never seem to have bad hair days.

Sensation Alert!

In airports, stores or other public places, one family with a knowledge of typology created a game they call "Sensation Alert!" Because a prominent Sensation function is the source of a certain *je ne sais quoi* in attire that is visible, Sensation types stand out in a crowd, like works of living art. Even when disembarking from an overnight flight, while other types look disheveled and haggard, a Sensation type's hair is coiffed, jacket, shirt, pants are unwrinkled, shoes are shined, makeup is still in place. Sensation alert!

Sensational Success

With their keen senses, pragmatic attitude toward money matters, and natural physical abilities and attractiveness, Sensation types rarely find making a living an issue, and they tend to be quite successful. They are almost universally adept in business, where their "Okay, what do we do now?" practicality of mind is needed. The list is long of professional areas where the Sensation function thrives and makes its contribution: corporate management, medicine and every area of health care, horticulture, animal care, sports and sports management, carpentry, clothing and textile design and retailing of all kinds. Good Sensation functions are important for designers of all kinds, structural engineers and builders, agricultural scientists, physical therapists, yoga and aerobics instructors, race car drivers, airplane and auto mechanics, cabinet makers and art and antique dealers, among many other fields.

Sensation types are omnipresent on television, video and movie screens. Sensation-type actors and actresses have the stamina for demanding days on the set and the physical abilities to be convincing, whatever the action on screen.

A particular sense may dominate in acuteness; a Sensation type may see, taste or hear with special keenness, leading to a specialty in art, music or cuisine. A Sensation type sales manager named Aiden, who has such keen eyesight he can recognize a restaurant sign several blocks away, became a prize-winning sharp-shooter. It is not uncommon for a particularly gifted Sensation type to face a choice: Do I paint? Sculpt? Cook? Sing? A remarkable example of the Sensation function's versatility is Italian tenor Andrea Bocelli. Blinded in a sports injury at 12, he nonetheless developed his musical abilities acutely to sing and play piano, leading to a wildly successful international singing career. As for his body's overall Sensation genius, though playing sports was not possible, he nonetheless can ride horseback through the woods, leap up the stairs of a Renaissance church two at a time, walk the beach with his young son on his shoulders and perform in lavishly staged operas.

Along with a highly placed Sensation function usually come exceptional physical energy, vitality and confidence. A prominent Sensation function allows Sensation types (and perceivers) to tolerate a high level of physical stimuli that go with a busy life. The business executive who flies to two or three cities a week, comes home, changes clothes and goes out to a show or dinner party as a matter of course probably has a high-ranking Sensation function. A Sensation type who works in the entertainment business listens to and reviews 40-50 new music releases every week; this same Sensation type at a dinner party also recognized that white pepper corns, not black, were used in a red sauce. A Sensation type is unlikely to thrive sitting long hours at a computer terminal in a graceless, windowless cubicle— and should not apologize for it.

Loving Hands

Sensation types tend to take very good physical care of their homes, themselves and the people they love and work with. Whenever they are picking color swatches, cleaning up the garage, planting a row of trees or cooking dinner, they are expressing their love for others and for the material universe. Sensation types and perceivers tend to be wholly comfortable with the hands-on aspects of caring. As parents, their sense of competence and comfort with physical tasks often gives their children a valuable sense of physical security, and parents often instinctively let the one with the more prominent Sensation function do more of the physical care-taking.

Come On! It's Easy!

Sensation types often distinguish themselves with physical feats that are beyond the rest of us, though they may not realize it. A Sensation type corporate manager named Susan went from New York to Boston to meet her boyfriend's plane from Europe – on her bicycle. "I don't know what makes you love gettin' on bulls and gettin' beat up, it's just the way it is," a bull-rider from Louisiana said. At times, "it feels like you can't fall off if they shot you off." Only a person particularly endowed in the Sensation realm has the physical awareness and stamina to last eight seconds atop an angry bull for a living.

This is because even the "average" Sensation type lives solidly in his or her body and registers more of its signs and signals. Sensation has a natural and often fearless interest and ability to explore what the body can do. Sensation types can push themselves harder and farther, and survive more extreme physical ordeals than most of the rest of us, and with less psychological wear and tear. Everyone can do a sport or exercise for fitness, but as a rule, only a Sensation type is endowed with the natural physicality and sustaining power to dance for six hours a day, go for an Olympic Gold Medal, do two hours of hatha yoga every morning, compete in annual triathlons or body-build for fame and fortune. Like Madonna, Pablo Picasso and Luciano Pavaroti, they tend to have more energy than other mortals for a life of high performance. Sensation-type Tom Cruise is known for doing some of his own stunts, Jane Fonda has offered her Sensation wisdom on best-selling workout videos and Reece Witherspoon plays sports and even rides elephants in her films. Another Sensation-endowed actor, Rachel Welch, past the age of seventy, does two hours of exercise, including aerobics and yoga daily.

Their psychological comfort with the physical also manifests in ordinary tasks, which they endow with special attention and care. At the end of a long dinner party, several weekend house guests were standing around the kitchen talking as coffee was brewing. "Let's do the dishes," suggested an introverted Sensation-type guest, a corporate marketing manager named Caroline. Seeing Caroline's boyfriend Jeff, an Intuitive investment banker, glance around in distress, their host reassured them that cleaning the kitchen could wait till the morning. As conversation continued, though, Caroline quietly went to the sink, turned on the water, soaped up a sponge and calmly went to work. Dishes and glasses were rinsed and put in the dishwasher. One by one, heavy pots and pans were scrubbed, dried and laid out on towels on the counter. By the time coffee was made, Caroline's cleanup was done, and with so little noise or fuss that the guests' conversation had gone on seamlessly around her. As she was finishing wiping the last counter top, someone exclaimed, "Caroline! Look what you've done!" Her introverted Sensation function had worked with an effortless, magic-wand quality. She shrugged amiably. "I couldn't stand the thought of getting up in the morning to see a dirty kitchen," she said.

Fashion Models

If Sensation types often seem especially gifted with good looks, it is due in part to an innate artfulness about how to enhance them. Looking so good takes focus, attention and effort. Even at a young age, they want their outfits to be perfect; they iron or hang and steam the wrinkles out of their t-shirts, where their friends are satisfied ironing them with their hands if at all. The opposite of unkempt, Sensation types look totally "kempt." Not a hair is out of place. No edge is frayed. No threads poke out of their buttons or down from their hem—they've seen them that morning and cut them off.

The cosmetics industry serves and indulges our Sensation functions to the most refined detail. The fashion world is populated with Sensation types, both designing and modeling next season's new collections. Supermodel Christy Turlington, earning her BA when she was over 30, gave herself a graduation gift—a trip to Africa to climb Mt. Kilimanjaro. Indeed, if one is not a Sensation type, however winsome one may be, the modeling profession might be daunting. A model's regimen is more than just eating carrots and non-fat cottage cheese. A fashion model named Dan was late for a dinner party because he had to work out, and he was going back to the gym after dinner. He drank nothing, not even water. "My face has to be ready for tomorrow," he said, matter-of-factly. Too many fluids before a shoot, he explained, and the bones would not show in his face. With the Sensation type's characteristically good business sense, Dan used some of his earnings to buy health clubs to back up his modeling career, and he went on, with his wife Julie, also a model, to found their own modeling agency.

Actress, model and photogenic Sensation type Elizabeth Hurley also enjoys intense physical experiences that would blow the circuits of other "types." She shoots guns for fun and once posed nestling into the fur of a live lion. Like many Sensation types, Hurley has an especially direct hands-on relationship with animals. When a friend gave her a German shepherd who had been wounded and stitched up by a vet, the stitches hadn't been taken out yet, so Hurley did it herself.

Money in the Bank

In general, the Sensation function relates us to money in a direct way, and Sensation types usually see money as a practical fact of life used in direct exchange for material goods. Ask a Sensation type how much cash is in his or her wallet and he or she will probably know. Valuing beauty, utility and quality, Sensation types like to make money and seem to make it relatively easily. Even on a student's salary, their environment and they themselves manifest the richness of their Sensation endowment. They are rarely extravagant. If they are spending money, they really have it.

They are often good with financial facts and figures, with or without business training. Sensation types know what they want done and what they can pay for it. In general, in business dealings, one can discuss money directly and frankly.

Extraverted Sensation Types

Extraverted Sensation types, with their hands-on competence and outgoing confidence, seem to be masters of the entire outside world. Whether they are cooking up six dinner entrees on a flaming stove top, embarking on a jet with their staff for a meeting halfway across the country, or selecting among fifty fabric samples for a client's sofa, extraverted Sensation types keep our world running well and looking beautiful.

Extraverted Sensation types have "a wide and accurate awareness of outer reality in all its differentiations," wrote Jung's close colleague Marie-Louise von Franz. [5] A "master at noticing details," and working with the physical environment, she continued, an extraverted Sensation type is "someone whose gift and specialized function is to sense and relate in a concrete and practical way to outer objects... Good taste is also generally present."

"[N]o other human type can equal the extraverted sensation type in realism," Jung wrote. [6] Extraverted Sensation allows a person to relate directly and with ease to his or her physical surroundings and to act on them. When it comes to outer conditions, they are naturally in command. Extraverted Sensation types have energy, often-prodigious amounts of it, and make things happen. They are like the generals engaged in the midst of their army. They often have a lot of projects going at once, such as a business deal, a house they're remodeling or building, a team or two they are coaching, a board meeting that afternoon, guests coming for dinner, their garden — their extraverted Sensation function embraces them all.

An Extraverted Sensation-al Life

Penny, an extraverted Sensation type, is the president and CEO of a jewelry-manufacturing firm. An MBA with years of corporate sales and marketing experience, she negotiates licensing agreements with top designer firms from Europe and the U.S. and manages a staff of over 200. With her Sensation-function stamina, she flies off almost every week to visit department stores in other cities and abroad, as well as drives to and from her company headquarters and its manufacturing facilities four hours away. Often socializing with business associates from all the top fashion companies and magazines, she shops enthusiastically with the same keen and gifted eye for fashion that she exercises for her product lines.

On weekends, she refreshes her energy by visiting landscape nurseries and riding around on a small tractor to supervise the creation of a three-acre garden of her design at her rural country house two hours out of the city. She drives there listening to music with her beloved Labrador retriever asleep on her lap. To feed her active mind, she reads a book a week, mostly non-fiction, and she eagerly discusses what she has learned at the frequent dinner parties she gives. Last seen, she had purchased a nearby house as an investment property, a fixer-upper where she was supervising renovations and which she planned to furnish and sell. "I had some spare time," she said with cheerful matter-of-factness.

Introverted Sensation Types

Introverted Sensation is a less obvious kind of Sensation perceptiveness. Introverted Sensation types tend to be men and women of few words but big impact. "If I talk about it, I won't do it," said Aiden, the visually gifted Sensation type sales manager, who is an introvert. Introverted Sensation types go about their business getting things done with little fanfare, but you can be sure they are noticing everything. They may be quiet, but they do not waste their time.

Jung's wife Emma, an analyst and an introverted Sensation type, described herself as being like a highly sensitized photographic plate. All that she saw made a very precise impression on her; every detail was absorbed and registered in great detail, while outwardly she seemed to be just sitting there.

An introverted Sensation-type painter named Thomas says that he can be having a conversation and concurrently be totally aware of the details of his environment. Even photographs, he says, do not record reality as he sees it. In his meticulously rendered still-lifes and landscapes he works to convey the vividness of colors he sees, the drama of depth from foreground and background. One winter day, he had to pull his car to the side of a road to take in the winter light as it turned a snowdrift pale apricot and the shadows of trees a deep purple. He rushed home to try to capture in pigment the scene just as he had seen it.

Japan, an introverted Sensation culture, is a living metaphor of this introverted photographic-plate psychology. A Japanese business-man was heard leaving the house in the morning noting, "It's an f/8 day," referring to a camera lens aperture opening. During their long train rides to and from school, his teenage children take photographs with their cell phones of what is going on around them and silently send them to their friends in virtual, real-time, introverted Sensation companionship.

An Introverted Sensation Hobby

On retiring to New Mexico, an introverted Sensation type

named Bill, who had maintained the heating and cooling systems of a New York skyscraper for thirty years, began creating silver jewelry of his own design. A specialty of his became a Southwest-style silver and turquoise cross, which he innovated with a slight vertical curve, so it would not turn over as one wore it. He soon made not only the crosses but also intricate silver-link chains to hang them on. A recent visit to his home workshop revealed a workbench covered with small tools, clasps, beads, stones, all organized and accessible in little boxes and compartments. Not a speck of dust was visible anywhere. Bill was polishing a silver pin he had made in the shape of a butterfly, carefully rubbing its silver wings between his forefinger and thumb with a jeweler's rouge. He had the pin in his hand for almost the entire visit, polishing and rubbing. At the end of the visit, he handed it to the visitor as a gift. The silver surface of the butterfly wings gleamed like mirror glass.

Fourth Function: Intuition

The Fourth or opposite function for a Sensation type is Intuition. "Sensation," according to Jung, "rules out any simultaneous intuitive activity. When I try to assure myself with my eyes and ears of what is actually happening, I cannot at the same time give way to dreams and fantasies about what lies around the corner." [7] But while Sensation types segue happily from sensation to sensation, their Fourth Function wants them to know more than what their senses tell them. Their Fourth Function's insights are often fresh, unstudied, unexpected, even pioneering. Driving home late at night after a day at a weekly wholesale market, a Sensation-type chef named Serge suddenly saw that adding a particular ingredient from Middle Eastern cuisine to a traditional French recipe would work. It became one of his most popular entrées and was described by a well-known food writer as "inspired" — by a sudden flash of Fourth-Function Intuition.

Sensation types and Intuitive types, typological opposites, can seem to live in different worlds, but in point of fact, each visits that other's world more often than they realize, opening their "other" eyes of perception to reveal a world of wonders and often true innovation.

Everyone has moments of insight from their Intuition function, but for a Sensation type, they can come with such clarity and force that they light up the landscape of their lives. After working for three different companies, a Sensation type named Kelly was searching for her true career path. Each position had left her dissatisfied. The companies themselves were in flux, her jobs barely tapped her artistic talents and she could see no future for herself anywhere. One day, walking home from the subway, Kelly saw in a flash her true work in a single distilled moment: *fabrics*. Her whole life she had loved the textures and colors of fabrics, and she could see herself working in the business of creating them. With this vision in her mind's eye, she turned toward her goal, with the Fourth Function's own distinctively influential participation. She happened upon a local adult-education magazine offering a night course teaching all about using sewing machines, and she enrolled. Then she found the perfect professional degree program in another city. She applied, was accepted and moved there. After a year of intense study, she graduated with highest honors and got a job with a prominent fabric manufacturer. This is how dramatically and true-to-course the Fourth Function of Intuition can work in a Sensation type.

Stepping deftly across stones through a small stream while on a hike, a young Sensation type suddenly announced, "Life is nature, nature is life!" This observation, so pertinent to their immediate surroundings yet transcending them, stunned his companions who still quote him years later. Though this spontaneous mediumistic quality can startle anyone within earshot, Sensation types themselves may pay scant attention to these sudden eruptions, if they even register them. When asked, "What did you mean when you said that?" they cannot readily answer.

Sensation types may not need to raise their psychic periscopes very often, but Intuition's messages burst through, not only in intimations of cosmic proportions or in visions of their life's work. Intuition may pick up a phenomenon in the *zeitgeist* around which to form a business, such as Sensation-Feeling type Gwyneth Paltrow's successful e-commerce empire built around health and beauty-enhancing Goop. It may suddenly reveal the meaning of a painful experience, uncover the motivation for what someone has done or said, even foresee the future. Though ordinarily they may find themselves somewhat baffled by the complexities of relationships and little inclined to ruminate for hours on the mysteries of life, their spontaneous "takes" are often astoundingly accurate. "He doesn't want to marry her," a Sensation-type told friends matter-of-factly prior to an ill-fated union that everyone else was trying to support. In a blast of truth, Fourth-Function Intuition said outright what others did not want to see or hear. His Fourth Function saw the troubles that lay ahead.

Spooky

Fourth-Function Intuition can sometimes seem to have its eerie side. A world-class chef and Sensation type says he dislikes driving by swamps. A Sensation-type company president admits she hates spiders and cobwebs. Though her Sensation talents have graced every other part of her home, she has never once been in her basement; her competent Thinking-Sensation-type husband does whatever needs to be done down there.

It is startling to witness an otherwise down-to-earth Sensation type reveal "otherworldly" fears or fascinations. "A type who is so accurate on the factual level can suddenly get melancholy, suspicious premonitions, ideas of dark possibilities... [of] dangers, misfortunes or illnesses," Jung's colleague Marie-Louise von Franz writes in *Jung's Typology.* [8] A Sensation-type New Yorker, for instance, found herself unable to enter Grand Central Station for many weeks after the World Trade Center attack, due to an immediate sense that a terrorist might be there at that very moment with a bomb. "[T]he Sensation type either surprises you by hitting the bull's eye, which you can only admire, or else he comes up with hunches in which there is no truth, just pure invention," von Franz continues. [9] In Sensation-rich California, for instance, one can find the world's widest range of experimental and alternative therapies, practices, sects, gurus, healers of all kinds, some of whom convey pure genius, while others exaggerate a grain of truth beyond its validity. A Sensation type may also project his or her hidden Fourth-Function Intuitive insightfulness outward onto someone else, worthy or not. As first-function Intuitives often come to learn, it can be helpful to seek corroboration for even an enticing intuition perception.

Fourth-Function Doubts

From the back of his or her mind, Fourth-Function Intuition may gnaw at a Sensation type. There may be a person they care deeply about or who intrigues them, but whose behavior they just don't understand. They might get a vague sense something "isn't right" or is missing in their lives. They may feel "uninspired" and like they are going nowhere, leading to self-criticism.

Such innocent-sounding questions as, "When are you two thinking of starting a family?" "Are you thinking of staying in the city?"

"What if your company is sold, what would you do?" pose challenges to a Sensation type's Fourth-Function Intuition. One Sensation-endowed New York couple, both Sensation-perceivers, were happily enjoying daily life together—working at jobs they liked, cooking delicious meals, caring for their two cats, decorating their apartment and traveling to visit family and friends. Questioned by loved ones, they thought from time to time that they should look ahead, make plans and preparations. They saw friends doing well with investments and wondered, "Why didn't we buy an apartment when they did?" Yet the one time they mustered their resolve and did go out to look at real estate, they became so exhausted, they came back home to their nice two-bedroom. "I had to take a nap," the husband said. "Are you worried about the future because you have been burned by not having planned ahead?" a friend asked. They looked at one another. "No!" they both said together. "I have the life I always dreamed of," the husband added thoughtfully.

Such self-questioning offers an opportunity to acknowledge the remarkable fact of Intuition's hidden presence in their lives. When they leave a mental window open to their Fourth-Function Intuition and trust it, even if they don't understand it, it can be rather uncanny and serendipitous. Some say that it is as if Sensation types have a guardian angel watching over them, and that they are lucky. An insight will emerge just at the right time, though it may represent a cliff-hanger for them (or for those who care about them).

Or what is needed next may simply fall at their feet. A Sensation-type college student named Elise was shopping in a grocery store one day and saw a $10 bill lying in the aisle in front of her. No one was around, so she picked it up. "This is my lucky day," she thought. "The show is starting." She decided she would simply watch what happened next. She went to class, and when her paper was handed back, she got an unexpected A. She was looking for part-time work, and she decided this was a good day to stop by the college job board. At that moment, a woman appeared and posted a new job. Elise read the index card and it was the perfect job she had been looking for. She called, got a prompt interview, and was offered the job. The story goes on. In the elevator on her first day of work, a man got on who took one look at her and said, "She's the one." A decade later, they are happily married with two children.

A Romantic Vision

Breaking through a Sensation type's usual focus on the practical activities of the here and now, Fourth-Function Intuition may sing a siren song—with an intuitive message. With a sense of yearning for something—or someone—to live for, the Fourth Function can call a Sensation type on a quest for meaning or change. One Sensation-type banker found his workday visited by visions and plans for a "dream house" outside of town (he eventually got land and is in the process of building it). A successful Sensation-type attorney plans trips to far-away places, most recently to Asia. "I always need something to look forward to," he says. He spent many weeks as an armchair trip planner doing research on hotels, restaurants and interesting sites he was inspired to visit and cooked Asian recipes. On a deep level psychologically, he was pursuing his imagination's intuitive vision of a meaningful and broadening life experience.

The Fourth Function also uses relationships for revelation. Sensation types are often happy and satisfied in their world of rich Sensations. There is a certain "what you see is what you get" aspect to Sensation types that is completely genuine, and when you are accepted by them, their commitment is a given. A relationship can cause them very painful confusion, however, especially when it takes them too far out of Sensation's solid grasp. It may be too "cosmic" an experience and, though a taste of heaven, require a retreat. A partner may want "more." This situation can trouble a Sensation type deeply, because he or she can't imagine what that "more" might be, or why it is needed. This too may mean an impasse, or even an ending. But a certain amount of that "more" might also be very important for the Sensation type's personal growth, as well as revitalizing to a relationship.

Sensation-Thinking Types

"Simplicity is the ultimate sophistication."
— Leonardo da Vinci

Elbert Hubbard, founder of the American Arts and Crafts Movement at the beginning of the 20th century, advocated having nothing in one's environment that is not both "Beautiful" and "Useful." He could have been articulating the credo of the combination of Sensation and Thinking. For Sensation-Thinking types, the top psychological priority is to perceive the material world in rich detail, then to relate to it using the ordered clarity and logic of reason. "This wine is too good for toast-drinking, my dear," Sensation-Thinking-type writer Ernest Hemingway wrote in *The Sun Also Rises*. "You don't want to mix emotions up with a wine like that. You lose the taste." Combining refinement of taste and practicality to make the world work and show its best, the Sensation-Thinking type's genius is evident nearly everywhere we look.

Focused on the sensory aspects of the here and now, Sensation-Thinking types observe the shapes, lines, proportions, colors and other physical properties of what is around them. Then they arrange it "just so," make it work well or clean it up so that it looks like new. They clear away clutter to make room for what is tasteful and essential. In their capable hands, the material world comes to order in a way that is both functional and beautiful.

Can-do Confidence

When true to nature, Sensation-Thinking types are the creators, providers and maintainers of a life of aesthetic quality, safety and security, not only for themselves, but for their loved ones, animals, homes and lands, offices and workshops. Consistent and dependable, they maintain clear boundaries and keep personal, emotional issues from interfering with practical matters. The extraverts in an obvious way, the introverts quietly and subtly, Sensation-Thinking types are men and women of action, goal setters and achievers. They waste little time on hesitations and routinely banish doubts.

While other types may rush through a task just to get it over with, Sensation-Thinking types don't want to "get it over with." They are interested in all the physical and mental challenges of doing the task efficiently. Whether it is a job they are doing or an aesthetic style they are creating, Sensation-Thinking types distill it to its essence. No-frills in attitude and approach, they do not go in for gewgaws or fanciful ornamentation. There is little disarray in their ways or in their world-view.

Because of their visual and sensory acuteness (Sensation) and the studied deliberateness and objective clarity of their decision-making process (Thinking), their style tends to be precise, calming and clean, like a Japanese garden or the ordered luxuriance of a French park. With their clear heads, dapper attire and clean desks and counter-tops, they bypass ancillary, frivolous concerns and go directly to the basic questions: how many, how far, what goes next, what is working, what isn't and how can we fix it? When they take on a task, they rarely get sidetracked.

No Fuss, No Muss

Sensation-Thinking types are right at home in the physical world of gardens, houses, vehicles, kitchens, bathrooms, stores, hospitals, ball fields, battlefields and all manifestations of nature, including their own bodies. Their Thinking function inclines them to be organized, reasonable, focused and interested in gathering facts, while their Sensation function with its observational powers rules their minds' priorities. The result is that they often accomplish a lot in a day because they do each task so simply and efficiently.

Being precise is both comfortable and pleasurable for them. In the Paris studio of Sensation-Thinking type painter Marcel Mouly, colorful still lifes and marine scenes lie against large neatly arranged bookcases and low white cabinets. Brush in hand before his easel, Marcel is dressed neatly in a pair of crisp khaki slacks and a plaid wool shirt. The oak floor of the studio is buffed and polished. "Don't you put a tarp down or anything?" asks a visitor. "The paint is supposed to go on the canvas, not on the floor," says the painter, as if it should be self-evident.

Endowed with exceptional energy, Sensation-Thinking types find the most efficient movements and perfect them with ease, strength and grace, whether painting a canvas or a wooden board, throwing a baseball, catching a ballerina or swing dance partner, adding a lobster to a steaming pot, operating on a patient, netting a fish, packing a box, mounting an art exhibition, polishing a motorcycle or driving a race car. As they cast their laser-beam attention on the needs and opportunities offered by physically doing the task at hand, things manifest, change and get done.

Coming Up With The System

Observing Sensation-Thinking types work is worthwhile: watch and learn. They are naturally systematic. Whether they are sautéing mixed greens, assembling a wind-surfer, wrapping holiday presents, painting a house or just getting dressed in the morning, they find the most efficient, skillful and artistic way of accomplishing the task. They approach every step thoughtfully, trying various movements, finding the most economical, productive ones and putting them together with precision—*voilà, la technique!*

Masters of method, their actions are careful and deliberate, yet, once they find the best and easiest way to do a task, they can keep up the activity for a long time, enjoying the elegant efficiency of movement that their distinctive creativity works to find.

Alpha Men and Women

Just as they dominated in strength, skill and courage on the hunts and battlefields of ancient times, Sensation-Thinking types (particularly extraverts) abound in leadership positions in business and government. Achilles, Hercules, Atalanta and other heroes and heroines of legend embodied Sensation-Thinking, as did Teddy Roosevelt leading the Rough Riders up San Juan Hill in the Philippines or Madonna taking on the rock music establishment.

Focused and clear-headed, Sensation-Thinking types take charge easily. Their natural life force and stamina, along with their frequent fashion flair, set them apart in any company. They convey, in an almost animal sense, that they are men and women to be reckoned with, and they can dominate their environment quite naturally. Often multi-talented, whatever their professional position, they will likely play piano, sing, paint, surf or cook gourmet meals on the side.

When they love you, a Sensation-Thinking type will move mountains for you because they can, and without breaking a sweat or without minding if they do.

The Life of the Body

Sensation-Thinking types are among the hardiest human beings on earth. They often give off a powerful physical immediacy. The more extraverted they are, the more forcefully their presence is communicated, but even the most introverted Sensation-Thinking types convey the impression of being more intensely and physically present than other types.

Whether extraverted or introverted, they are direct and activity-oriented. "Come on," they say in words or attitude, "let's get started, let's get it done." But they prefer to move at a sure-footed, steady pace, taking one step at a time, in order to accomplish the moment-to-moment experience of doing. A Sensation-Thinking type, if allowed to, can slow an activity down to a pace that feels comfortable and reassuring to everyone, and at which everything can be savored, while nothing is overlooked.

Sensation-Thinking types know the joy of using their body and testing their physical boundaries. Sensation-Thinking types populate Olympic Villages every four years, and they distinguish themselves physically at every age. Sick in bed, a Sensation-Thinking type is saying, "If I could only get up and get some exercise...." Many can endure physical hardship better than other types. "What would possess you to push yourself so hard for so little?" a *USA Weekend* reporter asked Robyn Benincasa, 35, a member of the winning team from the Eco-Challenge, a 24-hour race over tough terrain involving mountain biking, canoeing, running and climbing. "To find out amazing things about myself," Benincasa said. As trainers, teachers and executives, they transmit some of their can-do attitude to the rest of us.

Refreshingly fearless and forthright, Sensation-Thinking types dive into lakes and seas without imagining what creatures might lurk below the surface of the waters. In team activities, they go for results without interference from interpersonal "issues." "It's awesome, because rugby is the type of game where you can hit somebody so hard, or they'll put their shoulder into you as hard as they can," says the star of a recent Vassar College female rugby team. "Then, afterwards, they're like, 'That was a great tackle.'"

Impeccable Style Step by Step

Sensation-Thinking-type actor Laurence Fishburne III was once asked by *In-Style* what he would wear out if he wanted to impress a woman and her friends. "Day or night?" he asked. "Night." "What city are we in?" "New York." "What restaurant?" "An elegant Italian one." "What time of year?" "Fall." Having collected the information he needed, he proceeded: "I'd be in a custom suit. Either a herringbone or a Prince of Wales windowpane. If it's herringbone, it's with a simple brown turtleneck. If I'm doing the Prince of Wales thing, it's with a charcoal gray shirt with links ['cufflinks are the bomb'] and black-and-gray suede shoes. With the herringbone, I'd wear the shoes I have on now—brown suede. Cashmere coat. White cashmere muffler. Camel Stetson driving gloves..." [10] Sensation Alert!

Management by Results

To Sensation-Thinking types, money isn't a mystery or a problem; they seem to earn it easily and to know how and where to spend it with a focused and refined eye for quality. In a business deal, a Sensation-Thinking type may be tough-minded, but will have few hidden agendas. A Sensation-Thinking type knows, bottom line, it's simple: it's all about money. He or she knows how much a job is going to cost and how much he or she wants to make on it, and that's the price he or she will give you. Sensation-Thinking types may negotiate, but they know when it does not make financial sense and refuse to waste time on it.

Whatever might be happening in their personal lives, Sensation-Thinking types can give structural backbone to a team or organization and keep operations running efficiently, though high-stress environments can be unfriendly to them. As managers, Sensation-Thinking types tend toward a focused, no-nonsense style. They like to stick to the project or subject at hand and are disinclined toward discussions of a personal nature, such as how well people are working together or someone's "problems at home." They don't want long explanations from their staff, just succinct solutions and results. However suave and socially adept they are, personal subjects can be distractions when they want to get a job done.

This emotional self-control can allow for a startling pragmatism. One Sensation-Thinking type business executive, on being made president of a division, fired a dozen under-par managers in a single day, thus purging his division of dead wood, making his point about his expectations and consolidating his reign within 24 hours of his appointment. Those who remained knew they were on a tight ship going full-steam ahead with an experienced and no-nonsense commander. The division went on to break revenue records year after year.

They are most comfortable when interaction with people is simple, clear and direct. When confronted with manipulation, power plays and unpredictable behavior on someone else's part, they feel deep malaise, because they do not understand such behavior. Dealing with an emotionally chaotic, irrational person can be cause for sleepless nights. Faced with intractable or painful personnel issues, they may choose to defer to the human resources department. "There are no problems, only people," laments a Sensation-Thinking-type government administrator.

Grace Under Pressure

When faced with a mission impossible, however, there is no one better. With their focus on physical detail and precision and their minds processing with rational clarity, Sensation-Thinking types are gifted with remarkable sang-froid in a crisis. An introverted Sensation-Thinking-type Navy Admiral named Bill recounted his experience as a young World War II Navy pilot in the Pacific, where he learned to fly a small open-cockpit reconnaissance plane on pontoons as the fleet was preparing a D-Day-like landing on Okinawa. He was then assigned missions to take off from his warship and fly five miles, alone, to the shores of Okinawa with a map of the island overlaid with a grid on his knees. Once there, he was to find the gun emplacements on the shore to be targeted, note their location on the map grid and radio the coordinates back to the ship's long-range gunnery officers. A shell was then fired from the warship to test the gun settings against the actual location. As he flew evasive patterns over the shore, he observed where the shell hit, then communicated back setting adjustments. "That was pretty exciting," the Admiral said with a slight smile.

Angst-free

While others get immersed in the shifting tides of interpersonal feelings and worries, Sensation-Thinking types prefer life to be simple, clear and self-evident. Things have their natural causes, facts are taken at face value and a lot happens that they don't try to figure out. They can be guilelessly and disarmingly direct. "So, how's life after divorce?' a Sensation-Thinking type was heard asking a friend as others around them gasped. The startled friend answered him honestly, obviously grateful for the opportunity of cutting through layers of anger and confusion.

Psychologically, they hold to the certainty of both what exists right in front of them and their ability to interact with it capably. Consistent and dependable, they maintain clear boundaries and keep personal, emotional issues from interfering with practical matters. With such clarity and certainty in their worldview, they often take on responsibility willingly, are conscientious and devoted to their duties. Thus, they can provide permanence of an enduring structure, and be like the bearing walls, pillars and posts of a family, department or an entire organization.

"I Just Don't Get it"

Though he or she may enjoy helicoptering to ski the pristine trails of the Canadian Rockies, the real bugaboos for Sensation-Thinking types can be in their personal life. Sensation-Thinking types prefer to attend to a faucet dripping or a sore left knee before they try to fathom why their wife, brother or friend is frowning. Emotional confrontations can be as uncomfortable for them as a subzero wind in the face.

Behind the worldly competence provided by Sensation and Thinking, the realms of their Fourth-Function Intuition and Third-Function Feeling and can open up unexpected vulnerabilities. Nothing makes a Sensation-Thinking type more uneasy than the complexities of human motivation and interaction or the uncertainties of their life's purpose and future. As keen as their vision may be of outer-world details, the inner landscape of personal motivations and feelings can appear indistinct. Normally they do not sit around wondering why someone is as he is or does what he does, and it takes a deeply disconcerting relationship experience or sense of malaise to make them examine their own inner workings. Even the most intrepid Sensation-Thinking types may try to keep personal confusion at bay by maintaining their activity level and keeping a firm and objective attitude as a protective barrier between themselves and uncertainty.

Yet a Sensation-Thinking type will think nothing of driving miles, even hours out of his way to visit a friend. They may not be inclined toward long heart-to-heart ruminations on the vicissitudes of life and love, but their advice will be clear-headed and wholly grounded in pragmatic good sense. Though "out of sight, out of mind" may appear to apply to them, their loved ones reside permanently in their hearts. Sensation-Thinking types have their own way of expressing love and appreciation by making the environment, personal and global, a more beautiful, safer, better functioning place in which to live.

Sensation-Feeling Types

Two Sensation-Feeling types, while driving down a street, were heard saying, "I like that house." "I like the way they have cut their hedge." "I hate the color of their shutters, it gives me the creeps."

Meanwhile, their Thinking-processor friend exclaims, "How do you *see* that? How do you know how you feel so *fast*?"

Sensation-Feeling types evaluate what they see, touch, hear, taste and smell according to their Feeling function. Their instinctive-knowing responses direct them toward what is enjoyable and worthwhile in their lives and away from what is not. Sensations are experienced and embraced or rejected according to their feelings about them: "I like your new T-shirt." "I don't like abstract art." "I loved Thailand." "I hate that new color for cars." "I like that chair there."

Wherever they are, Sensation-Feeling types are all there, body, heart, mind and soul. Their senses and bodies are busy giving them their primary experience and their secondary Feeling function, the body's intelligence processor, is evaluating these messages. In a water-cooler conversation in Boston, as co-workers lamented how winter was dragging on, a Sensation-Feeling type sales manager agreed. "I am so tired of going out and having my face hurt!" he said.

Sensation-Feeling types do not analyze or categorize what their senses are telling them. Finding them pleasurable or disagreeable is all they need to know. "I am so glad to be out of college," a Sensation-Feeling type named Celine said. "I can go to a film and have my own experience and not have to run it through the ringer of analysis afterward."

As Jung observed, Sensation and Feeling are closely related psychologically, as both functions have their sources in the body. For Sensation-Feeling types, their moment-to-moment physical experience of life is BIG and frequently colored by their feeling state. Along with a rich sensory life, their instincts are also potent and highly intelligent. They "read" other people's emotional states with

exceptional clarity and accuracy. Just as animals respond to messages, organism-to-organism, from another creatures, the human
Sensation and Feeling functions, working together, take this ability
to its most refined and effective level. "If I were ever in a war zone,
I would want to be with my son," says a mother admiringly of her
environment-savvy Sensation-Feeling teenager. With Sensation-Feeling types, their first impressions are strong and they live from them.

Refined Lifestyles

Sensation-Feeling types are natural gourmets of life, with an
innate ability to sense the highest quality—what looks, feels and tastes
good, and at a price that "feels" right, too. They enjoy sharing their
quality world, and others enjoy going there with them. Those who
receive an invitation from a Sensation-Feeling type usually accept.
Sensation-Feeing types get along well with people, look great and
enjoy a good time, all the while making sure all the ingredients are
of the highest quality so that their friends, customers or colleagues
are happy. Using their keen senses as well as their Feeling function's
"phony-meters," they choose good restaurants, clubs, stores, resorts
and places to visit.

Sensation-Feeling types dress, cook, decorate, paint and otherwise create with a particular flair for color and texture, specializing in
the beauty of what is natural. They come up with lively, unusual, sen-
sually pleasing combinations that "just work," as nature does. They
go through their environment touching, tasting, sniffing as they go,
perceiving what is around them and relating to each item with *feeling.* "I love the brown *toile* with the mauve," says a Sensation-Feeling
type, raffling through a rack of blouses. She'll pay good money for
something that truly meets her Sensation and Feeling criteria and not
otherwise.

The combination of Sensation perceiving and Feeling process-ing can make their personal presence compelling, even downright charismatic. They are very hard to say "no" to, even if we wanted to. Sensation-Feeling types are so generous and relate in such a genu-ine manner that their exceptional creative gifts are never off-putting. Their eye-catching looks and creations are so naturally an expression of themselves that one cannot hate them for outshining everyone in the room.

Physically Related

With their Feeling function wanting to value and be valued and to relate to other people in a real and genuine way, their relationships are important and strong. In Sensation-Feeling types, there is usually a material or physical component. Instinctively generous, when they find something they like, they share it. They love giving and receiv-ing gifts, material representations of affection and appreciation. They enjoy nourishing their loved ones with good food. They naturally caress and cuddle with intimates old and young, and with their pets.

Their instincts have so much truth and integrity that Sensa-tion-Feeling types are probably the least likely people to go into ther-apy (although some are truly called to seek out its insights); usually other people want their opinion. They know viscerally what is real and true both for them and often for others as well. Sympathizing with a friend's anguished ruminations, they feel their own instincts clearly, and they can cut to the chase when it comes to the cause of emotional turmoil. When they themselves fall into deep emotional confusion from a heartbreak or disappointment, they are remarkably resilient. They follow their organism's natural healing process, which needs just enough time, no more, no less, to re-emerge into the flow of life.

A Morning with a Sensation-Feeling Type

A Sensation-Feeling-type fabric designer named Anna described a recent Saturday morning. She woke up with the image of the pheasant in her refrigerator. "So making a pheasant stew was a project to do in my imagination all day," she said. But first, the question was, Does she want to wear socks or no socks? She decided, no socks. Going out and walking up the street, she stopped by a butcher for veal stock, then into a cosmetics store to see if they had any new lip glosses. While she walked, she was thinking about whether she wanted the sunny side or the shady side of the street. Shady. Stopping in for a latte, she pondered, "Do I want cinnamon or sugar in my latte?" She wanted both.

Home again, she called her sister just to talk. While on the phone, she felt something sticky on the table. She grabbed a sponge, sponged it off, felt it again, sponged it again. Seeing her cat sitting in the window, she noticed the little longer hairs on his cheeks shining in the sun like dune grass and thought how soft they would feel.

Anna always has on-going projects. "When I see something, I immediately think, 'What can I do with it?" she said. "I appreciate the beauty of what I see, but I am immediately rearranging it or using it in some new way, or making it look better. I see an object, which becomes the point of an idea, and then I want to put things together with it to fulfill the idea. Then I see something else, and it becomes the focal point of another idea. I might have three 'ideas' going at once."

She particularly likes working with nature's own creations. When she brought home apples from a farmers market, she "liked how they looked with their leaves still on the stems." She put them in the perfect bowl and "liked how they looked there for a long time." Later that week, when she got home from work, she "liked smelling that sweet ripe fragrance," and that triggered her to think, "It's time to bake something with those apples" and baked them with butter and maple syrup. She had sensed, "liked" and created something with part of a whole cycle of nature.

Working Hard and Getting Paid to Play

In professional pursuits, Sensation and Feeling is a versatile combination, though it may take them time to experiment and narrow their talents to focus on a specific use of them. They have to enjoy what they do, which usually uses their Sensation functions. Sensation-Feeling types excel in product sales and marketing, retailing, interior and landscape design, fashion and textile design and manufacturing, hotels and restaurants (front of the house and in the kitchen), and other fields in which their Sensation functions can flourish along with their abilities to relate with people. A successful Sensation-Feeling type investment banker focuses on commodities. Working well with partners, customers or clients, they put together harmonious business deals. Some go into human resources in Sensation-friendly companies valuing style or industries like retailing. As capable and sensitive caregivers, they often enjoy careers in the health-care field, from massage therapy to nursing to veterinary medicine.

Portrait of Sensation-Feeling Type: Estee Lauder

Starting out in the cosmetics business, the young Estee Lauder cooked up little pots of face cream in her kitchen. "I always felt most alive when I was dabbling in the practice cream," she said. Sensation-Feeling sensibility went into her marketing, which she based on free samples. "If you put the product into the customer's hands, it will speak for itself if it's something of quality," she declared. In the late 1940s and1950s, she traveled to each new store that took her line and personally selected and trained the new saleswomen. Her successful approach was later discussed in business literature as "relationship marketing."

"I'll Take It."

Sensation and Feeling is a truly winning combination in sales. The combination of extraversion, Sensation and Feeling has brought former heavyweight champion George Foreman remarkable success in business, as it did in boxing, where his Sensation function gave him enduring physical awareness, strength and ability to be a champion both in his youth and again in his mid-life return to the ring. Meanwhile, his Feeling function gives him an innate sense of quality. Typical of Sensation-Feeling types, George Foreman knows a good thing when he encounters one. Retired from boxing and wanting to maintain a healthy heart, he found out about a small, healthy-cooking well-priced electric grill. Believing in this product, he used his extraversion to sell his message personally at every opportunity. His Sensation-Feeling sales philosophy: good quality backed by real relatedness and the genuine enthusiasm of a sincere personal recommendation from experience. "A lot of people, when they buy those grills, really are buying YOU," he explained in an interview. "And a lot of people think, 'You know what? I like that guy! I'm going to buy that!'" Over 100 million of his signature grills have been sold, making him a multi-multimillionaire. [11]

Portrait of an Introverted Sensation-Feeling Type: Brandon

Brandon is highly successful as an advertising sales representative. With his Feeling function, he communicates with great effectiveness in a very personal way and with a sensitivity and respect that customers and prospects respond to. He reads their body language instinctively and responds in genuine ways that bring a positive reaction. An introvert, he most often uses email, texting and telephone. When he has to make presentations in person, however, his Sensation function helps him expend effort on the details of his appearance, so he always makes a special impression on clients. When he entertains customers, his choice of restaurants with stylish ambiance and good food always makes a hit. Socially, Brandon's taste in clothes, clubs, wines and places to go is unsurpassed among his friends. He also cooks well using the best quality ingredients.

As an introvert, Brandon found early in his work life that he must regularly take time for himself. On Sundays, he turns off the phone and other devises and claims a day of quiet at home.

And Looking Ahead

Sensation-Feeling types may be able to see a few days from now, but their future disappears into an impenetrable haze, and it is fine with them. As a Sensation-Feeling-type put it, "I must have a calendar in front of my eyes, and then I can fill in the little squares."

In truth, Sensation-Feeling types do not need to plan or live by a strict schedule. "Magic happens in the moment," says an extraverted Sensation-Feeling type named Jim, describing his work as a sales representative for a printing company. "I make a call and go out and meet with the person. She says I should talk to someone down the hall, so I go to his office. He picks up the phone and calls someone else, so I drive over to his company. That's how I get customers. The hard part is calling for that first appointment and getting myself out the door—I can spend a morning just straightening up my office. Once I'm out, everything just starts happening."

Relating to Sensation Types

Stay in the present…and enjoy it! A Sensation type's comfort zone encompasses their immediate circumstances. Everything else tends to be off their radar screen. If Sensation types do not see it right in front of them, they do not easily imagine it. They are not made psychologically to imagine it. If a Sensation type seems dismissive or uninterested in what we are saying, he or she may simply not "see it," and cannot readily even try to. It may be too far beyond the immediate situation, where Sensation wants to focus.

Don't push the planning button. Theoretical possibilities or visions of the future will not hold much interest, as they are not Sensation's "business." Sensation types are not likely to be thinking of next week, or even what is coming up that evening. Sensation deals with concrete actualities, not with plans and possibilities; with what is, not with "what if." How things used to be or what might happen "when" is not on their mind. Strategizing—"if we do this (or this happens), then we can do that (or that may happen)"— does not pertain to Sensation perception. While Sensation types may set goals, they move forward using what is right at hand, and there are plenty of benefits to letting them.

Slow it all down. Because they perceive so many of the details of doing a task, Sensation types should not, indeed will not, be rushed without protest. It takes time to process all the sensory information they are taking in. Too tight a schedule or too many activities causes stress and confusion, because Sensation cannot do its job in a rush. And Sensation types really want to do a good job and enjoy the doing of it.

Clean up. Sensation types have a lower threshold for visual or other sensory disorder. Walking into a room strewn with toys, piles or last Sunday's newspapers can really disturb a Sensation perceiver. Picking up says, "Come in, you are welcome here." De-cluttering, a quick vacuuming or adding fresh flowers can do wonders to facilitate a relationship with a Sensation type or perceiver. Spending a little extra effort with your appearance is a way to honor his or her Sensation function. Your efforts will be noticed.

Be spontaneous. Feel free to be spur of the moment. What might seem "last-minute" to other types is a Sensation way of life. Sensation types prefer to live without too many plans. They move forward deliberately, purposefully, while "the future" just appears—"falls at their feet." They will decide Friday evening to have a dinner party for ten on Saturday night. Their guests may forgo other engagements, knowing their senses and palates will be treated so well.

Be specific. Sensation types are not mind readers. Don't say, "At one point, we are going to need to..." When you need something done, call them in and give them concrete details, and they will take on the challenge then and there. Ask specific questions about concrete facts, such as, "How many feet of lumber will we need to do the job?" Give them a problem to solve, stating your needs precisely and simply. "We need more light over the work table." "Would you consult with me on the roast?" "Where is the best place to put the new printer?" Then watch them go to work. Sensation types and processors like more "show" than "tell." With them, a picture is truly worth a thousand words. To teach them to do something, let them watch you do it. To convey information, show them a photo, graph or illustration of what you are talking about. If you are making a point, give a pertinent example.

Let them be Sensational. Sensation types like and need not only to attend to material details, but also to be physically active. They express themselves and learn by doing. Their extra energy and stamina often allow them to do more or go farther the rest of us. Their limits can often take them to apparent extremes. It is easy to project one's own personal apprehensions, concerns or limitations onto Sensation-type friends, loved ones or colleagues, when they are quite confident and able. If a Sensation type is serious about wanting to do a triathlon or climb Mount McKinley, it may be appropriate just to enjoy watching him or her make the preparations for the adventure and listening to his or her tales afterwards.

— 6 —

The Intuition Function

"Now we know. But we do not know why. That will take a long time. But when we do know why, the knowing will be so full, there will be no more questions."

The Log Lady, *Twin Peaks*, Episode 16.

A MOTHER IN College Park, Maryland, wakes up in the middle of the night, minutes before receiving a telephone call that her daughter has been in a car accident.

In the dim light of dawn in Rochester, New York, a daughter "sees" her mother standing at the foot of her bed and learns later that morning that her mother, who lived thousands of miles away, has died.

A brother and sister taking a walk in rural France, get lost in the woods as the golden afternoon light dims, and they make their way through the trees and underbrush, turning right and left following an inner sense of direction to the safely of a road.

Striking examples of Intuition perception like these become personal and family lore. We are fascinated when aspects of reality that we otherwise cannot see suddenly appear so clearly. The Sensation-oriented, scientific viewpoint of modern thinking tends to eye such experiences with skepticism, while some consider them to evidence rare and special "psychic powers." But according to C. G. Jung, every human being is endowed with an Intuition function. Far from an exceptional faculty, each one of us has Intuition built into our psychological hierarchy, attesting to the importance of perceiving not just what things are, but what they mean and the possibilities they contain. There is a universal necessity to incorporate this sense of inner knowing into a full human life.

Some people have Intuition as their First Function; these are Intuition—or more commonly called Intuitive—types. This chapter may pertain especially to anyone who goes often to their Intuition function to perceive. Yet we all have an Intuition function and use it many times a day, perhaps without realizing it. Intuition gives us a spirit of inquiry, a natural impetus for meaning and a vital creative curiosity that is supremely and excitingly human. Not just in the middle of the night or in the midst of the wilderness, but at any moment we may suddenly apprehend not only with our physical senses, but also with our inner sense of significance, potential, inspiration and guidance.

Elementary

We all have at least a little Sherlock Holmes in us. Something "occurs" to us, and we say "I get it!" An answer or solution comes "out of the blue." We realize, "Oh, that's why he did that," or "Uh, oh, I can see where this is going." This experience of seeing and knowing spontaneously shows our Intuition function at work.

Many of our so-called thoughts are in fact insights of Intuition perception. An intuition can be rather like an idea that has not been thought through. Our Intuition function sees the meaning of signs and symbols, from stop signs to flags, from glyphs to computer code, and helps us learn foreign languages. "Intuition has that quality of conveying a tremendous amount of meaningful content simultaneously," Marie-Louise von Franz writes in *Jung's Typology* [1] An intuition can come in a flash, though it may take a week or even a lifetime to describe and understand it.

Getting the Message

What is our Intuition function and how does it work? Even Jung, who was an exceptionally perceptive Intuitive type, found it hard to describe. "Because intuition is in the main an unconscious process, its nature is very difficult to grasp," he wrote in *Psychological Typology.* [2] Intuition is the ability to "see around corners," he continued, and to register "subliminal perceptions" that are beyond our intellectual processes. Intuition, Jung explained, is "an inexplicable 'knowledge,' or an 'immediacy' of psychic images'" with "no recognizable foundation," but having "an analogous or equivalent (i.e., meaningful) relationship to objective occurrences."[3] In other words, our Intuition function is there to tell us something significant about what is happening that we otherwise would not know.

Intuition gives us access to a primal sense of knowing that bypasses our Thinking function and from a source yet to be found. Modern science cannot explain it, but Intuition perception is an empirical fact of human psychology that serves deep and important purposes, including the gift of insight and purpose about our lives and our world, as well as an inner sense of direction, context and comfort in the face of all that we do not know intellectually. Whether it leads us on a treasure hunt or on a deeply serious journey of survival, our Intuition function wants to show us the next important clue and its meaning.

Not Just a Cigar

Intuition is the psychological function that perceives phenomena not picked up by our physical senses. Intuition makes connections and sees contexts, patterns, similarities and synchronicities that resonate with us personally or seem to be part of a larger picture.

As an Intuitive himself, Jung had special insight into the workings of this powerful and mysterious psychological function. Its essence, for him, was the ability to see the possibilities and potential within reality, and to "surmise," which allowed him a century ago to explore and map uncharted territory inside the human mind. "[I]ntuitive activity is not concerned with the present but is rather a sixth sense for hidden possibilities," he wrote. [4] "[A]ctual reality counts only in so far as it seems to harbour possibilities which then become the supreme motivating force, regardless of the way things actually are in the present." [5]

While Sensation asks, "What is here, really?" Intuition wonders, "What's this about?" While a Sensation type is noticing the layout of a room or the colors of a person's clothes, an Intuitive type is searching for significant details about what is happening—an anxious expression on someone's face, a toy left on a chair or two people talking intently. The Intuition function sees not just that something is, but that it has meaning. A cigar is never just a cigar, to para-phrase Freud; it was smoked halfway down or its scent infers it is of expensive quality or the smoker evidently had permission to smoke indoors. A whole picture begins to appear about the cigar, its owner and its context like pixels resolving in the mind. Moreover, for our Intuition function, if the cigar weren't somehow significant, we would not have noticed it.

Welcoming Intuition

The human Intuition function evolved increasingly intelligent ways of noticing our surroundings that led to making superior choices. Primitive humans had to "know" where food was and what or who would cause problems or be of aid, just as we must today. Where we used to face perilous physical conditions, we now come face to face with an unprecedented variety of people and contexts, as well as nearly insurmountable amounts of information from lit-tle-known sources. We are almost constantly entering new territory and must know what to do, or make our best guess.

Nevertheless, most modern people discount their intuitive per-ceptions far more often than their sensory ones. Our Sensation func-tions are well educated and much is demanded of them. We know that red is red, water is wet, a good desk is 30 inches high, horizontal is across and vertical is up and down, all represented as scientifically observable facts assuring us of what is real in a concrete sense. Intent on proof and certainty, we learn to downplay and distrust our Intu-ition perception with its evanescent quality. Yet we thereby deny our-selves access to this powerful function within us that, in the midst of sensory impressions, perceives all-important intimations and hints of what might be ahead and picks up guiding messages hidden in what we can see, hear and touch. We also lose the thread of meaning, sig-nificance and purpose that runs through our lives.

Inner Scanning

As a perceiving function, Intuition is a *receiving* function, like inner radar. As a "sixth sense," it is receptive in particular to a sense of special significance emanating from things, just as the eye, ear, nose and taste buds receive sensory information. The color purple, the sound of a saxophone, a step on the stair or the smell of garlic can all *mean* something to our Intuition function.

While scanning our surroundings and circumstances, Intuition's inner eye is on the move, looking for meaning, relevance, connections or incongruities and highlighting items that stand out. A lot can be taken in at a glance, as it were, bits and pieces of information—a frown here, a slip of paper there, a door closing, the scent of perfume—fragments that form a partial but intelligible picture of reality.

Intuition helps us make a "first sort" in a panorama of options or possibilities. Scrolling down web pages or emails, it notices information of particular interest. We can pick out just the right book from a library shelf or a pile on a bookstore table.

Everyone's Intuition function, with its ability to oversee, imagine, expand and connect, gives us a valuable sense of perspective. Looking for hints of significance or special importance, Intuition perception goes inward like a Russian egg within an egg within an egg, or outward to ever-larger contexts seeking the ultimate context, the Big Picture. Not bounded by the here and now, Intuition sees along the time continuum from past to present and into the future. It gives us hindsight and foresight. A far-distant goal can suddenly appear with clarity and certainty. We see a solution or recognize our next step. Intuition sees links and commonalities across cultures and national boundaries, even seemingly into other dimensions or worlds.

Spider Sense

We frequently face the question of how seriously to take an Intuition perception, or what we should *do* about it. An object or a comment seems to appear out of context; it hangs briefly like bubble in our consciousness, then fades and is forgotten. Later, an event occurs that confirms or relates to it, and we are reminded of what we had noticed hours or days before.

Fans of the comic-strip superhero Spider Man know that he counts on his "Spider Sense." When it "tingles," he pays attention. Using our Intuition function, we get to know our own personal "Spider Sense," come to recognize it and develop confidence in it.

Whether it sees a relevant detail or senses something "in the air," an Intuition perception comes as a hunch, a hint, a partial picture, a prompt. Something gets our attention as new, significant, energized or noteworthy. Scanning inward, Intuition brings something to mind. Perhaps it "connects the dots" between seemingly unrelated objects, people or events. Perhaps we get an impulse to do a particular task, such as tidy up the living room or send an article to a friend.

Some intuitive "tinglings" are clear and strong and take over one's mind completely, others are more subtle and tentative, though the more we listen, the more confidently it speaks. Intuitive film and television director Allen Coulter *(Sex in the City, The Sopranos, Hollywoodland, Vinyl)*, says that he is keenly aware of "the little flashes," such as, "'She should kiss him now," or "The camera should be lower." "I always say to myself, 'Try it!'" he says. "Not that it is what I'm going to do in the end, but I have learned always to give them expression. I always come to regret it when I don't." Soon to start demanding work on a new network TV series, he adds, "I can hear the rapids up ahead." He has heard them in his Intuition function.

Intuition perception is far from a flight of fancy, but a vital infor-mation- and intelligence-gathering activity with a purpose. In fact, "knowing" purpose, knowing "why." is one of its specialties. Whether it comes as a "still small voice" or a thunderbolt, the Intuition func-tion is always connected to the meaning and potential in our life circumstances.

Seeing into Human Nature

One of the Intuition function's most useful purposes is for psy-chological intelligence. It is our own personal view into the intangi-ble but influential world of human motivation and behavior, both our own and that of other people. From its earliest days, psychother-apy gave the Intuition function an uninterrupted "therapeutic hour" to journey unimpeded through the inner landscape, using its "stream of consciousness" or "free association" technique. For everyone, as we follow the progress of our own life along its natural continuum of growth and change, our Intuition function provides us with aware-ness and insight. We are all psychologically equipped to be "insight-ful" so that our relationships as well as our own lives work better and have more meaning, harmony and depth.

Just Coincidence?

Intuition notices events that seem related but not necessarily as cause and effect, events that Jung called synchronicities. We pick up a magazine and read a sentence. An hour later in the post office, we overhear a conversation about the same topic. A bus goes by with a billboard featuring a key word we have just read and heard. Some-thing seems to be trying to get our attention.

Intuition perceptions often accumulate around a developing sit-uation and give us a sense of timing when "opportunity knocks."

"Most of the time, I get a notion of what I should do," a Intuitive high-technology entrepreneur named Andrew says, "then I sit with it for a while. I wait and see if it gets clearer, or if another associative idea comes to flesh it out. It's as if I have a mental bulletin board where I put up an idea and keep it in view. Then all of a sudden the time arrives and I act. My intuition knows the time is now, and I'm ready." As he takes action, "new factors may appear that influence what I do or even determine it, but they are not really out of the blue. I recognize them as being part of the whole situation."

Little Sages

According to Jung, Intuition "counterbalances the powerful sense impressions of the child ... by mediating perceptions of mythological images, the precursors of ideas." [6] Before the Thinking function develops and the full capacity for rational processing emerges, Intuition perception is vivid with these "precursors of ideas." Following Intuition's lively inner imagery, young children superimpose magical meaning onto their world of toys, clothes, beds and car seats. Stories, pictures and objects come alive. Imaginary friends accompany them. Santa Claus really eats the cookies left out on Christmas Eve.

Especially at around four years of age, the human brain goes through a neuronal growth spurt, in which new neural connections fire up our capacity for Intuition perception to a new level. This is the age when parents find themselves writing down amazing things that come "from the mouths of babes." Children ask naturally all the fundamental questions explored by world's most intuitive grown-ups: "Where do I come from?" "What is life?" "Where did Grandma go?" and always "Why?"

To do well in school, our Intuition function often must recede into the background as "just our imagination." Nevertheless, Intuitive children, like the adults they later become, can be seen scanning their environments with their eyes seeking meaning and the vital significant details by which they orient themselves.

A Chameleon Function

Where do Intuition's insights and experiences actually come from? From somewhere "other" and ineffable? Will we ever know for certain? What we do know is the psychological fact of an Intuition function built into every human being, indeed into human nature itself, to perceive meaning and direction via an inherent, spontaneous and seemingly inspired way of knowing. What Intuition shows us, we simply *experience*. We know it empirically, and it is often exactly what we need in that moment. All we have to do is pay attention. But to what?

To perceive with Intuition, the Sensation function is switched off and sensory experience becomes highly selective, even quite dream-like. "When I try to assure myself with my eyes and ears of what is actually happening," Jung wrote, "I cannot at the same time give way to dreams and fantasies about what lies around the corner...[which] is just what the Intuitive type must do in order to give the necessary free play to his unconscious."[7]

While most of us can readily use our Sensation function to be aware of what we are physically seeing, hearing, tasting and touching, Intuition perceptions are harder to recognize. This is in part because the Intuition function communicates unseen information via the seen, the unknown appearing within the known. It is ingenious in the forms and ways it selects, often using the language of our other functions. It may communicate to us as a mental image, a sound or a voice we hear, a smell we pick up or a sudden emotion. A thought or idea or feeling may pop into our consciousness that seems unrelated to the conversation or to what we are reading. We may feel an inexplicable hankering or desire, which inspires us to take an action. We unexpectedly turn physically toward a friend's house or reach "automatically" for someone's hand.

Opening the Channel

Most of us are more intuitive than we may think—in fact, too much thinking may be the problem. To pick up Intuitive signals and cues, both the habitual reasoning activity of Thinking processing and the usual personal evaluative reactions of Feeling processing need to be held in slight abeyance. By suspending our processing functions, our Intuition function is free to range far afield and to scan, speculate, extrapolate, anticipate—to be purely *perceptive*. An Intuitive psychotherapist named Anne calls it "opening the curtain." Before long, something significant appears on the blank screen of her mind, perhaps a detail, an image, a word, an idea, a feeling, or a directive to speak or act. "It's like bird watching," Anne says. "If I wait quietly and alert, something always comes."

Intuition perception requires mental space. Given the constant barrage of facts and messages coming at us every day, we need to create distance, at times literally stepping back, moving back our chair or getting up and walking away, so we can see what is really significant and important.

50% Right

To envision the future creates a nest for the egg of the new to hatch, though to assume that what we envision will always happen may be going too far. Intuition gives us a hint of a truth or of the direction of things, but an Intuition is not always a guarantee. The path of reality may turn and go another way, and often does.

With a characteristic glint of humor in his eye, no doubt, Jung is said to have described Intuition as "50% right." This quintessentially intuitive observation is both ambiguous in meaning and profoundly true. One's intuitions may be reassuringly accurate half the time and at other times seem to miss the mark. Intuition may see half of what is happening, while the other "half" is still unknown, undeveloped and in the process of "becoming." What Intuition sees might well occur, but in an unforeseen form or version.

Our Intuition function knows what it sees in the moment. As a signal or hint in the vicinity of Truth, it is at the very least more than we knew before. We can use these perceptions as guidelines or directional signposts, as good working hypotheses, while keeping our inner eye vigilant for other possibilities. For gifted astrologer Eric Frances, intuition is "listening to the still, small voice within yourself. This way to distinguish this sublime thing is that it's not accompanied by fear, and it doesn't push you around. Intuition is not suspicion of any kind; rather, it is a subtle but noticeable tug, with the freedom to choose."

That not all insights are bullets that hit the moving target of developing events encourages an open-minded experimental attitude without self-judgment, criticism or having to be "right," as in the best "brainstorming" sessions. Even when we do pay attention to our intuitions, we can find that they aren't precise, or that actions we take do not seem to lead anywhere. This is business as usual when working with Intuition perceptions.

Part of the 50% rightness of Intuition perception is an attitude of both/and—both to value and take it very seriously and to understand that we may "only know the half of it." Intuitions in the mind are like seeds in nature, each one with the potential to become a flower, tree or vegetable, but not all seeds sprout and even fewer grow to fruition. There is a natural mystery connected with the Intuition function, which we are made to enter. Perhaps a wise attitude toward an intuition perception is, "*Possibletively!*"

A Noble Gift

"The function of unconscious perception," Jung stated, is "the noblest gift of man" [8]. Our inner perceptual radar may be rusty or overshadowed by rational biases, anxieties and doubts, but by clearing our minds of all processing for a while, we have the opportunity to get information "from the source." When we acknowledge our insights, we can nourish them with our attention, corroborate them and express them in order to get their full benefit. Thus our product gets launched, our investments rise, our article or book gets written and published, a work of art is created, a teaching point works with a struggling student, someone's unhappiness is eased or a play idea provides for a child's delight.

tWe all have an Intuition function, and the more we know about this all-important faculty of perception, the better our lives can be. Seeing into the future from what is salient in the present, we can keep our bearings and maintain an open mind for directives on life's leading edge. Our Intuition function gives us the width and breadth of perception about our world that is vital to guide us safely through today's realities, and to give us the inspiration of a vision for the future based on these realities.

Intuitive Types

"...every ordinary situation in life seems like a locked room which intuition has to open."

—C.G. Jung, *Psychological Types* [9]

For a person with Intuition as his or her First Function, the primary psychological inclination is to look for the possibilities that are rooted but hiding in the actual situation. It is as if they see with a kind of psychological infrared vision what is significant or potential, like the first indications of an event, trend, emotion or action "trying to happen." Intuitives tolerate ambiguity and uncertainty, even see them as opportunities. The Intuitive is the one whose eyes are often scanning the environment seeing connections, meaning, hints of direction and always *more*.

The Unusual as Usual

Daily life for an Intuitive might seem unusual to others, even slightly uncanny. Here are some examples from normal life for an Intuitive:

*While visiting friends for the weekend, an Intuitive high school teacher came down for breakfast and told them of a dream she'd had in which they had sold their house, and she was visiting them in another city. Her friends gaped at her. Just that week, they had indeed decided to sell their house and move, but hadn't yet told anyone.

*Thirty years ago, against the advice of nearly everyone he knew, an intuitive writer named David put all his savings into gold coins. "'You'll get no interest,' people said to me. 'It's not reasonable,'" David said. "I had to fight myself about it. But my intuition was so strong, sensible or not, I had to do it." While many fortunes have been made and lost since then, those gold coins have gone up in value more than 800%.

*An Intuitive real estate broker named Henry often had lunch in the same restaurant as a local store owner named Sam. One day, upon leaving, Henry handed Sam his newspaper. "Here, I want you to have this," he said, and walked out. When Sam got back to his store and read it, he found a crucial piece of information affecting his business. Henry had no way of knowing this connection; he merely had the impulse to hand Sam his newspaper.

Living with the Spirits

Intuitives can be visionary leaders, both canny and savvy. According to poet Beth Brant, the life of Pocahontas is an example of Intuition's influence. The daughter of a powerful tribal chief in what is now Virginia, Pocahontas was given a name meaning "getting joy from the spirits" in the language of the Powhatan Confederacy, the Indian people who lived around the Jamestown Colony. Her "spirits" guided Pocahontas to argue to her tribe to spare the life of captive Englishman Captain John Smith, thus avoiding the retribution of her people's genocide. When Smith returned to England, Pocahontas married another British settler, John Rolfe, whom she proceeded to make wealthy by encouraging him to grow tobacco. Learning to read English from a clergyman and agreeing to be converted to the Church of England, Pocahontas cemented the "make-money-not-war" working relationship between the Powhatan Confederacy and the British that kept her people alive. Likewise, muses and "spirits" speak to all of us via our Intuition functions, and Intuitives are especially able to listen.

Cues and Clues

An Intuitive's first psychological priority is to look around—for information, signals, messages, something out of the ordinary or about the ordinary, the signs or seeds of opportunity or trouble. "What's happening here?" "What is he thinking?" "Who is really in charge here?" "Has anything changed?" "What is going on, what has gone on, what is about to go on?" "What needs doing?" "What is the next move?" Needless to say, Intuitives make natural-born detectives, both in fiction and film and in real life as private eyes and police investigators, for whom the material world is like a stage set in which to search for evidence.

Intuitives, like Sensation types, do not immediately judge or assess what they see, but rather initially just register it. One or two items may be enough to provide them with a quick orientation, but scanning for clues may go on for a long time before doing any processing or coming to any conclusions.

Intuitives watch what is going on with people and navigate social and work situations by taking signals or soundings from others. When he gives speeches, an Intuitive businessman named Dan says he "listens to the room" as he talks and adapts his speeches as he goes along.

Like dolphins reading their renowned sonar, this perceptiveness is a natural part of Intuitives' relationships. One-on-one, Intuition helps them to "sense" where another person is coming from—to "step into someone else's shoes." Psychologists call this perspective taking. An Intuitive social worker named Melanie says she uses her Intuition function to do an initial scan of her clients as they walk in and sit down. "It gives me an over-all reading of how they are," she says.

When Intuitives meet someone, they have a particular way of scanning the person with their eyes, looking for meaningful details in his or her face, hair, clothes, shoes, perhaps his or her stance. This can be done obviously or subtly, even while talking congenially. Their inner eye might land on a furrowed brow or a down-turned mouth and "see" worry or displeasure. A quick scan of a torso tells them the person looks fit, or perhaps the shoulders are slumped with discouragement or the burden of some bad news. A scan of a person's clothes may point out that the jacket looks new, indicating the person has good self-esteem or has some disposable income. From these and other details, Intuitives know how to approach and relate to a person. When not appearing to sweep the surroundings for clues of special import, Intuitives may be looking at nothing, deeply intent, as if trying to penetrate "elsewhere" to an ultimate meaning or truth.

"It's Like..."

However strongly or vividly an intuitive "hit" comes through, Intuition perception is cognitively rather imprecise and therefore difficult to convey. Intuitives often use analogies, comparisons, metaphors and other devices that describe or explain what they mean by referring to something similar. "It's as if…" is a typical Intuitive phrase.

There are other telltale phrases, such as "I was wondering…" "I wonder if…" "I wonder why…." "What if…" The mental activity of wondering is Intuition perception, as it envisions what might happen "then," or what might be true "if." Intuitives have a special talent for imagining options and possible scenarios. They leave voice mail messages speculating about what you might be doing instead of answering their call, like, "Hi, you're not there, I'll bet you're out to lunch with your sister or out having a cappuccino…"

Processing Intuitions

In order for it to be productive and ultimately satisfying, intuitive exploration needs to be guided from time to time by processing what one is seeing. Even the most wide-ranging and perceptive Intuitives eventually must ask: what is it all for, how does it relate to my initial question, my life, my work; what exactly is my Intuition trying to put me onto? In other words, they consult their processing function.

When intuitive messages come in, Intuitives have access to both Thinking and Feeling processing in second and third place in their psychological hierarchy, though they tend to process using one more often than the other.

INTUITION	THINKING	FEELING	SENSATION
First	Second	Third	Fourth

or

INTUITION	FEELING	THINKING	SENSATION
First	Second	Third	Fourth

Intuitives *think* in their own distinctive way. Their first priority is to scan for ideas, concepts, clues or subjects of special interest; *then* they may think about what they might mean, categorize them, analyze their characteristics, or compare them with their knowledge base.

They also *feel* in their own way. Once they have gathered enough perceptions, their Feeling function helps them assess and prioritize them according to how they feel: "What is really important or valuable in all this? What do I like about what I'm seeing? Do I really want to be doing this right now?" "What am I really relating to personally?" "Whom could I share this insight or information with?" A feeling may get their Intuition's attention, and they suddenly "realize" they are feeling something. A feeling becomes an intuitive discovery that they feel happy, peaceful, upset, apprehensive or restless, or they may get a "gut feeling" about a person or situation.

If people or circumstances require quick decisions or opinions right *now*, Intuitives may try to steer themselves directly into Thinking processing, but it isn't their natural way. Intuitives prefer to allow their intuition enough freedom to roam and not to process too soon. Intuition perception needs to take in sufficient information to see a direction or get signals of significance. If an Intuitive tries to be too "scientific" by trying to give proof, expert citations, examples or arguments for every insight that appears, their Intuitive vision gets stymied and dulled. Likewise, if an Intuitive responds with a Feeling reaction to every intuition, he or she may get too carried away with enthusiasm or pulled down into discouragement. Intuiting requires and deserves its own time.

A Beautiful Mind

An Intuitive's mind is like the airspace over a busy airport, with half-ideas and images circling in holding patterns, some of which may land and others may fly off the radar screen. An Intuitive's perspective seems to come from an overlook as they survey the situation. This may include their own thoughts and feelings. He or she may get a distracted look that makes you want to ask, "Where did you just go?" An open-minded, purposefully vague state of awareness is an Intuitive's necessary modus operandi.

Intuitives add two and two and get seventeen. A fact or idea or situation emanates so many possibilities! Whether surveying a work project, marketplace, industry or personal life situation, their minds naturally extrapolate and expand to a larger context, then into an even larger one. They make connections and synthesize. Favorite college courses have titles that begin with "Comparative."

Led by their Intuition function, Intuitives' awareness follows a labyrinthine and circuitous route. They may not end up where they initially intended or even wanted to go, but that is what Intuition is for, to explore new territory and see and report on what is there.

Buddhist scholars tell the story of Shantideva, a bodhisattva in ancient India, who as a student was considered lazy and uninterested in his studies by his teachers, who were trying to teach him to learn by rote the traditional scriptures of Buddhism. Hoping to humiliate him and force him to leave the school, his teachers invited the boy to give a talk, an honor reserved only for Buddhist masters. Shantideva spoke of what he knew intuitively. Thinking must be "tamed," he said. If the mind is trained to be open and steady no matter what happens, one remains in the immediacy of one's experience. His talk became a classic of Buddhism called *The Way of the Bodhisattva*. Though viewed as "lazy" or "uninterested" in the usual step-by-step education process, this long-ago Intuitive was simply using his Intuition function to perceive reality more deeply and directly by keeping processing at bay, a useful definition of meditation.

Intuitives are always looking for a new and better way. Once again, Jung describes an intuitive mind from personal experience: "The intuitive is never to be found in the world of accepted reality-values, but he has a keen nose for anything new and in the making. Because he is always seeking out new possibilities, stable conditions suffocate him. He seizes on new objects or situations with great intensity, sometimes with extraordinary enthusiasm, only to abandon them cold-bloodedly, without any compunction and apparently without remembering them, as soon as their range is known and no further developments can be divined. So long as a new possibility is in the offing, the intuitive is bound to it with the shackles of fate. It is as though his whole life vanished in the new situation. One gets the impression, which he himself shares, that he has always just reached a final turning-point, and that from now on he can think and feel nothing else. " [10]

Intuitives' Delight

Two Intuitives encountering one another almost immediately recognize a kindred spirit. Just as two athletic Sensation types might take off running down a mountain leaving everyone else trudging gamely behind, Intuitives can be seen taking off on the wings of their Intuition like two *Fantasia* milkweed-seed dancers twirling and leaping through the air. Even if it is just a brief exchange at a meeting, in an airplane or at cocktail party, they perceive with increasing delight and exhilaration that here is someone else who can actually follow them. They don't have to "make total sense;" their minds can loosen up, and they can go "tripping the light fantastic" sharing and comparing what they see.

Intuitives' Delight can seem to be an exclusionary activity that leaves others feeling baffled, abandoned or rolling their eyes and saying, "Here they go again!" Despite its effects on others, however, Intuitives' Delight can be important and purposeful, as in brainstorming for story ideas, marketing strategies or a vision for a new organization. Or Intuitives' Delight can be just for the fun of it. It is encouraging and inspiring for two Intuitives to share what they have been observing or "thinking about" in their special way, and to explore where their Intuition functions might take them together.

Rare Birds

Though Intuition is rewarded when it leads to finding a useful solution or making money, it can be a lonely vocation at times. Intuitives can feel out of the mainstream, or like voices crying in the wilderness. They may have to dare to be unconventional. In order to perceive via Intuition's rules and conventions, even logic must be temporarily suspended. To be who they are, Intuitives are often drawn to exploring all kinds of subjects of broader interest, such as mythology, world religions, anthropology, psychology, quantum physics or mysticism. Some Intuitives are inspired to study dream interpretation or traditions of humanity that survive from eras before science and rationality took precedence over intuitional insight.

With their perception functions directed toward the Unknown, they are no strangers to personal risk. Intuition is both experiential and experimental. Experimenting with intuitions creates some spectacular "failures," but for an Intuitive, taking risks can become second nature. Intuitives naturally seek the adventure of variety. "I never do the same thing over and over, and never do anything the same way over and over," an Intuitive computer engineer says. To follow one's intuition requires trial and error, as well as perseverance and patience—at times, all alone.

Caring for Little Intuitives

"I would not give an Intuitive-type child a pair of scissors and ask her to cut out all the cardboard angels for the classroom holiday displays," a psychologically savvy Boston teacher named Cate says. "But I would ask her to help with the story for the school play, like what the dramatic situation should be, how the characters should be portrayed and who in the class should play them." Intuitive children may have less interest in Legos, blocks, erector sets or other "hands on" playthings, though they might play video games for hours. They tend to love anything from outer space or from the distant past, from legendary characters to dinosaurs.

Intuitives of all ages can zero in on finding an answer or solution to a problem that intrigues them. However, if forced to focus on one subject in the Thinking function's way in a classroom or a meeting, they can get bored or distracted. Others may attribute this to an attention "deficit." But Intuitives' attention naturally ranges far broader and more comprehensively than for others. Intuitives are "idea people;" in whom every idea is bursting with implications. They may be seeing the subject from different angles or in different contexts. Focusing is not Intuition's job.

Recently in some quarters there is a misreading or misunderstanding of the primacy of the Intuition function for some children that can result in prescribing focusing-enhancing medications. But are these children simply Intuitives? Psychologically it is important to make sure that the Intuition function doesn't get sidelined from doing its own important work and from making its insightful and creative contribution.

All the sights and sounds of a busy classroom, as well as the many activities of contemporary family life, can pose a challenge to a perfectly healthy and normal Intuitive child, for whom Sensation is his or her remote Fourth Function. This is just as true for an Intuitive parent trying to get everyone breakfasted, outfitted and out the door on time every morning. With little Intuitives as well as big, keeping the activity level moderate, and sensory and physical stimulation within bounds, will help avoid assaulting or overwhelming their Fourth Function which only invites confusion, resistance and complaints, even an accident or two.

Library Camp

An Intuitive librarian named Doris in a New York City library became legendary for her uncanny practice of greeting library users with, "I was just thinking of you this morning." She would hand them just the book or magazine article they did not know they needed and that launched their inquiry into a fruitful new direction.

Given how much they enjoy following an idea back to the source and out to its many permutations, Intuitives tend to have an affinity for libraries and archives, both virtual and brick-and-mortar. "So much learning is done on line now, but an actual library, with its smells and possibilities, is my idea of heaven," Cate, the Intuitive teacher, says. Our Intuition function is made to explore and browse with open-minded purpose. Indeed, research is an Intuition-function specialty. Many scholars from academe to law offices have Intuition as their First or Second Function. Intuition perception helps them to put ideas and issues in a larger context and scan massive amounts of information to find pertinent examples or cases to illustrate their point.

Intuition at Work— Tuning into the Zeitgeist

Through our Intuition functions, we have our fingers on the pulse of the living "spirit of the time"—the *zeitgeist*—showing itself in common patterns throughout a culture and even across the globe. Intuitives are especially aware of the manifestations of this *zeitgeist*, which runs through thoughts, general mood, events, values, social and political movements, even fashions and fads, as they arise and fade. Trend-watchers, futurists and consultants have created professions out of their Intuition functions by conveying their perceptions of what is going on in the *zeitgeist* and where it is headed.

Most organizations have strategic planners and advisors whose Intuition functions report on what they see happening in their company, field, market or industry. "In looking at a new business," an Intuitive consultant named David says, "I see who could be the different players, what their roles are likely to be and how they would play them." Intuitives specialize in picking up cues in situations that others miss and in envisioning the possible implications of events. They see indications of change and envision ways to take advantage of future opportunities. In the 1970s, an Intuitive corporate executive named Gerald Levin saw and understood early on that satellites newly launched by Western Union and RCA envisioned mostly for transmission of voice and data for telephone companies, could also carry television signals, giving enormous growth to a media-business breakthrough called Home Box Office.

Many non-fiction books and articles are by Intuitive writers and journalists reporting on the living pulse of meaning and significance on the world scene, while Intuitives in the publishing business pick the manuscripts that will likely appeal to a particular segment of readers in the future.

Intuitive media phenomenon Oprah Winfrey's success is attributed to her "instinctive knack for taking the nation's pulse."[11] Millions look to Winfrey for substantive explorations of leading issues of the day. "I'm a communicator, a catalyst through which information flows," Winfrey told *Newsweek*.

Intuition guides financial investors, marketers and analysts as they survey economies, industries, companies, and all kinds of complex financial instruments, intuiting where money might be made. Intuitives abound in the financial world, from visionary individual investors like Warren Buffet to many of Wall Street's most successful players.

The advertising industry attracts many Intuitives, who can see market trends for clients, as well as scenarios that turn a product into an image with meaning. In their tag-lines, jingles, ads and commercials, Intuitive copywriters come up with words that resonate intuitively; that is, they mean more than they say, such as, "Reach out and touch someone" (AT&T) "Where's the beef?" (Wendy's) "We try harder." (Avis) "Just do it." (Nike).

Many therapists, social workers, guidance and career counselors and organizational consultants are Intuitive types, who can see the direction of someone's career or psychological growth, or how an organization could run more productively and smoothly.

Visionary Artists

With its ability to imagine and envision what is "there" but cannot be seen in other ways, Intuition creates art in which individual visions materialize. Intuitives' paintings manifest highly individual visions. From William Blake, Edvard Munch and Joan Miró to today's animation, multimedia, skateboard and sneaker artists, Intuition offers up raw material for beautiful, expressive and enigmatic imagery from an inner landscape. Architects too are often Intuition perceivers, such as visionary architects Frank Lloyd Wright, Frank Gehry and Louis Kahn.

Many Intuitives try to express in words what they sense subliminally. A high school friend once described novelist Philip Roth, as "a dreamy, creamy kind of guy. He didn't go by facts, but he always seemed to know what was going to happen." The writing talents of Virginia Woolf and James Joyce were unleashed using Freud's "stream of consciousness" technique to access the flow of their inner perceptions. Intuitive visions have fired the creative powers of poets Rainer Maria Rilke, Emily Dickinson, Edna St. Vincent Millay and T.S. Elliot.

Intuition in Hollywood: "I've got a What-if...'"

Hollywood could be called Intuitionville. The Intuition function in any context is always seeing plots developing, characters evolving and significant themes building. Hollywood's success is dependent on long-range projections of what audiences will want to watch in the future.

Hollywood is the only town in which there are so many Personal Assistants to take care of all the Sensation details of daily life— Hollywood's Fourth Function. "I'm a mess!" Intuitive actress Angelina Jolie once lamented. "I have three pairs of pants and I rotate. I'm so bad at shopping." Despite the glamour of the Academy Awards, the daily uniform in Hollywood is typically Intuitive: tee shirt ("when in doubt, wear black"), jeans and athletic shoes. "The greater the stature of a film-industry male, the less formal is his attire," humorist Dave Barry noted. "I imagine Steven Spielberg goes to premiers in his bathrobe."

Acting is another specialty of Intuitives, who seem to "channel" and embody their characters. "As an actor, I am a conduit, I give a voice to a soul that has no voice," says Intuitive-type actress Meryl Streep. "You have to understand the character…what is behind the words," Intuitive actor Benicio Del Toro told interviewer Robert Lipton on "Inside the Actors Studio. "You could make up a language, and still be able to communicate to your audience." Their Intuition produces inner visions that inspire and direct acting "in character." Intuitive actor Johnny Depp, also on "Inside the Actor's Studio," said that he is always wanting to go deeper; his favorite word is "Why." When he reads a script, images appear in his mind, which he uses to guide him as to how to play the character. For scenes in *Edward Scissorhands,* for instance, he pictured his dog cowering in the corner upon being punished, then leaping back with love and devotion.

Finding the Cheese

Jung pointed out that Intuitives tend to "abandon every situation in which no further possibilities can be scented." [12] In Spencer Johnson's best-selling parable for the current economic climate, *Who Moved My Cheese?,* mouse characters live in a maze in which the cheese they eat keeps disappearing. Waking up to find the cheese is gone, two of the mice, Sniff and Scurry, immediately go out into the maze of their world and, navigating through twists and turns, find a new source of cheese. They do not cling to what was, but with utmost focus and sense of urgency, scurry off sniffing the air for hints of cheese somewhere ahead. (Interestingly, Intuitives often have a particularly alert sense of smell, the most primal of the senses, as if inwardly able to "sniff out" valuable clues.) They find it, too. When the others arrive, Sniff and Scurry have been there feasting for hours.

The Cassandra Lesson

Born to anticipate, Intuitives see possibilities and consequences, con as well as pro. An intuitive "feeling-sense" of foreboding, is worth noting, keeping an inner eye on, and perhaps investigating, or else it can degenerate into worrying. Much anxiety comes from allowing our Intuition function to look ahead without grounding it in the current situation, where there is always guidance if we pay attention.

This said, an Intuitive's insights and understandings can come so fast and with such power that, when expressed, others cannot take them in right away. A poignant example of this dilemma is Cassandra of Greek mythology, the Trojan princess who was granted the ability of special sight, but whatever she saw would not be believed. When she "saw" all the Greek warriors hidden inside the Trojan Horse, the people of Troy wouldn't listen. The horse was pulled inside the city gates, and the city of Troy was destroyed.

Many Intuitives suffer from Cassandra's problem to some degree. It is very difficult to convey clearly to others the information Intuition brings, even to use it fruitfully in one's own life. Intuitives often hear impatient comments like, "Get to the point!" or "What are you trying to say?" and learn to keep their insights to themselves or to ignore and dismiss them.

The manner of delivery requires a measure of art. If Cassandra went screaming through the streets of Troy beseeching everyone not to open the gates and let in that horse, few indeed would take her rantings seriously. Any Intuitive eagerly relating insights may broadcast them in a scatter-shot way "too fast, too soon" and lose her or his listeners, whose gazes wander or brows knit in resistance.

Recognizing the ineffable and profound nature of Intuition perception and the importance of its mission, even when misunderstood, is an Intuitive's special challenge. The ancient mythologists saw how dangerous it could be when an Intuitive was not heard. Intuitives themselves need to acknowledge their gifts and role and find their own way to convey what they see in order for all to benefit from it. Communicating the wisdom that comes through them and selecting the right people to hear it are part of their purpose. Clear reasons and genuine feeling for its importance can carry an insight powerfully to its audience. When an Intuitive says, "I can be wrong, but here's what I see," others are likely to sit up and take notice.

Extraverted Intuitives: Making It Happen

While introverted Intuitives, according to Jung, are "directed inwards, to the inner vision," extraverted Intuitives direct their intuition "outwards, to action and achievement." [13]

Extraverted Intuitives try to see what is "really" happening in their organization, community, culture and the world. On the lookout for interesting trends and information in their business or their field of interest or expertise, they want to share and discuss their perceptions with others, sound them out, then refine them from the feedback they receive.

Extraverted Intuitives are often found among the world's "movers and shakers." "Many business tycoons, entrepreneurs, speculators, stockbrokers, politicians, etc., belong to this type," Jung wrote. [14] They see what needs to be done, and they can get the right people together to do it. Aware of the important issues and trends of the day, extraverted Intuitives are often politically involved and network on behalf of a cause they believe in. Their intellectual interests range widely, and their interest in people does, too. As psychologically astute observers, they put this special ability to work in many ways, both in their work and in their relationships.

Extraverted Intuitives come up with many significant activities for their family, friends, schools, and communities. Being both organized and able to anticipate what will be needed, the extraverted Intuitive-Thinking types particularly are superb at planning events. Meanwhile at the event, the extraverted Intuitive-Feeling types are making sure all the people who should know one another do.

Some of the most insightful journalists, interviewers, commentators and authors are extraverted Intuitives. Extraverted Intuitives are also likely to be among our favorite teachers from high school, the "cool" ones who gave us really interesting ideas, memorable projects and a lot of laughs.

Introverted Intuitives: Exploring Inner Space

"You need not do anything. Remain sitting at your table and listen. You need not even listen, just wait. You need not even wait, just learn to be quiet, still and solitary. And the world will freely offer itself to you unmasked. It has no choice; it will roll in ecstasy at your feet."

-- Kafka, "The Great Wall of China"

Introverted Intuitives both embody and teach others about "the interior life which is so painfully wanting in our civilization," Jung wrote in *Psychological Types*. [15] Introverted intuition is the ability for *introspection*, to explore ourselves, the rich landscape of our thoughts, feelings, motivations, dreams, creative impulses and imagination. Everyone's introverted Intuition can come alive in solitude, where we can commune with our inner reality of feelings, inclinations and perceptions and see what to do next from this ever-changing inner picture. Introverted Intuitives especially like to stay and roam in their inner world, quietly scanning, looking for patterns, building up inner "files" on what they see going on, noticing interesting new developments or ways of responding to life. With their inner vision, they gaze beyond the horizon of their lives.

"The world always looks outward, I turn my gaze inward; there I fix it, and there I keep it busy," wrote French essayist Montaigne in the 16ᵗʰ century. "I have no business but with myself." Introverted Intuitives often express their insights in writing or art. Montaigne's pioneering inward observations on the rich life of the human mind still fascinate readers 400 years later. Another introverted Intuitive, Marcel Proust, expressed his insightful ruminations as fiction and transformed the modern novel.

"The introverted intuitive has the same capacity as the extraverted intuitive for smelling out the future," Jung's colleague Marie-Louise von Franz writes. "But his [or her] intuition is turned within, and therefore he is primarily the type of the religious prophet, of the seer...the shaman who knows what the gods and the ghosts and the ancestral spirits are planning, and who conveys their messages to the tribe." [16]. Whatever they appear to be on the outside, introverted Intuitives are wild visionaries on the inside. Often loners with only a close circle of trusted intimates, people with introverted Intuition experience a stream of inner impressions that are constant, abundant and interesting, and they are likely to be writing or painting or otherwise creating something really new with the insights that come to them.

In order to be true to themselves, free time alone is essential, so they can wander through their inner world and not have to relate and respond to other people. "I don't want to seem anti-social," an introverted Intuitive computer systems designer says, "but when I'm working, I can't have anyone interrupting me." He is wholly focused on "seeing" into a problem and envisioning options, possibilities, connections or solutions and figuring out what might work.

Social life may not come easily for an introverted Intuitive. While encouraged by society to develop a gracious persona, introverted Intuitives may try to be outgoing, but in crowds secretly they prefer to see, not to be seen.

Intuitives' Fourth Function—Sensation

For Intuitive types, the Fourth Function looms large, as it is the Sensation function, which includes all the perceptions coming in through their five senses and their bodies, indeed the entirety of the material, physical world. While they are extremely perceptive about the underlying meaning and significance of what is going on, when it comes to the Sensation realm, Intuitives may not notice what is right before their eyes. As Jung explained, for Intuitives like himself, "Sensation is a hindrance...[I]ts intrusive sensory stimuli direct attention to the physical surface, to the very things around and beyond which intuition tries to peer." [17]

Managing the practical, hands-on material aspects of life, such as meals, getting dressed, housekeeping, shopping, staying healthy, even safely driving and walking down the street, all require relating somehow to the Sensation realm. Though they may not give themselves credit, Intuitives come to terms with the basics of Sensation experience in unique ways, through acts of will, devotion and some ingenious workarounds.

No one experiences life on planet Earth quite as an Intuitive does, psychologically configured as they are to bypass Sensation perception. There are many tasks that others perform easily and as a matter of course, which Intuitives struggle with or want to avoid as seeming too Sensation-intense. Yet, at any moment, a Sensation perception can break through, putting them into a state of amazement, even bliss. In a recent cartoon, a woman in curlers and a bathrobe stands by her refrigerator, holds out an ice tray and says, tears in her eyes, "Oh, God! Perfect ice cubes yet again." For an Intuitive type, the fundamentals of the material world that others take for granted can constitute a realm of marvelous occurrences. Yet Intuitives can be also heard banging and crashing their way through a task, as if every object they must handle is a mortal enemy. An Intuitive's understanding of his or her Fourth Function often holds the key as to whether the Sensation realm is experienced as a daunting obstacle course or as a world of wonders.

The Blind Spot

On a practical level, having Sensation as one's Fourth Function can present some significant challenges. Arriving home at her townhouse on a residential street in San Francisco, an Intuitive writer named Katherine pushed her garage door remote and nothing happened. Annoyed that its battery must have died, she noticed that the porch light wasn't on, her husband Dan's usual signal of greeting. Leaving her car in the driveway, she walked to the front door and opened it to see candles lit throughout the living room. Confused and concerned, she called out, "What is going on?" Her husband Dan appeared from out of a dark corridor. "Didn't you notice?" Dan said, "The electricity is off everywhere; the lights are out along the entire street." No, she hadn't noticed.

The blind spot in Sensation perception of an Intuitive can be downright startling. An Intuitive graduate student in New York City was so deep in discussion with a friend as they walked along the street that she walked right into a no-parking sign. Fourth Functions in general do not specialize in creating funny situations, but not seeing what is so "obviously" there inspires a particularly Intuitive sense of humor about their life's absurdities, and comedians are often Intuitives.

Too Much Santa — A Christmas Story

Fourth Functions quickly overwhelm, and a little bit of Sensation stimulation is a big experience for an Intuitive. Sensation overload is often close at hand—at any age. An introverted Intuitive child named Anna, three years old, came downstairs on Christmas morning to see the tree lit and surrounded with presents. The sheer visual stimulation of the sight blew her little fuses, and she burst into tears and collapsed onto the floor. Her mother sagely scooped her up and carried her back up to bed, while "Santa" removed all but two or three presents. When the child was aroused and brought back down to a more manageable sight, she responded happily and Christmas went on as planned, one gift at a time.

Not Burning the Omelet

St. Teresa of Avila, a medieval saint who was head of a large and influential Spanish convent of her time, was renowned for mystical experiences from visions to levitation. Legend had it, however, that she never burned the omelet she was cooking. For an Intuitive, attending to the task at hand requires exceptional concentration, akin to meditation. In fact, it can be the ultimate challenge for an Intuitive to "be here now."

An Intuitive's gift for seeing possibilities can be tricky where the practical Sensation aspects of life are concerned. "I think of doing so many things, but I get around to actually doing only a few," laments an Intuitive-Thinking-type software designer. St. Teresa offers a useful clue: eggs. Legend does not report that St. Teresa never burnt the paella or the caramel flan. In their material needs and ambitions, Intuitives do well to keep them relatively simple, basic and within reason.

The St. Theresa story suggests another clue about the Fourth Function. It helps to approach it with an attitude of devotion and mindfulness. When exercise or cleaning up is approached as a kind of ritual in your life that honors you as a human being, you may invoke surprisingly pleasurable, even sublime, moments.

A sense of levity and humor also helps, but the Sensation realm for Intuitives is actually no laughing matter. If they push their limits, they can get reckless or angry, break things, hurt themselves, even become ill. Sharp knives can emanate danger. Mechanical things can stop functioning, as if the Sensation realm is declaring, "Enough! Time to stop!" Done simply and mindfully, however, Sensation tasks can bring Intuitives enjoyable feelings of accomplishment.

Task Evasion

It is normal for an Intuitive to have a natural resistance response to the prospect of a Fourth Function task. In fact, all physical effort involves approaching using his or her Fourth Function. Intuitives see what needs to be done and may enjoy thinking up ideas as to how to do it, but when it comes to actually doing it, they can come up with all kinds of reasons not to launch into it. "Nobody sees behind the couch anyway...Why do a garden? It's supposed to be a rainy summer...I might hurt my back if I try lifting that..."

Intuitives may suffer from accusations of laziness, sometimes self-directed, but even doing the laundry or taking out the trash requires making a psychological leap into their Fourth Function. Intuitives experience a certain strangeness while doing hands-on tasks, as if they are watching themselves from a distance: "Hmmm, here I am, sweeping the floor..." or "washing a crystal glass..." or "trying to take a fish hook out of a fish's mouth." Sensation tasks are never routine. Strenuous or exciting, they become tiring.

One of the most important psychological skills for an Intuitive is remembering that he or she is a physical being in a physical body with physical needs and limits. Each fundamental area of life in the Sensation realm, such as food, clothes, their body, their homes, cars and material possessions, presents its own special kind of Fourth Function challenges. It may take a big switch in psychological gears, but adding a drop of Sensation awareness helps tether Intuitives to the "real" world of the practical aspects of life.

What is more, a small amount of Fourth-Function Sensation can bring a touch of magic. Putting fresh flowers in the living room can be thrilling. A rainbow or a big storm can inspire a kind of religious awe. A swim or float in a lake can be ecstasy. Even a stroll around the back yard can be more than enough to swell an Intuitive's senses to the brim. Cooperating with their Fourth-Function, not forcing it, Intuitives experience the miraculous aspects of the Sensation world.

They can also "materialize" things creatively that reflect an influence or purpose, and in a style, that is beyond the ordinary.

Food — A Free Lunch!

An important task of an Intuitive type is to make sure to eat. Intuitives can work right through the lunch hour without even noticing that they are hungry. An intuitive art dealer named Alex is known for walking to his office refrigerator and grabbing a carton of something—he scarcely knows what—and a fork and proceeding to eat without interrupting his conversation with the customer. Anyone eating standing up is quite likely to be an Intuitive.

It is no surprise that Google, Inc., one of the largest gatherings of Intuitive types and perceivers in America, is known for its free, chef-created gourmet breakfasts, lunches, afternoon sweets, and dinners, plus snack racks on every floor and a "grab and go" selection of prepared foods. "The whole point is to keep employees here, to keep them happy," Google chef Darin Leonardson told the *Seattle Times*. "So that's my job, to keep them happy."

An Intuitive Colorado college professor named Carey observed that many Intuitives love muffins, as if their Fourth-Function Sensation knows the "good" in baked goods. Muffins pack nutritional energy into a convenient size and shape which can be eaten while standing, walking, or driving.

Although they like to eat, there are few Intuitives working in Sensation-intense restaurant kitchens (unless they are writing a book about the experience). As Carey proudly asserts, "I'm a dinette." Intuitives may prefer to set the table or help clean up, sighing to themselves, "I love dishwashers."

And You Can Freeze It

Convenience is a mantra for an Intuitive's life-style. Intuitives often choose convenience over price, in fact, over just about anything. They like to strategize and streamline the Sensation aspects of life from fixing meals and cleaning house to running errands. They prize ease of operation and want handy what they use regularly. They are good at organizing their immediate environment for the least amount of effort.

For their Fourth-Function Sensation needs, Intuitives often think ahead. Many Intuitives put things in plastic bags and containers and freeze leftovers "for later."

Clothes — What To Wear?

"I buy expensive suits. They just look cheap on me," Intuitive financier Warren Buffett once lamented. Buffett's brilliance in investing has made him one of the richest men in the world, yet standing before his closet his Sensation function daunts him.

"It's like writing a novel to get dressed in the morning," an Intuitive writer named Veronica says. "I have to imagine what I am going to be doing, who will be there, what the weather is going to be." She is grateful she works at home. "I have two fashion modes," she says. "Sweats or standing in front of my closet saying, 'Oh, help.'" As they can find the sensory overstimulation of stores bewildering, Intuitives love the ease of dressing in a simple uniform, whether officially required or not. Though Silicon Valley, California, is full of multimillionaires, everyone is wearing a company T-shirt.

"It's not fear of flying…it's another, perhaps less commonly discussed travel-related anxiety: fear of packing," novelist and children's book author Yona Zeldis McDonough once confessed. (Footnote 18). An Intuitive program director for a global Non-Governmental Organization named Alice said she loves her trips to Pakistan, in part because all she needs to pack or wear is what all the women wear there, the *shalwar kameez*, a long tunic over matching pants that is the daily attire.

The Body — So Near Yet So Far Away

According to psychology pioneer Abraham Maslow, "Knowledge of the body, respect for the body, love of the body, these are paths to peak experience." Intuitives such as Maslow have a unique relationship with their bodies as with physical experience in general. An Intuitive might say, "I am my body," but they don't really believe it. Their body is "something other," full of mixed signals, surprises, long periods of silence, but also eloquence.

Romantic poet Percy Bysshe Shelley may have rhapsodized over the dirt under his fingernails—this "bit of earth" which might have "been men like myself, towns, civilizations"—but an Intuitive's personal physical perceptions may more often loom ominously. Intuitives can be as healthy as anyone else, but they often feel physically vulnerable. An ache or pain can sound an alarm, and he or she imagines the worst. Taking their child to the doctor can hurt them more than it does the child.

While Intuitives often enjoy exercise as a regular routine, they are not happy campers. At the suggestion of a hike, they can suddenly get anxious; it seems awfully far to go, or it might rain, or they don't have the right shoes. They prefer physical activities to be familiar, moderate and free of hazards and bad weather. They are not usually fans of creeping crawling things.

In a pleasurable environment, however, their senses can take them over. Out on the dance floor, an Intuitive can be seen "coming alive", moving his or her body to the music with beatific abandon. An Intuitive advertising copywriter named Nathalie says, "I can lose all my troubles at a fragrance counter." For Intuitives, such Sensation moments as these are paths to peak experience.

Things — The Fourth Function Strikes Again!

A writer named Alexis described her relationship with the material aspects of life from an Intuitive's point of view. "Things act up," she said. "They bump right into me!" An item disappears for hours or days at a time. When such a thing happens, she says, in her bafflement and frustration, "The Fourth Function strikes again!"

Existentialist philosopher Jean-Paul Sartre wrote of the "troubling materiality of things" and of their "latent energy." Their Sensation function can cause Intuitives consternation many times a day. Objects do strange things. They often vanish. "I am always saying, "What did I do with that?'" an Intuitive history teacher says. "I just had it." "If something disappears, I've learned to say, 'It's hiding,' and go do something else," an Intuitive psychotherapist named Arnelle says. Some things show up years later, and often at a significant time.

Arnelle recognizes another phenomenon of her Fourth-Function Sensation, however: surprises. When she is getting dressed for an important event, the perfect outfit seems to appear item by item at the last minute from things she may not have worn in years. A delicious dinner is assembled from a seemingly empty refrigerator. "So Fourth Function!" she says, marveling.

Intuitives are unlikely to be Mr. or Ms. Fix-its around the house, but they know what needs to be done and often how. "There's got to be a way!" is their motto, as their intuition leads them to the right icon to tap, the right information source or the right person to do the job. A new gadget may remain unprogrammed for weeks, or they will do it in a fit of inspiration, pushing buttons until somehow it suddenly works, as if by magic. Maybe it is by magic.

Everything Plus the Kitchen Sink

If objects are not annoyingly "hiding" or "in the way," they *mean* something, and an Intuitive can get very attached. It is hard for an Intuitive to throw anything away. Moving out of her home of twenty years, an Intuitive named Amelia had to get rid of years of accumulated "stuff." "It was a deep personal experience," she said. "I felt I had to pick up each thing, see where it fit into the trajectory of my life, thank it and say good-bye."

"I can't throw anything out, it's so wasteful," another Intuitive says. "It might be useful some day." Even the neatest Intuitive has a corner of a closet filled with clothes that do not fit, a pile of magazine articles they might want to read or a box full of extra buttons. An Intuitive child routinely piled every doll, stuffed animal and toy into a little baby buggy and happily wheeled it wherever she went—just in case.

The special delight in holding onto things really does at times provide just the item needed (if they can only find where they put it). The problem comes in approaching the hands-on, decision-making process of weeding out and getting rid of things, preternaturally avoided.

Another Sensation object that acts mysteriously is money. Intuitives can suffer from a money "blind spot," feeling anxiety about not having enough, yet suddenly spending extravagantly. Intuitives may see how to make money in a strategic or conceptual sense, but when it comes to what is in their pockets, the check-out items flowing through a scanner, adding items to a website shopping cart, getting an actual check in hand or monitoring their bank balances and cash flow, they may have to make a special effort to pay attention.

Calling on the Mediators: Thinking and Feeling

To tend to life's material needs, Intuitives can turn gratefully to their Mediator Function of Thinking or Feeling to make the connection.

INTUITION   THINKING〉   SENSATION

Using their Thinking function as mediator, Intuitives can plan, organize physical tasks, make lists, research facts and set up a schedule. An Intuitive-Thinking type teacher and mother of three named Catherine managed her Sensation-intense home-life by cleaning a room a day. Monday, she cleaned the living room; Tuesday, the rec room; Wednesday, the bathrooms, and so forth. Thursday, she also did the laundry. Saturday, she planned the next week's meals and did the shopping. As for providing the family meals, she says, "Anyone who can read can cook."

Thanks to Thinking as mediator, neatness can be a hallmark of many Intuitive-Thinking types. Tidiness—"everything has a place and everything in its place"—is their bulwark against ever encroaching disintegration into an unmanageable mess. Organizing the things in their environment is actually a talent. When an Intuitive named Rachel supervised extensive renovations of her New York apartment, her Thinking function mediator served her well. The result appeared sleek, stream-lined and uncluttered. There were seven closets filled with hanging racks, built-in drawers, countless shelves and vertical storage units. Kitchen cabinet doors hid hooks, shelves and Lazy Susans. Counter space was pristine, not an appliance in sight, as every gadget was put away in its designated place in this Intuitive-Thinking type's dream kitchen.

The Feeling function as Mediator can provide the energy of motivation.

INTUITION   FEELING ▷   SENSATION

The Sensation function can be approached on a current of enthusiasm or personal relatedness. If Sensation effort will further a relationship, an Intuitive can be inspired to push past resistance. Intuitives, particularly Intuitive-Feeling types, can "get to" their Fourth-Function Sensation simply through really *caring*. When they feel what tasks are the most important to them, they can make them a priority. Using the Feeling Function Mediator, Intuitives can cook a dinner, buy a present, do a load of laundry, knit a scarf, even build a tree house or deck for someone he or she really cares about. An Intuitive's labors of love may not happen daily and may take a while to accomplish, but they all evidence a special quality. The husband of an Intuitive-Feeling type says that the best soup he has ever eaten was made by his wife when he was sick.

The Feeling function can connect an Intuitive with Sensation through music. An Intuitive-Feeling writer named Suzanne says she can approach Sensation tasks more easily thanks to her iPod and stereo. "Playing music while cooking or cleaning actually makes them fun," she says.

There can be a certain amount of anxiety faced with Fourth-Function Sensation situations, however. The Mediator Functions can at times over-mediate and become part of the problem, psychologically, rather than the solution. An Intuitive-Feeling type, for instance, while immersed in the Sensation-intense atmosphere of a Trader Joe's, was relating with his Feeling function Mediator to the clerk at the busy check-out counter. Though full of feeling and enjoyable, their interaction caused the distracted clerk to double scan an item. Meanwhile, the Thinking function as Mediator may go into high gear and over-research or over-manage a task until the Intuitive's energy is exhausted and her physical limits are exceeded.

Sensation Overload: "In Extremis"

Another word of warning: Intuitives have a special need to ration their energy and time spent in Sensation activities. Intuitives may hit "tilt" in Sensation-loaded situations that others simply find fun and exciting; going beyond "tilt" leads to a state one Intuitive calls being "in extremis." Intuitives often learn through painful trial and error that too much sensory stimulation can overwhelm or exhaust them, causing them to be short of energy and short of fuse.

To avoid becoming drained or "in extremis," a condition hard to recover from, Intuitives must engage in a kind of triage. They have just enough Sensation focus and energy to take good care of the Sensation-realm basics and necessities, done slowly and with care and special alertness. When faced with an activity or task in the Sensation realm, here are some tips for Intuition perceivers:

Slow way down. Don't rush into a task. Think or feel your way into it. Then take it slowly, so you can pay better attention. Daunted or overwhelmed, Intuitives tend to rush through a task to "get it over with." Because Intuitives don't necessarily see details, if they move too quickly, things can start "acting up" and obstructing their efforts. Then they get frustrated or exhausted or feel like giving up. Almost any necessary Sensation task can be done slowly.

Breathe. When faced with a Sensation task, from folding laundry to packing a box to taking a shower, Intuitives can learn a lesson from children. Focusing on an activity, a child's breathing can be heard becoming deep and regular. Intuitives can breathe in the same manner to help them focus on what their hands and body are doing. Sensation tasks can then almost feel like "child's play."

Stay in the moment. Looking ahead is an Intuitive's forte, but when all the future steps of a task loom in the imagination, Fourth-Function anxiety arises, and it is easy to feel daunted or reluctant. In a Sensation-intense crisis, it is easy to lose one's usual composure. By focusing on real conditions each moment, doing each next step and breathing, Intuition can continue to work. In a mysterious First and Fourth partnership, the Fourth Function itself seems to lead one through its domain.

Do things in small batches. Intuitives easily see everything that needs doing, and it is tempting to want to get it all done at once, but the Sensation effort required would put them on overload and reinforce their resistance response. Set about weeding only one row of the garden. Go to one store. Have a dinner party for four or six, not twelve. Also, an Intuitive may not pick up the physical signals that it is time to stop and rest. Take breaks.

Have mercy on yourself, keep it simple. Keeping the Sensation aspects of life as simple as possible is a smart practice for any Intuition perceiver. Sensation energy and attention is best meted out. Intuition can always present exciting possibilities, but most take Sensation effort to accomplish. Unless you are *really* inspired, keep your ambitions reasonable. Do not try to do things the same way a Sensation type would. And be sure to praise yourself: "I did an entire load of laundry tonight!"

Intuitive-Thinking and Intuitive-Feeling Types

An Intuitive normally uses the Thinking function or the Feeling function to process and respond to their Intuition's perceptions. Encountering a friend looking fit, for instance, an Intuitive-Thinking type might ask him for information, such as what he does for exercise or where he works out. An Intuitive-Feeling type seeing the same friend would respond in a personal way, perhaps with an enthusiastic, supportive comment like, "It's good to see you, Jim. Wow, you're looking really fit!"

A Word About Intuitive-Thinking Types

"The discovery of the laws of nature requires first and foremost intuition, conceiving of pictures and a great many subconscious processes. The use and also the confirmation of these laws is another matter...logic comes after intuition."

—Eugene Wigner, Nobel Laureate in Physics

With their minds firing in bursts of inspiration and insight, Intuitive-Thinking types see more in what is there than just about anyone. Intuitive-Thinking types, such as Jung himself, are found among the most visionary of people. They peer far into the future for possibilities and penetrate to the far-reaching implications of what they notice in the present. Behind their keen gaze, we can expect to find highly original observations and ideas.

Intuitive-Thinking according to Jung is "philosophical intuition systematizing its vision into comprehensible thought by means of a powerful intellect." [19] This perceive-then-process sequence is the natural way an Intuitive's mind works. For an Intuitive-Thinking type, logic serves their insights. The Thinking function refines and clarifies their hunches and organizes their perceptions, puts them in logical order, compares and contrasts them with what is known, combines them into concepts, analyses options and verifies and corroborates the patterns and trends they see.

The Intuitive-Thinking mind is a think-tank of possibilities. They can take a few facts, numbers, pieces of research, events, behaviors, and let fly with extrapolations, permutations, experimental combinations, "what ifs," "and then we could's." The air seems to crackle around them.

An Intuitive's way of thinking is slightly different from the logical step-by-step Thinking process of a First-Function Thinking type. Intuitives are more interested in scanning and picking up information from a situation than with processing it, that is, before needing to know what they think of it all. Intuitives have a particular ability to tolerate the ambiguity of not knowing, as they keep an open-minded awareness always scanning for new images and impressions. Ever curious about a new way to do things, they can't help trying to push every envelope. Intuition aided with Thinking specializes in looking ahead and preparing well for what's ahead. Science-fiction writers and fans are often Intuitive-Thinking types, as are visionary trend watchers.

Innovators

Sitting in their offices, Intuitive-Thinking types envision strategies and come up with breakthrough ideas for investments, companies to buy, ways to promote a product, what software might do, what films people will want to see or books they will want to read, what treatment strategies to try, which political candidates will get the votes and what campaign issues to focus on.

The financial world abounds in Intuitive-Thinking types seeing opportunities, from financial wizard Warren Buffet to many of the investment bankers of Wall Street and The City in London.

The high-tech industry is distinctive for the sight of introverted Intuitive-Thinking types staggering out of their cubicles into the blinding light of fortune, power and even some fame for doing what they do best: seeing what technologies, products and services will be needed, designing them and investing in the companies that will create the future. An interviewer described introverted Intuitive-Thinking type Bill Gates, founder of Microsoft: "His manner doesn't betray a lot of softhearted emotion; he rocks slightly as he talks, using eye contact only as punctuation. He speaks more freely of strategies than goals and seems more moved by numbers than by anecdotes." [20] Other notable Intuitive-Thinking types include legendary Apple pioneer Steve Jobs, mythologist Joseph Campbell, cosmologist Carl Sagan, visionary media magnate Oprah Winfrey and America's visionary Founding Intuitive Thomas Jefferson.

Psychologically astute, Intuitive-Thinking types make good counselors, as well as consultants and advisors. They can see consistent themes and patterns and possible courses of action and their consequences. Intuitive-Thinking perceives the underlying structure of things, the way everything fits together. Every detail becomes part of a larger picture. They can see and think out a game plan.

Writer and filmmaker Woody Allen has made an Intuitive-Thinking type's poignant wonderings about the human condition into an art form. Combining wit and penetrating insight, Intuitive-Thinking types often write easily and compellingly, and also make popular and effective teachers. As friends and family, Intuitive-Thinking types are inventive, knowledgeable and a lot of fun, and their advice is often sought.

Masters in Planning

Intuitives-Thinking types are generally forward thinking, making them experts in scheduling and planning, from travel to marketing and tax strategies. Cate, the Intuitive-Thinking type Boston teacher, is known in her extended family as Vice President of Planning. In the dead of winter, Cate is sending emails and trying to coordinate everyone's schedules for August, so they can enjoy a favorite annual weekend together at a lake house. "My mind naturally works six months out," she says cheerfully. "I often think of a large calendar in my head, similar to a large desk calendar that has all of the months at the top. I can see the weeks and months ahead of time, and can fairly easily make appointments and plan dates."

Keeping a perceptive overview of what is happening, Intuitive-Thinking types often make influential networkers. In his book on *The Tipping Point*, New Yorker writer Malcolm Gladwell, a highly intuitive thinker, describes the crucial role of "Connectors" in creating a sudden exponential leap in popularity of a product or idea. Connectors are interested in details and facts about people and their lives, he writes; they know what each person does and where they are at the moment, and can put people together according to potential common interests. "They see possibility," Gladwell writes about these masters of the powerful "weak tie." "We rely on them to give us access to opportunities and worlds to which we do not belong."[21]

A Word About Intuitive-Feeling Types

Individuals of unusual sensitivity, Intuitive-Feeling types quickly find another person's wavelength and can communicate on it. Their psychic antennae are always up. As their Intuition scans people's expressions, movements and interactions with others and pick up significant details, their Feeling function feels others' states of discomfort or pleasure, their wants and needs. Intuition with Feeling puts out "feelers," "feels out" situations, picks up the "feeling vibes," and finds the response that will encourage, assuage, heal, enthuse or bring people into harmony.

If Intuitive-Thinking "knows" what we are thinking, Intuitive-Feeling sees into the mysteries of the human heart. In *Stranger in a Strange Land,* science fiction writer Robert Heinlein explains his resonant word "grok": "Grok means to understand so thoroughly that the observer becomes a part of the observed—to merge, blend, intermarry, lose identity in group experience. It means almost everything that we mean by religion, philosophy, and science." [22]Though often under society's radar, Intuitives using their Feeling function are "grokking" the human landscape in order see how best to further the wellbeing of the people around them and of the general atmosphere. Their insight into human nature helps them relate deeply to people; they process their perceptions by *feeling* them "with every bone in their body." When they say, "I can empathize," they really can.

Expressing and Guiding

Intuitive-Feeling type actress Meryl Streep brings such a depth of emotional truth to her characters that she seems practically to channel them and bring them to life on the screen. Some of the world's great novelists from F. Scott Fitzgerald and J.W. von Goethe to Jack Kerouac have brought the insights of Intuition perception together with Feeling processing in their novels. As writers, they saw into the emotional and psychological dynamics of their contemporary society and allowed their Feeling functions to resonate, empathize and create. We can relate to the characters in their novels and to what they are experiencing.

Able to make a felicitous Feeling connection brought about by Intuition's messages, Intuitive-Feeling types often find themselves working with people. They use their insightfulness in the fields of organizational management, human resources, executive search, guidance and counseling. Intuition processed with Feeling helps them sense people's true feelings and "intuitive-feel" who would work well with or for whom.

Creative advertising and marketing departments benefit from their insight into human nature. Those with enough extraversion do exceptionally well in public relations and corporate communications. Churches and service organizations can be natural homes for Intuitive-Feeling types, including priests, rabbis and ministers. Despite their popularity, however, Intuitive-Feeling types are usually less enamored with organizational leadership than to being insightful guides or consultants in the background, getting things going in the right direction and then bowing out and moving on to their next calling.

When they are more introverted, Intuitive-Feeling types relate especially well one on one; many become therapists or pastoral counselors. They see the valuable qualities in people even before the people themselves can. They sense feelings, unconscious motivations or conflicts, and often know what people are likely to say or do next. "My therapist knew that I was going to cry before I did," a former therapy client of an Intuitive-Feeling type said. They usually have a contemplative, visionary or mystical side and have insights inspiring feelings of wonder, awe, ecstasy and sublime love.

At a dinner party, though they may let others make the food, Intuitive-Feeling types contribute an inner connectedness that will send everyone home nourished in spirit as well as in body. This subtle interpersonal "gluon" works in organizations as well. Claire, an Intuitive-Feeling type working in an international organization, acts as a bridge connecting disparate points of view in numerous projects going on around the world. "I know I am different from my colleagues, who are mostly experts," she says. But Claire sees what is most important in what everyone is saying, and she is able to bring it all together in a synthesis that everyone can agree on and support. She has Intuitive-Feeling's special ability to pick up what is "trying to happen" for people, as individuals or in a group, and to help everyone surmount resistance, conflict or self-interest in order to achieve it.

Relating to Intuitive Types

When encountering Intuitives, whether as friends, family and colleagues, it is helpful to remember two things: the wide-ranging, perceptive nature of their minds and the possibility of a tentative, ambivalent attitude toward physical tasks and Sensation-intense experiences. Here are some other suggestions:

"What are you seeing?" It's an Intuitive's favorite question. You are sure to learn something interesting, and the Intuitive will be surprised and glad to be asked to offer what they are doing so naturally. An Intuitive can enjoy speculating about almost anything. To launch an Intuitive's First Function, try a comment like, "The situation has certainly changed. What's your take on our best way through it?" According to an astute manager at a start-up technology company, "I always allow an Intuitive's mind to roam unfocused around a situation. There's a wild card in there that may make the winning hand."

Bring the lunch. When you are with an Intuitive, he or she will appreciate your subtly attending to Sensation aspects of whatever you are doing. Take care of lunch, remember an umbrella, bring the directions, offer to do the grilling, take note of where the car is parked, help them with their packages and keep track of the suitcases. You'll be a real godsend.

Intuitives are…intuitive. Trying to hide something you are thinking, doing or feeling from an Intuitive doesn't work very well. "I can't get away with anything with her!" jokes the son of an Intuitive mother. Intuitives can't help suspecting if something is amiss or being withheld, and their Intuition function will keep trying to guess. Better to give them the facts and let them help you solve your problem, so you can both move on.

"Can't we just toss that thing?" This, it is said, is arguably the most frustrating thing about living with an Intuitive. "There are things in our attic that haven't been used in 25 years and still he won't throw them out!" an exasperated wife of an Intuitive says. If you throw something away and don't tell them, they will probably miss it – Intuitives are uncanny that way – and you risk their being very upset. Yet, if you ask, the initial response is, "No! I might need that!" It is helpful to remember that your request has brought out their resistance response, for no one is comfortable suddenly presented with a Fourth-Function task. "No!" really means, "You're making me confront this object that I've not even noticed! I need *time!*" If you don't make a confrontation out of the issue, going at loggerheads with their Fourth Function, and if you convey how important it is to you that something be done, the item will be dispensed with or the task will be done, albeit in the Intuitive's own way.

Keep it simple, and be patient. An Intuitive confronting a Sensation-intense task or experience is vulnerable; the Fourth Function in everyone is an area of unknowns and deep self-doubt, however masked. Something in the person is saying, "I can't do this!" Limit requests to the basics. When an Intuitive must "perform" using his or her Fourth Function, it is better to be encouraging and helpful, not critical and impatient.

— 7 —

The Thinking Function

HUMAN BEINGS, as Shakespeare wrote, are "noble in reason." When it comes to the prodigious and unique human capacity for reasoning and intellectual processing, we have our Thinking function to thank.

The Thinking function focuses our intellect to produce rational, directed thought. It takes information, ideas, sense perceptions, insights and personal experiences, breaks them down into their component parts and makes them comprehensible. Thinking processing organizes, categorizes, compares, defines and systematizes our perceptions in order to understand the world. It is our innate ability to detach from our emotions and differentiate this from that. Using our knowledge base, it takes a problem, defines it, analyses it and follows a logical sequence of steps to a solution. It creates theories, formulates concepts, finds procedures and figures out how to improve on them. The Thinking function works diligently to get the facts and the proof and the rationales to support them.

From the time the morning alarm clock rings until we fall asleep at night, the human Thinking function reigns supreme in modern life. For centuries, the Thinking function has worked hard and well to create our high civilization with its technological, medical and scientific advances, its global transportation, communications and financial systems, its governmental organizations and corporate enterprises, as well as its social and intellectual principles. It brings organization to our minds and our ways of doing things. We cannot manage our lives today without utilizing at least some Thinking processing, and wherever we have Thinking in our hierarchy of functions, we can be quite sure it is as developed and refined as it could possibly be.

Will the World Please Come to Order?

In every situation, no matter how chaotic it may seem, there is an order, form or logical arrangement of things. Our Thinking function is in us to find and work with this intrinsic order and to organize aspects of our reality into a coherent and understandable pattern in our minds.

Our Thinking function may be First, Second, Third or Fourth in our own personal hierarchy. This determines how often we are naturally drawn to using Thinking processing to understand and interact with our world. But everyone's Thinking function works in the same way. It gives us the ability to form and understand concepts, organize our perceptions and thoughts and put our ideas into words, sentences and paragraphs. Thinking allows us to follow an intellectual process that leads to accomplishing tasks efficiently. At its best, our Thinking function is able to bring some rational structure and consistency to our grasp of objective reality in a constantly changing universe in which all things down to the infinitesimal level are in perpetual movement. Noble indeed!

Step by Step

As a processing function, Thinking analyzes, categorizes and orders the physical stimuli coming in from our Sensation function and the spontaneous insights, notions and flashes of significance provided by Intuition perception. Our newest function, Thinking processing allows us to abstract, to process one step removed from our visceral reality. It takes an idea, fact or perception, works on it on a mental level, then "decides" what it is and what to do or say about it. Even when a lot of things seem to be happening at once, our Thinking function distinguishes among them and focuses on what makes logical, rational sense.

Thinking comes up with the "next thing" to be considered or done, by following the steps in a logical sequence as it moves through time. It helps us structure papers, articles, memos and presentations and participate in logical discussions. Thinking allows us to come up with and follow orderly procedures, formulas, recipes and directions, all of which respect Thinking's deliberative process.

All too often, the frenetic pace of modern life keeps the natural step-by-step Thinking process from being honored, creating a less satisfying experience and often a less effective result. Thinking processing is methodical and thorough. No step is skipped, or the chain of logic is broken, and the Thinking function loses its way. It cannot and must not be rushed. What should we do about the lost shipments problem? What department handles which part of the project? What kind of car should one buy? Would a Thinking type like some more lasagna? "Let me think about it..." is the response.

A Thinking World

Thinking is the Lion King function of the Western world. Ancient Greece prominently featured the emerging human Thinking function in its classics of written literature and philosophy. Ever since 17th century French philosopher René Descartes declared, "I think, therefore I am" and launched the Age of Reason, the Western mind has held human rationality to be its highest achievement. It is also its workhorse. A lot of Thinking function is needed to keep the global-market economy operating, and the contributions of Thinking types and processors are vast and considerable, as are their responsibilities.

The Thinking function devises laws, organizational structures, efficient production and transportation schedules, computer systems and code, medical and scientific research projects, as well as centuries of theological, political and economic thought and theory. In every culture today, Thinking types excel in educational systems and workplaces teaching, using and maintaining advanced technology and communications. Thinking types abound among the "experts" in many fields.

Thinking types often rule and govern their countries, their cities, their communities and at times even their families. Whether a Thinking type knows best may be subject to debate, but when it comes to debates, guess who will win?

Managing modern life seems so complex that it can be easy for many to lose confidence in their powerful and innate capacity for Thinking processing. It is tempting to leave the thinking to other people or even to machines. Yet we abandon using our own Thinking function at our peril. Even if we may not call on it as easily or as often as a Thinking type does, we can be sure that a good understanding and working relationship with our Thinking function, wherever it is in our psychological hierarchy, will help the quality of thinking everywhere.

It's About Time

In its ability to order and sequence logically, the human Thinking function has an affinity with the notion of time, and it is our innate timekeeper. Attentive to dates and times, the Thinking function helps us schedule our days and weeks and take command of our year. Thinking keeps track of events and memories. It connects us with the past and helps us logically and systematically to schedule the future.

Asked what was the world's most important invention, W. Daniel Hillis, the conceiver of massively parallel computing, answered, "clocks." The clock, he said, represents objectivity. "It converted time from a personal experience into a reality independent of perception. It gave us a framework in which the laws of nature could be...quantified..." [1]—an example of a fine Thinking function at work.

Words: A Thinking Function Art Form

Where the Thinking function is concerned, in the beginning really is the word. We first use words as toddlers to identify important people and objects. Our Thinking function begins to develop as we recognize the significant features of our surroundings and try to communicate what we want and care about, as well as what we do not want. With the emergence of language as mental symbols of what we see and do, we take our first step toward abstract thought.

Words—and their definitions—are part of the human Thinking

function's role and its genius. In its work of giving order to thought and making phenomena intelligible, the Thinking function takes charge of word-smithing—*logos*, "word" in Greek, is the foundation of logic.

Words are names that the Thinking function ingeniously "thinks up" to represent and describe objects, concepts, principles and situations. When a client comes in for a consultation, a therapist defines the "presenting problem," which might be "misoneism" (the ego's instinctive hatred, distrust and fear of the new and unfamiliar.) Computer programmers devise "workarounds," when they encounter a "glitch." Pilots become alert to clutching the controls lest they create "pilot-induced turbulence." When the Swiss engineer George de Mestral invented Velcro by imitating the burrs that attached to his hiking pants, he also invented technological "biomimicry." Thinking has coined an intellectual universe of evocative terminology in every known realm: swarm logic, thermal mass, exoplanet (planet outside our solar system), sharing economy, polar vortex (on the top and bottom of ours), emoji, sustainable business model, cognitive overload, eye candy, predictive text, differential diagnosis, soft power, at-grade median crossing, trophic cascade, informatics, freezer burn, social engineering, panpsychism, wintry mix, rebound headache, pop-up dinner, collateral damage, metro sexual, identity theft, symbolic capital, tropic weight, idiosyncratic volatility, threshold of toxicity, scientism, anagram, palindrome, price adjustment, Frequently Asked Questions (FAQs), and naturally occurring retirement communities (NORCs), all kinds of –isms and –ologies, just to start.

Music styles are categorized by the Thinking function and terminology invented, from jazz, rock, pop and alternative, to jazz-fusion-funk, dub-step, ska, techno, lounge, trance, house, electro, Eurodisco, urban rock, and more. Painters and other artists are organized by Thinking into "movements" and their styles differentiated, defined and named, such as Impressionism, Post-Impressionism, The New York School, Pop Art, the Pre-Raphaelites, ukiyo-e, The Ash Can School, the Hudson River School. More than just jargon, these words and names define phenomena with precision and add to our knowledge and choices.

Thinking types and Thinking processors especially appreciate knowing the names of things, from cocktails and culinary entrées to manufacturers or designers of clothing. Brand names for them are more than just a matter of status, they help them identify and distinguish clearly among items, styles and qualities.

In fact, for the Thinking function, words define and make something real. In the Thinking world, until there is a word for it, it isn't yet real; indeed it cannot even be conceptualized. In science, the practice of naming has brought order to the profusion of natural and physical phenomena as a kind of shorthand identifying a recognizable creature, pattern or syndrome.

This ability to identify and name things has deep psychological importance. "A word is helpful in medicine," a Thinking-type physician said. "It gives meaning, makes it seem that we have an understanding, so the patient can better tolerate the condition." Psychotherapy has long used Thinking processing in a very creative way through the cognitive process of putting inner experiences into words. Freud's "talking cure," as we now know from the work of Nobel prize-winning neuroscientist Eric Kandel, modifies brain circuitry and harmonizes brain chemistry. Using the Thinking function to come to clarity and understanding through words helps heal the entire human organism.

Thinking Types

As Jung wrote in *Psychological Types*, "When the life of an individual is mainly governed by reflective thinking so that every important action proceeds, or is intended to proceed, from intellectually considered motives, we may fairly call this a thinking type." [2]

"Real life" for Thinking types is the life of the mind, and a vast, rich and varied life it is. A powerhouse of mental activity, the Thinking type's mind is resolutely at work organizing, deliberating and analyzing thoughts and information and making logical sense of what is going on. Anyone with a "steel-trap mind" is probably a Thinking type. Grabbing bits of information from their perceiving functions like snacks on the run, Thinking types are often obviously busy *thinking*.

The memories of Thinking types are unusually good, because memory is important to the Thinking function as an inner organizational tool. A Thinking-type grandmother, who had come to the U.S. from Ireland in her teens, still knew all the families of her home county by name and the towns they came from, as well as who had married whom and where they had settled. She kept the whole geography of her homeland alive in her mind as a grid of family connections, intermarriages and locales spanning several decades.

Far from the interference of their switched-off Fourth-Function Feeling, Thinking types' minds are clean, well-lighted places. Starting with their earliest days in pre-school, people with high-ranking Thinking functions are configured for success, and professional and career opportunities— good psychological "fits"—abound. Thinking types thrive in corporate management, banking and finance, law, accounting, computer science and technology, government, academia, engineering, medicine, research, library science, psychology, film-making, theology, consulting, publishing, journalism, the military—the list goes on and on. Indeed, career planning for people with prominent Thinking functions can pose the challenge of too many options, as Thinking is needed so widely in our intellectually complex, efficiency-oriented world.

Wherever Thinking may be in our personal hierarchy, much is demanded of our rational intellect in current-day life. If you are a Thinking type, you may not have considered your Thinking function as the especially powerful psychological processing faculty that it is, nor sought to place it in context of a society that encourages use of it so often. You might have assumed that everyone uses his or her Thinking function just the way you do, when many use Feeling processing or Intuition or Sensation perception as their first psychological priority. This fact poses special challenges and responsibilities for Thinking types, as well as opportunities.

Cool Heads

It appears that the cooler the climate, the more prominently Thinking processing is said to feature in a culture. Northern Anglo-Saxon mores, for instance, discourage emotional display as undesirably messy and unseemly — too southern and steamy, perhaps? Thinking types do appear "cooler" in comparison with Feeling types and processors, and are often the "cooler heads" around. Thinking types appreciate the "coolness" of jazz, which gives structure to the wild spirit of improvisation. Just saying "cool" brings emotional decibels down into a manageable range.

In a personal or professional crisis, a Thinking type's Thinking function goes to work as an intrepid instrument of information gath-

ering and analysis. Even if they are privately torn by emotional conflict, Thinking types can act as the voices of reason, analyzing the
circumstances, making decisions and coming up with solutions. In
situations of heightened distress, a clear-headed Thinking type, emotions on hold, can save the day.

Immersed in a busy home and family life, Thinking types can
maintain their professional focus and career activities more easily
than some other typologies, thanks to their natural ability to "compartmentalize," be organized and not easily led off course by disturbing interpersonal or inner concerns. Indeed, any household benefits
from a Thinking type in its midst, even if that person is only three
feet tall.

Thinking of Everything

A "detail person" usually has a high-ranking Thinking Function.
A Thinking type named Jim, for instance, was the best traveling
companion imaginable on a recent family trip to France. An experienced world traveler in his work as an education consultant, Jim
had accumulated considerable know-how to add to his natural gift
for detail. He started by making the travel reservations for everyone.
Are people coming from different cities to meet the same plane in
New York? Not a problem. Do they have to fly home on different
days? Okay. During the entire trip, he kept account of the luggage at
hotels, train stations and airports. He figured out the times to leave
to catch trains, buses or planes, and arranged for taxis. He packed
several guidebooks, well studied, and had interesting suggestions for
what to see in each place. It was soon evident that Jim was also the
source for whatever was forgotten, as he had thought ahead of nearly
every possibility. A wrap-around bandage for a sprained ankle? Jim
had brought one. Neosporin for a cut finger? Jim had it. A beard

trimmer? No problem, Jim had that too. The last night of the trip, the group gave Jim an award and a big round of applause.

Time on Their Minds

Thinking processors, as we have mentioned, have a respect for time as an essential ordering and measuring tool of life. Using their good memories, they can be counted on to remind us of an appointment with the accountant or dentist today or what you and your friends did on New Year's Eve in 1995. They celebrate not only their wedding anniversary but also the anniversary of the day they and their spouse met. The past is not over and gone, but remains very much alive in the Thinking function and is often inextricably entwined with the present. Certain dates can be especially painful if they are anniversaries of unhappy events. Thinking types can find it hard to let go of unwanted memories.

In their fascination with the past, however, positive influences from history, their own or the world's, appear in their full and rightful glory. Someone with a good Thinking function thrives studying history and revels in its dates, names, events and places. Thinking types flock to the History Channel. Thinking types study and visit hallowed ground where history was made. Thinking types take history personally. A Thinking-type physician has done so much research into the life of a family ancestor from the 18th century that the gentleman seems virtually alive to her, and she herself could step right back into Revolutionary War-era New York City to join him.

A Not B

The Thinking function differentiates and contrasts things, so we know this is not that. Then it makes selections and decisions.

When someone says, "I've decided that...." the person probably has a high-ranking Thinking function. One must not expect a "snap decision" from a Thinking type, however—there are too many considerations!

Innately objective, logical and reasonable, Thinking types may seem to be doing some heavy lifting when it comes to making a decision. Other types might make a choice spontaneously for reasons they can't cite or prove, but Thinking types must deliberate; they must know their reasons and take them logically one by one. A Thinking-type landscape designer says he finds eye exams nearly impossible. "The doctor keeps asking, 'A or B?' 'A or B?'" he says. "I want to say, 'Wait! I have to think about this!'"

Me Not Them

Our Thinking function helps us experience ourselves as individuals separate from family or society. Thinking distinguishes by identifying and defining certain unique characteristics and by comparing and contrasting them. With the emergence of our Thinking functions as small children, we are able to discern our separate selves from our mothers, fathers and siblings, and to begin to build a sense of our own individual identity and self-definition.

Inevitably, in its very nature, our Thinking functions bring a sense of separation from others, of being unique and different. Indeed, too much Thinking processing in our life can cause painful isolation, one of the hazards of a Thinking-intense contemporary life.

True Blue

In their relationships, the crown jewel of Thinking types' psychology is their loyalty. When they find a good thing, they stick with it. Once they give you their trust, it can be for life. They are loyal not only to family and to friends who have proven trustworthy, but also to traditions (even radical traditions), styles, brands, retailers, organizations, teams, schools, as well as to ways of operating and approaches to situations that have proven themselves. They can overlook many transgressions for the sake of loyalty, but when their trust is betrayed, the wound goes deep.

Thinking types understand the power of enduring concepts like fairness and justice, and attributes of character like "principled," "honorable," "ethical," "equitable," and "dependable," which often pertain to them.

Rapid change to the established order of things is generally unappealing, perhaps even suspect. Overall, if one wants to propose a change to a Thinking type, it is best to give a good rationale and expect at least some skepticism or resistance. And be sure to give them time to "think about it."

"First, Second, Third" and Other Organizing Principles

The Thinking function orders not only by time and logical sequence, but also by number. Quantities and percentages are important to the Thinking function. Mathematicians have good Thinking functions. Thinking types often enumerate. When someone says, "This is a good idea for the following four reasons," he or she is probably a Thinking type. Dewey of the ubiquitous decimal system was doubtless a Thinking type, as are many fine librarians.

A sure sign of a prominent Thinking function is the presence of a list. Whether it is to elicit from their minds what food they need to buy or what qualities they want in a partner, lists serve to clarify, order and objectify. On returning home after a month working on a Habitat for Humanity construction project in rural Georgia, a Thinking-Sensation type named Adam called a friend to come over. "Come help me make a list," he entreated. "I want to figure out what this meant to me."

First, in any project, they make an outline.

Feeding the Mind

Thinking types love to learn and are constantly reading, studying and researching subjects they want to know more about. Thinking-type film director and actress Jodie Foster, as a mother of two young sons, found herself in the garage listening to NPR "because I want to have a stimulating side to my life." [3] A large majority of PhD candidates in all fields are Thinking types. Even their leisure avocations usually involve lively mental activity, such as crossword puzzles, "who-done-it" mysteries or games such as bridge, chess, Scrabble and Trivial Pursuit. In fact, scratch the surface of a normally "rational" Thinking type and you may find an intensity of passion for a field of interest amounting to a "magnificent obsession."

Using the Thinking function's special art form of words, a Thinking type is often impressively articulate. He or she uses words thoughtfully, at times pointedly, and speaks in complete sentences, complex ones with dependent clauses and modifiers, like the members of British Parliament. Talk shows depend on Thinking types.

The Thinking function can contribute a healthy dose of skepticism against unconsidered naiveté and illusion. Matter-of-fact Thinking types want evidence and proof before they will accept something as true, despite what their own instincts and intuitions may be telling them. In Sinclair Lewis' 1925 novel *Arrowsmith*, the physician-hero prays, "God give me a restlessness whereby I may neither sleep nor accept praise till my observed results equal my calculated results or in pious glee I discover and assault my error."

Rules of Decorum

"When the English do something twice, it's a tradition," as the saying goes. Thinking types everywhere take delight in customs withstanding the tests of time. They are not ones to say, "Oh, that old thing..." They are often enthusiastic appreciators of "vintage" anything, from ancient cashmere mills and battlefields to single malt distilleries to generations-old vineyards.

A respectful nod to tradition rules socially, as well. Thinking types are most comfortable with a certain level of formality and tend towards rules of politeness and non-invasive subjects such as books, local issues, sports scores, professional matters or items in the news. A discussion can even appear heated and opinionated without getting "personal." Thinking types star in courtrooms where they can fight gladiatorial battles on points and issues and then go to lunch together and talk about their weekends with the kids. Any talk about the family, however, will focus on activities, not emotional dilemmas. Facts and ideas reign in the Thinking-function realm.

Lawyers, who are usually Thinking types or Thinking processors, have a gift for giving safely dispassionate and objective language to the flagrant interpersonal issues tackled by our legal system. Thinking types can maintain a presence of mind in situations where emotionality could rule out justice. Even in court, where crimes are being discussed that have involved the most intense emotions, lawyers ask, decorously, "What was your *state of mind* at the time of the incident?"

Thinking types have a direct, reasonable communication style. They exchange information. Step by step, they state their position, allow other people to state theirs, permit all sides to revise their positions. They argue, retreat, come closer until they reach a point of consensus or agreement, all on an intellectual level that never intrudes.

In order to process what is happening rationally, they keep emotion at a distance, seeming formal and, to some Feeling processors, even chilly. But their sincere connection with people must not be underestimated. The psychological standpoint of Thinking processors lies naturally at a slight distance from emotional scenes, however moved they might be. They can have the compassionate objectivity of a good psychoanalyst or Buddhist master. They lend solidity to relationships by giving plenty of emotional space, while remaining steadfastly and devotedly loyal.

A Few Words about Extraverted Thinking Types

World-class communicators with a naturally firm grasp of external events, extraverted Thinking types run large sections of the modern world. Experts at ascertaining the facts in outer-world situations, they can cut through obfuscations and conflicting arguments, see what's what, establish clarity, make a decision and get the job done.

They can be untiringly generous with their ideas, time and energy, and the world gladly takes as much as they will give. Extraverted Thinking types can be tireless community organizers, government leaders and committee chairpersons. Gifted with a natural sense of authority, they convey information with impressive clarity and reassuring certainty, are at ease expressing themselves before an audience and are stimulated by having one. Their eloquence can be heard in the halls of Congress, Parliament, *L'Assemblée Nationale*, in court-rooms and classrooms, at pulpits and podiums, at conferences and convocations. Meetings of all sizes are natural forums for extraverted Thinking types.

Jung wrote that the extraverted Thinking type determines an ultimate "ruling principle" for himself or herself, as well as for his or her whole environment. Extraverted Thinking types are often the ones who establish order in families, groups, businesses, churches, and governments and throughout society. In the finest extraverted Thinking-type minds, external reality crystallizes every moment to reveal an orderly structure, which they then set to work explaining and implementing.

A hallmark of an Extraverted Thinking type is friendliness that nonetheless maintains a decorous distance from premature intimacy. Extraverted Thinking types are devoted to their families, who are always encouraging them to get some rest.

A Few Words about Introverted Thinking Types

While extraverted Thinking seeks to establish order in outer situations, introverted Thinking works towards achieving an inner sense of reasonableness and rationality. Researching diligently in libraries, on the Web and in the quiet study-rooms of the mind, introverted Thinking goes straight for the facts, ideas, concepts and logical structures, whether in mathematics, science, history, horticulture, physics, philosophy, or in relationships. Introverted Thinking is "thinking about philosophical principles or abstractions or basic questions of life," writes Jungian analyst Marie-Louise von Franz, herself an introverted Thinking type. One must "first clarify one's ideas," she writes. "[I]f one is muddle-headed from the very start, one will never get anywhere." [4]

These introverts truly think in order to talk, and sometimes do not bother with the latter. Introverted Thinking goes on all by itself, invisibly, seemingly without any outside prompting, always sorting and organizing, like internal software. When they are ready, introverted Thinking types present their thoughts in a precise, condensed fashion like gemstones, all mined, cut and beautifully set as in a piece of intellectual jewelry.

Socially they can manifest the awkward charm of a Jimmy Stewart or Mr. Darcy; small talk is not their forte. If broadsided with too much enthusiasm or effusiveness, introverted Thinking types often close down like the Batmobile. While introverted Thinking types will be deeply comforted by the "idea" of family, they might secretly dread the prospect of a large family gathering with its intensely extraverted Feeling aspects. Nevertheless, introverted Thinking types are warmed by family bonds to the depth of their hearts. Romantic attachments and ties of friendship run equally deep. As Marie-Louise von Franz writes, "When an introverted Thinking type loves, there is no calculation in it. It will be totally for the sake of the other." [5]

The Thinking Type's Special Dilemma: Too Much Thinking

Carrying a mantle of reason, logic and clarity, Thinking types are encouraged, and encourage themselves, to take charge. Indeed, they can see responsibilities everywhere they look and take on the complexity and weight of them. Back surgery cases seem to focus with cruel regularity on Thinking types.

The Thinking function in everyone has a tendency to create an increasingly complex matrix of procedures, facts and requirements, until one is lost in a mental labyrinth and has forgotten where one was trying to go—a common post-modern experience. In a Thinking-intense culture, keeping an awareness of the other three functions and their realms, both within ourselves and in the people around us, takes effort, imagination, determination and practice. But human life is fundamentally too complex for one function to bear alone. It requires a cooperative partnership among all four functions to be balanced and well lived, which is just as true for successful organizations and society at large.

Realizing that one need not "think" of everything may be a disorienting experience, but also a relief for Thinking types, particularly as they discover their other three functions. With the constant daily demands made on Thinking, they must bring this powerful processing function to a halt every so often to avoid intellectual exhaustion. With the Thinking process stilled, the perceiving functions of Sensation or Intuition can come to the fore to provide fresh input of impressions from the immediate environment or insights from the creative imagination.

Fourth Function: Feeling

"...for as it nears the object of its yearning our intellect is overwhelmed so deeply it can never retrace the path that it followed."

— Dante

On two important occasions, a Thinking type may have an uncharacteristically personal and emotional reaction: if he or she has been hurt deeply in some way or if he or she has fallen in love. When the Fourth Function of Feeling is activated, rational rules of logic no longer apply.

With Fourth-Function Feeling, we introduce a momentous subject with a powerful influence on Thinking types and on their relationships. The Fourth Function in everyone poses challenges. But it must be said that as a Fourth Function, Feeling is arguably the most powerful psychological force to be reckoned with, both for Thinking types themselves and for those close to them.

However robust and competent someone's Thinking function may be, Feeling, as its typological opposite, is at significant times fully its equal in impact. Indeed, the Feeling function's influence on a Thinking type's life can be as important as the ability to reason logically, and at times appears to be more so. An eruption of Fourth-Function Feeling from the depths of the unconscious can render the primary Thinking function all but useless and ineffectual. Fourth-Function Feeling experiences can bring a Thinking type's most agonizing heartaches, but also his or her most ravishing moments of rapture and creativity. In their Fourth Function is the wellspring of his or her feelings of self-worth and deepest personal values and priorities; it nourishes them with a profound sense of emotional security and wellbeing, a beauty and sweetness in life beyond words.

A Thinking type's relationship with his or her "toggled off" Feeling processing can be confoundingly indirect, as if it were the dark side of the moon. "If you ask a Thinking type what he [or she] feels, he generally either replies with a thought or gives a quick conventional reaction," psychoanalyst and Thinking type Marie-Louis von Franz observed in *Jung's Typology*. [6] Von Franz gives the example of a Thinking type man who, on hearing that a friend has died, weeps deeply in sorrow, but on meeting the widow, he can't come out with anything to say. "They have the feeling somehow and somewhere, but not just when they ought to produce it," she writes [7]. Thinking types and processors are grateful senders of greeting cards. With them, it is truly the thought that counts.

The Human Factor

In organizations, where the Thinking function often prevails, Feeling is often referred to as the "human factor." The founding editor of *National Geographic* knew his readership well when he set the magazine's main editorial goal as "mental relaxation without emotional stimulus." In order to maintain unsullied rational clarity, the psyche of a Thinking type holds Feeling processing at a distance, though it doesn't always stay there. "Thinking, if it is to be real thinking and true to its own principle, must rigorously exclude Feeling," Jung wrote in *Psychological Types.* [8]

But while the spotlight shines on the work of objective reasoning, the subjectively oriented Feeling function is very much alive deep in a Thinking type's heart. Seen or unseen, Feeling is a Thinking type's constant companion in the realm of personal relationships, enthusiasms and values. It colors his or her immediate visceral responses to people and situations, and provides the richness and warmth of their intimate human attachments.

Feeling is the psychological function that processes how much one values someone or something. Feelings of appreciation, caring and devotion are felt without any intellectual or rational components. Feeling as the Fourth Function in a Thinking type is an especially pure, untouched, undefiled kind of Feeling, with an open-hearted quality, as well as a raw heart-on-sleeve vulnerability. For a Thinking type to "go there" voluntarily, he or she must feel very safe or very impassioned.

When approaching and relating to Thinking types, keep an inner eye out for the appearance of Fourth-Function Feeling. In truth, their Feeling function can deeply motivate them, though they may not be aware of this. For an observer, Fourth-Function Feeling can be like a glimpse of a rare bird or animal or a precious jewel. When a Thinking type suddenly comes out with an expression of tenderness, it can be breathtaking; it's best not to say a word.

On in the Background, the Psyche's Weather Channel

The Feeling Function is our psychology's processing of our aliveness, our organism's natural responses to life-in-progress. Like the weather outside, sometimes we feel serene and sunny inside, sometimes sultry and stormy or anything in between. When Feeling is the Fourth Function, it is as if these emotional weather systems are moving through at the deepest levels, normally registering only as a slight change in inner pressure, a dimming of their usual clarity, or as a vague and distant mood.

Under certain conditions, however, the usual clarity of the Thinking function is eclipsed and Feeling comes bursting through. As an inner force of nature, a sudden appearance of Fourth-Function Feeling can be deeply disconcerting experience. A Thinking-type writer named Leslie with an interest in Africa went to see a movie by Italian filmmaker Bernardo Bertolucci on an African political theme. The film opens with a woman in an African country seeing her husband arrested and taken away to prison. Leslie watched in the dark of the theater as the woman escapes to Rome in order to find work to earn money to buy her husband's freedom. In the intricate plot, the woman lands a job as a housekeeper in the home of an expatriate Englishman, a pianist and composer. He falls in love with her, and, unbeknownst to her, he quietly starts selling his belongings one by one in order to send money via a priest to her home country to purchase her husband's liberty. As the furniture disappears, the housekeeper slowly realizes what the Englishman is doing for her, and to the strains of the passionate piano music he has been composing and playing for her, she falls in love with the Englishman. One day, inevitably, the husband, now freed, shows up, suitcase in hand, at the door of the Englishman's house in Rome to reunite with his wife. At this climactic point in the film, Leslie's objective, rational mental circuits flooded. She was so overcome, she had to leave the theater, unable to bear witnessing the outcome.

Thinking types who excel at running departments and organizations of all kinds may, once home, convulse in agony over personnel matters that touch their Feeling functions. The prospect of firing an employee can distress them for days, and they may feel awkward doing it. In family life, Fourth-Function Feeling can cause disabling emotional confusion and pain. A Thinking-type professor and father of a teenage daughter, for instance, suffered torture witnessing the inevitable mother-teenage daughter conflagrations. The emotionality of these confrontations between the two people he loved most in the world caused him such anguish he had to leave the house.

Our psyche always strives toward balance; too much First Function focus or activity is certain to provoke a protest from our Fourth Function. "'He knows his feelings very well,' Jung wrote of an extraverted Thinking-type man he knew, "but he denies them any validity and declares they have no influence over him. They therefore come upon him against his will..." [9]

Hot, Don't Touch

Supremely competent at managing jobs and the practicalities of everyday life, Thinking types in tender intimate matters may see themselves as highly vulnerable, at times inept. Not quite trusting their instincts, they fear that if they make a mistake the relationship will be destroyed. Separations can feel terrifying, stark and isolating. They may try to distance themselves from the so-called personal side of life, labeling it as "drama," unimportant or a hindrance to the work they want to do. When relating to the Feeling processors in their lives, Thinking types may be impatient or critical, without realizing that they may be using their rationality to maintain a safe distance and control, in order to shield themselves from hurt or confusion.

Underlying their objective facades, however, the Feeling function of Thinking types is of a rare and intense nature, clear as a mountain lake, tender and delicately beautiful as a spring flower, or as searing as molten lava. A Fourth-Function event might cause pain, but just as often an eruption of ecstasy. "I have realized something!" a Thinking-type college student announced breathlessly to his mother in a quick phone call. "The purpose of life is to be happy! And I *am* happy! I am enjoying everything I am doing in my life!" Then he hung up.

Returning from a week spent on a silent retreat, an extraverted Thinking-type artist was greeted by her husband of thirty years with home-baked bread and an embrace that clearly expressed how happy he was to see her. She was overwhelmed. "Aren't we lucky to be so in love at our age?" she exclaimed. No human feeling could be more exquisite.

Love-struck

"Everybody loves a lover," the song claims, and no one is more amazed by experiencing this phenomenon than a Thinking type, who suddenly finds himself or herself dancing down the street whistling

"Zippity Do-Dah." The Feeling function gives Thinking types in love a visceral, emotional connection with another human being that feels organic, as if sharing a single nervous system. He or she suddenly feels vibrantly aware and alive. There is nothing like love to part the veil of mental processing and reveal the hyper-real Technicolor world of Fourth-Function Feeling. Thinking types can fall in love fast and hard. They want to worship at the altar of the Feeling function and to testify to their love.

Fourth-Function Feeling is uninhibited when it connects. When you hear that someone has met the love of his or her life and they were co-habiting two weeks later, it can well be an enraptured Thinking type having a Fourth-Function epiphany. The relationship might last, too, thanks to Thinking types' remarkable gift for steadfast loyalty.

A Thinking type in love experiences his or her Fourth Function in all its primal power. The Feeling function, surging up unbidden, transforms. Suddenly, a person (or a place or an era) takes on the highest value in the Thinking type's life. The beloved carries a quality that is almost mystical, mythical. It's hard to ignore the feelings of intense attraction and other vivid feelings that rock his or her world.

If you happen to be on the receiving end of a Fourth-Function Feeling attachment, you too can feel its power. It is a great privilege, but also a responsibility, and must be handled with utmost care. Along with the adamant warmth, generosity and fervency, there is a quality of unpredictability to a Thinking type in the throes of his or her Fourth Function, as if he or she could take flight or crumble at any moment.

The Fourth Function on the Big Stage

Music is a quintessential expression of the Feeling function. Opera may have been born in Italy, where the Feeling function is quite at home, but opera houses all over the world would close down without Thinking types, whose Fourth-Function Feeling can live there safely, voluptuously projected onto the grand stage. Under the intellectual guise of following the libretto, studying the history of great singers and tracking down obscure recordings, Thinking types flock to opera to nourish their Feeling functions and give them a "voice." "The fact is, we need opera," novelist and opera lover Ann Patchett wrote in *The New York Times Magazine*. "It is an enormous, passionate, melodramatic affair that helps put the little business of our lives into perspective. The more dire things get these days, the more we look to comfort ourselves with facts... But ... [o]pera, more than any other art form, has the sheer muscle and magnitude to pull us into another world, and while that world may be as fraught with heartache as our own, it is infinitely more gorgeous. Through voices like Pavarotti's, we are lifted up, temporarily transformed. Opera reminds us of the enormous beauty we are capable of, and if there's a good cathartic sob at the end, well, we probably needed that too." [10]

Fourth-Function Feeling's Best Friend

The natural world often holds a special fascination for Thinking types, and some of their most profound relationships are with animals. A Thinking type's Fourth-Function Feeling resonates with animals. There would be no humane societies without Thinking types. The local pet stores would be empty. Horse shows would not exist, and dog shows would not be the elaborate, passionate and delightful extravaganzas they are. Thousands of top dogs are lovingly trained and organized into their categories and groups by Thinking types, for whom dogs are often their teachers. For a dog, to *be* is to be *with*: the Feeling function at its most fundamental.

A holiday card featuring the picture of a sloe-eyed hound wearing a Christmas wreath is probably from a Thinking type or processor in the loving embrace of his or her Fourth-Function Feeling. Indeed, a Thinking type's pet is arguably among the luckiest creatures on earth. The most sophisticated Thinking type with a number of advanced academic degrees can be totally besotted by a Labrador retriever or cocker spaniel, a dressage horse, a Maine Coon cat, even a pet iguana or Norway rat. Watching a Thinking type relating with his or her favorite animal, one glimpses a more natural and emotional side of the person. A Thinking type who has lost a pet is almost inconsolable. A friend says she is convinced that her father, a Thinking-type banker and mathematician, put his hunting dog King on a par in importance with his three daughters. King is buried in the family cemetery.

Emotion Recollected in Tranquility

Among the best ways for a Thinking type to "process" feelings that either hide or threaten to be overwhelming is creative self-expression. Contemplating life's unpredictable, unfathomable emotions and sublime inspirations, Thinking types and processors allowing their Fourth Function wellspring to flow creatively have written some of the world's most beautiful poetry, music, philosophy, metaphysics and theology. In art, poetry and music, Fourth-Function Feeling is "invoked" so it can reveal its power transformed by human effort into a beautiful, moving and graceful form. Bach was a Thinking type. True also of Beatles John, Paul and George (with Ringo providing the grounding beat of Sensation).

Thinking-type biographer and memoirist Laurie Lisle (*Portrait of an Artist: A Biography of Georgia O'Keeffe; Four-Tenths of an Acre*) uses the first hour in the early morning to sit quietly with a cup of tea, a book and her journal. "I have to set up the right conditions," she says. "Then feelings and insights just come up. It so hard to capture them." By devoting the effort first thing in the morning to finding the words and phrases, Lisle brings vitality and remarkable depth of understanding to her books and essays.

Two Kinds of Thinking

According to Jung, there are two different kinds of "thinkers": those who depend on Sensation perceptions to orient themselves—Thinking-Sensation types—and those who more often think about Intuition perceptions—Thinking-Intuitive types.

THINKING	SENSATION	INTUITION	FEELING
First	Second	Third	Fourth

or

THINKING	INTUITION	SENSATION	FEELING
First	Second	Third	Fourth

Using perceptions from their Sensation function, Thinking-Sensation types tend toward a logical, practical, procedural thinking, which focuses on the concrete aspects of a situation. For them, a thought follows upon another thought methodically and systematically addressing the material facts at hand. Pragmatic, deliberate and organized, often hands-on capable, Thinking-Sensation types have a direct, tactile relationship with the workings and characteristics of whatever exists before them. Thinking-Sensation types take good care of their wardrobes and home environments, and their style is neat, classic, well-considered and of high quality. They make decisions based on practical, logistical or aesthetic issues, and they can come up with clear procedures to follow in the midst of current circumstances. About the past, they are interested in the facts of actual events and lives. Thinking-Sensation types make excellent historians, teachers, doctors, engineers, government leaders, attorneys, corporate managers, and computer programmers, among a host of professions compatible with their typology.

The other kind of thinking is the spark-plug, synapse-popping kind of *intuitive* thinking. Thinking combined with Intuition, sometimes called associative or metaphorical thinking, takes care of strategy, options and new directions. It is as if Thinking-Sensation types think vertically and Thinking-Intuitives think horizontally. In their thinking process, Thinking-Intuitives take a set of facts and immediately think of their meaning, context, possible relationship to other facts. They follow ideas, concepts and possibilities step by step *outward* into theories. With their curiosity going in many directions, Thinking-Intuitive types are thinking, "What if this happens? " "What if we try that..." Strategic thinkers, Thinking-Intuitives are often found among think-tank members, economists, journalists or political commentators and college professors, especially the brilliant "absent-minded" ones.

Thinking-Sensation Types

The combination of Thinking processing and Sensation perception thrives in the modern world and makes many contributions to it. Just watch a crisply attired bank manager flip from screen to screen on the bank's website, enter information into a succession of complex forms, then arise extending a firm handshake and a smile —Thinking-Sensation expertise in action.

Thinking with Sensation is like the preponderating O-positive blood type of Western culture. Thinking-Sensation types keep so many aspects of our modern world functioning it is easy to take them for granted. That is, until you need to get a certified foreign-currency draft to pay an overseas vendor, find the leak in your plumbing system, write a manual, organize the annual library book sale, build an extension onto the house, want a teacher of arithmetic for a room full of six-year-olds, or find someone to run an organization. No wonder so few of them are unemployed for very long. Truly, where would we be without them?

Their clear, practical minds and hands-on competence lead them to an interest and expertise in all kinds of things in the Sensation realm. Martha Stewart is a Thinking-Sensation type. They process many facts and ideas easily and can discuss or write about them knowledgeably, making their points clearly with good supporting arguments and examples.

Sensation gives them a gift for physical hardiness and for looking debonair, as well as a practical "just-do-it" attitude. They enjoy direct and tactile relationships with children and animals. There is often a special animal in their life.

Order and Form

While Thinking with Intuition pushes thinking "out of the box," Thinking with Sensation is thinking *about* the box. Thinking-Sensation makes sure that everything necessary is in it, that it is kept in good working order and that procedures for its use are effective and clearly articulated. Thinking-Sensation types know the exact kind of tool for a task, from a knife for cutting tomatoes to the authentic rum for a true mojito cocktail. They love projects. Step by step, they read and research to find out what works best and then set about doing it.

Thinking-Sensation types are interested in facts about the real world, practical facts, such as the proper thread count of comforter covers, the capabilities of a piece of sports equipment, the type of seed that attracts goldfinches, the procedures for processing digital photographs. Other facts may pertain to the past, such as how the railroads were built or aspects of Alexander the Great's successful military campaigns. They often know a lot about favorite sports team or a particular band, artist or category of music.

Thinking-Sensation types tend to read a lot, and their books are all arranged by subject, century, author and title and shelved a half-inch from the edge.

The combination of Thinking and Sensation creates some of the world's greatest gardeners. With their natural sense of nature's timing and the beauty of orderly design, they create luxuriant, well tended gardens that flower all season. They remember all the plants' names.

They keep an appointment book to organize every waking minute productively, and when the exact hour comes, they'll appear, mentally prepared, equipped with all the necessary materials and dressed appropriately.

Thorough

"I'm slow, but reliable," says a Thinking-Sensation-type teacher named Jessica modestly, straightening her classroom at the end of the day. One can indeed count on Thinking-Sensation types to come through. More tortoise than hare, a Thinking-Sensation type persists until the job is done and done well.

Thinking-Sensation-types can make good carpenters; they measure twice and cut once. While a Sensation type named Pam was busy redecorating her living room with vibrant fabrics of contrasting patterns, her Thinking-Sensation-type husband Randy was meticulously applying three coats of high-gloss paint onto all the woodwork, its subtle gleam contributing to a flawless and finished effect everywhere one looked.

When you ask a Thinking-Sensation type for directions, you will get street names, the number of lights, precise landmarks, and how long it might take you, and they will be right.

Conservators and Collectors

Greatly valuing tried-and-true tradition, Thinking with Sensation perpetuates red phone boxes, taxicabs and private clubs in London, as well as historic towns, houses, gardens and monuments everywhere. Thinking-Sensation types seek out what works well, maintain it and preserve it.

They are among the world's most devoted collectors. They get an enthusiasm or favorite theme, whether it is old maps, family photographs, first editions, vintage postcards, a china pattern, art by a particular artist or figurines of fish to create veritable mini-museums. Gift and antique shops and auction houses would be quite empty without Thinking-Sensation types.

Thinking-Sensation Style

Appearances aren't everything, but they can be revealing. With their good Sensation functions, Thinking-Sensation types have a neat esthetic (Sensation) that follows logical fashion rules (Thinking): "The shirt placket, belt buckle and trouser fly should all line up." "Shirt trouser bottoms should break on top of your shoe, so that the crease on the leg rumples just slightly." "Your tie must reach your beltline." "You can now wear white after Labor Day." They know what designers are correct for the milieu they will be in. They don't "decorate" themselves as a work of art the way a First-Function Sensation type would, but they always look very "smart."

Fashionistas might call the Thinking-Sensation look "permanent style." Thinking-Sensation types are made for tuxedos, and vice versa. (Think Gregory Peck, Jack Kennedy, Barak Obama, Hugh Grant and Annette Bening.) Otherwise, fashion trademarks include a slightly formal, pragmatic, freshly laundered, old-school wholesomeness. Colors are neutral or rich and pleasing without being flashy, such as "Nantucket red". Their classic crew necks and V-necks, clean khakis, comfortably worn, but their loafers are polished. The original "preppies" of the 1920s had Thinking-Sensation-type style. More "midtown" than "downtown," they don't bother with temporary fads, but tend toward abiding and classic lines and looks. Astute shoppers, they find a store and designer and stick with them. Fabrics and accessories must be of good quality.

Their wardrobes are thoughtfully color coordinated and mix-and-match. Their clothes fit them well and are kept washed, pressed and in good repair. In their closets, clothes and shoes are meticulously arranged by season or category on shelves, in bins and boxes, clearly labeled. One Thinking-Sensation type investment advisor keeps every dress, jacket, pair of pants, blouse and skirt in a cleaner bag so it is free of dust and doesn't wrinkle in her closet. It works.

Great Educators

As a Thinking-Sensation type, Jane possesses an ideal typology for all the activities that fill a teacher's life in and out of the classroom. With her strong and diligent Thinking function, she develops and conveys lessons clearly, accomplishes myriad school administrative responsibilities and completes frequently required courses and seminars on curriculum, education theory and child psychology. She is both entertaining and in command in front of 30 children every day, produces and acts in children's theater productions, engages parents skillfully in conferences and parent-teacher association meetings. She uses her secondary Sensation function constantly in the daily pageant of classroom activities, from moving around desks and tables to creative classroom projects. Her children always notice her earrings or her shoes.

An extravert, Jane keeps in touch with children she has taught, and gets invited to their high school and college graduations, then to their weddings. She also stays connected with many friends, some of whom she has known since grammar school. Outside her packed school days, Jane maintains a busy schedule of tutoring, art classes, kayaking and long-distance swimming.

Thinking-Intuitive Types

"I began to suspect that thought, which I had always before looked on as a cart-horse,…might really be a Pegasus, so suddenly did it alight beside me from places I had no knowledge of."

— Joanna Field, *A Life of One's Own*

Thinking in partnership with Intuition is quite different from the step-by-step, practical, solution-oriented kind of Thinking that works with Sensation facts and perceptions. Enhanced by Intuitive insights, Thinking takes off into new realms of imaginative concepts, theories and possibilities.

For Thinking-Intuitives, ideas are not just useful and a means to an end, they are *fun*. Thinking-Intuitives are inspired to put thoughts together in exploratory, original, unorthodox, even revelatory ways, yet they can convey their intellectual discoveries with riveting precision.

Thinking-Intuitives are arguably the most mentally inquisitive of human beings. They have a special talent for intense and lively interest, whether in their current favorite subjects or their work, which is usually mentally challenging. They research aspects of a situation, event, person or set of facts, and immediately try to push the frontiers of thought. What is their significance, their connection with other events, their likely future development? They probably just read something else that relates to these very thoughts.

Thinking-Intuitives can make superb students and often go on to be professors and teachers. For Thinking-Intuitives, to live is to research. Irrepressible sleuths, they have hundreds of browser bookmarks and their bookshelves are full, side tables piled high, file cabinets bulging. Thinking-Intuitives try to gather enough information on a topic so they can *understand* it. They have the intellectual confidence that, if they look long and hard enough, they will.

Indeed, Thinking-Intuitives personify the delights of scholarship. Two Thinking-Intuitive type professors, one in America, one in Europe, found out that they were working on research on the same subject, which was Spanish paintings in 19th Century France. At a summit meeting held in a restaurant in Paris, they discovered that one of them was more interested in the Romantic era and the other in Impressionism, so they decided to divide up the intellectual territory. One would take Spanish paintings in France prior to 1838, the other would study Spanish paintings in France after 1838. Then they called for the waiter and ordered a good champagne.

Exceptionally articulate in speaking or writing or both, many Thinking-Intuitives become writers and make excellent editors. They also fill the ranks of mathematicians, physicists, philosophers, legal experts, political commentators and strategists, and other professions all along the cutting edge of thought.

Both analytical and insightful, a Thinking-Intuitive's lively mind can be truly formidable. Thinking-Intuitives can be provocative theorists and incisive critics. Brilliant cultural essayist Susan Sontag may serve as an example, but all Thinking-Intuitives are born intellectuals. Clear-headed, astute and well informed, they have prodigious mental stamina. They make great chess players. Keeping their wits about them long after other personalities tire, Thinking-Intuitives leaven the intellectual life of our culture and expand the boundaries of our knowledge.

Furthermore, with their laser-beam minds and subtle, intuitive sense of the absurdity contained in many situations, Thinking-Intuitives are among the world's funniest people, using words that others quote for laughs for years afterwards. W.C. Fields, Jerry Lewis, H. L. Mencken, Whoopi Goldberg, Lily Tomlin and Billy Crystal are examples. Even among the introverts, keep an ear cocked for wry-flavored comments, made *sotto voce*.

Extraverted Thinking-Intuitives thrive in a classroom, courtroom or drawing room. They love stimulating conversation and argument. They work an audience with dazzling presence of mind. They remember discussions with you from six months ago and pick up where you left off. They also make wonderful dinner party hosts—after first engaging their favorite caterer. They keep the conversation lively and pertinent to all the guests, whose various interests and expertises they remember and ask about. They are often ready with the perfect *bon mot*. These extraverts network and socialize widely, often globally, with people who share their enthusiasms.

As for introverted Thinking-Intuitives, their minds can be so completely occupied, they can be standing right next to you and barely seem to register you are there. As trepidatious students know who have approached a professor deep in thought, it can be daunting to interrupt their ruminations. But from behind their notebooks, tape-recorders, computer screens, lecterns or desks, introverted Thinking-Intuitives are almost universally tender-hearted, and they make considerable contributions to the world as scholars, jurists, historians, teachers, writers, astrophysicists, mathematicians, news editors, research librarians or members of any number of intellectually rich professions.

Mind Over Matter

For Thinking-Intuitives, "Where there is a will, there is a way" is not a cliché. They can do almost anything they set their minds to. Read Plato? Learn ancient Greek. Enter a marathon? Start training. Discover a unified theory of the Universe? Worthy and exciting work. Be another Sherlock Holmes? Elementary, my dear Watson. Leave home and become a great Hollywood actress? Just do it, like Katharine Hepburn. Amelia Earhart was a Thinking-Intuitive, as was her friend Eleanor Roosevelt. The Thinking-Intuitive type has a genius for total conviction free of any doubt whatsoever. A Thinking-Intuitive named Barbara went to medical school in the 1930s, a gender-breakthrough she dismisses. "I wanted to go," she said. "It never occurred to me not to." She practiced medicine into her 90s pioneering in the field of geriatric medicine.

A Thinking-Intuitive magazine editor-in-chief named Susan, a marathon runner at 40, got married at 41 and at 45 got pregnant — with twins. "Lucky for me," she said, with characteristic wry mirth. "They'll entertain themselves."

A Thinking-Intuitive's creative life is highly original, with their minds keeping an inner window open to feelings coming in from their Fourth Function. "And I want to write like Michael Jackson would write—instead of writing parts on the instruments or humming melodies, you think of them," singer-songwriter-musician Jack White told interviewer Alec Wilkinson at *The New Yorker*. "To do everything in my head and to do it in silence and use only one room." [11]

Sports-minded Thinking-Intuitives, though they may be rare on professional football or Olympic teams, specialize in athletic endeavors requiring focus and strategy. Sailing is an example, or running. They can also make formidable tennis players. A Thinking-Intuitive government administrator and tennis player was able to stand in the middle of the court and direct the ball anywhere he wanted to, causing his daughter to run all over the court, until she grew skillful enough to aim strategic shots of her own.

A Thinking-Intuitive tends to approach his or her body as an intellectual issue. He or she does medical research, then simply makes a decision. Pain is merely an annoyance and can often be canceled out mentally. A day after major surgery, the person is up and walking around, telephoning colleagues and friends who insist, "Hey, this can wait, get some rest!" British astrophysicist and Thinking-Intuitive Stephen Hawking continued exploring the laws of the universe despite being almost completely immobilized with Lou Gehrig's Disease; his Thinking-Intuitive genius operates independently of his physical limitations.

The Power of Positive Thinking

Thinking-Intuitives can have the most indefatigable and resourceful of spirits. On a weekend with friends in the country, facing a second day of wet weather, a Thinking-Intuitive magazine publisher piped up, "But it's a bright rain!" prompting them all to set off on an excursion anyway, during which they explored antique shops and discovered an excellent Mexican restaurant.

They are happy to leave the haute cuisine to others in order to converse with their guests. But one Thinking-Intuitive, fascinated by soufflés, studied a number of recipes and learned to make the perfect cheese soufflé, which became her signature contribution on any occasion.

The Joy of Being Quirky

Thinking-Intuitives can be as pleasingly, ingeniously eccentric as the proverbial Oxford don. They inspire respect, affection, even reverence, because they are so original and so darned smart.

You can intrigue them into a life-long friendship. There is no need to make small talk, nor to hide how smart you are. Just tell them what you've been reading and thinking about or bring up a question you have been pondering. They may challenge or argue with you— smart Thinking-Intuitives enjoy a good argument—but they'll help you cut through any fuzzy thinking and maybe send you in a new direction. They admire intellectual integrity, including someone who says, "I don't know."

If you see a Thinking-Intuitive as an ivory-tower intellectual, just get him or her talking about an intellectual passion. Their sheer conviction and intellectual energy, along with the unusual details they have accumulated, will very soon have you fascinated. A Thinking-Intuitive entrepreneur named John says he likes nothing better than to sit and "noodle" a new economic model he has designed, testing it and trying different scenarios, plugging in growth rates and interest-rate projections and shaping the yield curve. His description of the model is so lucid, he makes you see your grocery budget or car payments in a new way.

Many Thinking-Intuitives are passionate about genealogy. Tracking down ancestors, following the trace of their heritage back through time, across oceans, throughout states and counties, grounds them in life itself.

Thinking-Intuitive Anti-Style

With Sensation in third place and their minds engrossed in their work or other interests, they are unlikely to seek out the latest fashion trends when there is so much else to think about. The colors don't quite match? Oh, well, it's not important, when their manuscript awaits, an interesting guest has arrived, an equation beckons or a rare book is waiting for them on reserve at the library. With an affinity for traditional looks and "old favorites," they are attached to the tried and true and have little need for the new.

Dressing up may mean putting on a bow tie with their brown tweed jacket, one of many white blouses or a very nice scarf over their comfy black sweater. A successful Thinking-Intuitive entrepreneur has a favorite London tailor make him his entire dapper wardrobe. When they find a style of shirt that works, they buy it in several different colors. When a Thinking-Intuitive's favorite shoe store closed, she wore her last pair of shoes for months until debilitating foot pain drove her to a doctor. At his recommendation of another shoe store, she was henceforth happily ensconced in "a new shoe situation."

As for their living environments, once their nest is made, they tend to settle in. An armchair remains in its place for years. Their signature decorative accent may be piles of books and magazine, all scrupulously organized by topic. One Thinking-Intuitive lived with the same appliances until they became valuable antiques of Mid-Century Modern. Her motto is, "If it ain't really, really broke, why fix it?" Even amidst luxury, Thinking-Intuitives live with the familiar as simply as possible by changing as little as possible, so they can enjoy an elaborate and eventful life of the mind.

Having to dress for a special occasion or pack for a trip can cause a Thinking-Intuitive considerable anxiety. They show up at the door looking perfectly presentable, though their real attractiveness is their impressive erudition and genuine curiosity, their eyes sparkling with wit and the light of firing synapses. Who needs to make a fashion statement when you keep everyone one fascinated and laughing?

Relating to Thinking Types

Here are some guidelines for interacting with Thinking types:

Give them reasons. With a Thinking type, give him or her a few good reasons for your decision or point of view, such as, "I can't come to your party because I will be on call all weekend and have to keep my wits about me," or "Investing in that office complex is smart because it is accessible via three major freeways and because First National Bank just came in on the deal." Thinking types and processors are disturbed by imprecision. They are uncomfortable with a casual "ball-park" approach to factual detail. Be as precise as possible, and substantiate.

Give them time to "think it over." Present your idea, proposal or question, and then honor the step-by-step deliberative process of their Thinking function. Do not demand or expect an "on-the-spot" answer. Their consideration process may in fact take several days. If a Thinking type seems to be overly, laboriously thorough, be patient. Impeccable logic may be needed in the situation. Give him or her time and space to process what is presented. Don't call back or pester for at least a week.

Be on time. Respecting their acute sense of time honors Thinking types and processors. A Thinking type loves to hear, "I want to get on your calendar." Thinking types and processors appreciate promptness. Show up when expected. Honor deadlines. Confirm a meeting. Definitely let them know if you're going to be late. If you are traveling with a Thinking type, offer to leave with plenty of time to get to the airport.

Don't gush. Keeping a polite and decorous emotional distance respects the boundaries of a Thinking type's comfort zone. There is no need for expressing all your personal feelings on the matter, no matter how heartfelt. Less can be more. Thinking types and processors instinctively create psychological distance to protect their natural standpoint of rational objectivity. The extent of their agreement with you, or their pleasure at seeing you, may not be effusive—a nod and a handshake will express it all. Tact and rules of politeness are a balm to a Thinking type, who appreciates the orderly, predictable relatedness of following established or traditional social codes.

Do not *ask, "How do you feel about...?"* Thinking types cannot honestly tell you what they are feeling, and they don't know readily what others are feeling. Flummoxed by being asked, they may put up defenses, such as changing the subject abruptly, even walking away. It's not that they are rejecting you, don't like you or respect what you have to offer, but feelings confuse them and they don't know how to respond. Their feelings might be strong, but they aren't comfortable openly experiencing or expressing them. Best not to ask, "How did you like..." the movie, the meeting, Saturday's game, the new neighbor, your proposal; Thinking types and processors don't immediately like or dislike things. Instead, ask, "What is your opinion?" "Do you want to weigh in on this?" or "What did you think of..." the idea, candidate, book or recipe.

Hear them out. Thinking types are rarely heard out to the end of their logical deliberation process. This can make extraverts compensate by over-assertiveness and introverts react by fading away into muttering self-effacement. Thinking types are often interrupted and even interrupt each other. We all want to be listened to, but it is a special gift to listen to a Thinking type and to take those mental steps with him or her to their conclusion. Logic is beautiful, and the results may surprise you.

Give your credentials. While Feeling processors often evaluate others by an instinctive personal response to them, Thinking types use facts about people in order to assess and evaluate them and their opinions. When relating to a Thinking type, presenting your credentials are not necessarily boasts; these are important facts that orient the Thinking function to who you are. Job titles, degrees, affiliations, publications, home town, travel experience or other attributes stated simply as facts help Thinking types to situate you in their minds and process what you have to say.

Avoid surprises. Thinking types thrive on the predictable. They don't like "unpleasant surprises." Alert them of changes early, so they can be prepared. You can't keep the unexpected from happening, but the fewer surprises that come from you, the easier your relationship will be.

Be thoughtful. A call, email or card on their birthday, a thank-you note, a genuine and spontaneous message saying, "I've been thinking about you," will move a Thinking type to their very soul. Your "thoughtfulness" will nourish them profoundly. (But don't overdo it, or they will become overwhelmed and shut down.)

Just value them. No one needs more to "feel" valued and accepted than a Thinking type, though they can be the last one to show it, or even know it. If you cannot "keep up" with their rational discourse or detailed arguments, simply be there and value them. Your valuing will be "felt" by their Fourth Function, which can have profound effects.

—— 8 ——

The Feeling Function

"People will forget what you said, people will forget what you
did, but people will never forget how you made them feel."

—Maya Angelou, poet

Most of us are well acquainted with Thinking processing, what it
is, when it is required and what it does for us throughout the day. The
Feeling function is an entirely different function and faculty we have
within us to process our life in a very different and equally important
way. Thinking gives more weight to logical thought to understand
our circumstances and make decisions, while Feeling gives more
weight to what is *felt*. Feeling is a *subjective* process based on the
intelligence of our instinctive visceral and emotional responses. It
is the source of our EQ, allowing us to relate to the people we meet
and to our life circumstances and to take action with this valuable
personal information in mind.

One of the chief difficulties in writing about the Feeling function is our language itself—the word "feeling" is used in so many different ways. As Jung wrote, "We must recognize that a 'feeling' of regret is something quite different from a 'feeling' that the weather will change or that the price of our aluminum shares will go up." [1] Feelings such as regret, contentment, unease, delight and "feeling just great" properly fall under the Feeling function. A feeling that is a look into the future or a hunch, as about the weather or the direction of financial markets, is actually Intuition perception. There are also "feelings" that pertain to Sensation perception, such as feeling cold or the soft fur of a cat.

The Feeling function, however, is how our psychology processes for understanding what our organism's responses are telling us about a person or situation. Jung observed that when we "feel," there is a Sensation component. The Feeling process is often very physical, as every Feeling type knows after a day of stomach jumps, shoulder cringes, swoons and little joyful leaps, and other "body language" accompanying their feelings. The Feeling-Sensation connection's intelligence can be as basic as when we feel out of sorts because we are hungry or depressed because we need rest and as sophisticated as the lowered eyebrow of skepticism or the sinking feeling in our chest of dread. We even use Sensation language for what we are feeling: we know the truth of something when we "feel it in our bones" or we feel like we have been "hit in the solar plexus."

The Feeling process is the heart's language—an experience can live in our hearts or be heart-fluttering; our heart can "sink" or "break." When we feel something powerful, our hand often spontaneously moves to our heart, a sure sign that the Feeling function is activated.

Feeling may not lend itself easily to words because it doesn't use or need them. When we are happy or scared, we might not have the words for it, but we *feel* it. Our Feeling function makes our instinctive responses intelligible for us. It is able to interpret the signals of our biochemistry, as it were, thus giving us an understanding of life gained from our on-going personal responses to it.

The Feeling function performs two vitally important psychological activities for us. One is to feel how much we *value* people, things and situations as a way of sorting them out and guiding our behavior and choices. The other is to *relate* in a personal way, allowing for deep and genuine relatedness with people, in fact with whatever life presents to us. This is not the "Have a nice day" kind of relatedness, but a direct, real and sincere personal connection with the people we know and care about, as well as those we simply encounter in the course of daily life. This aspect of our intelligence to evaluate and relate according to our personal responses is built into us to further the quality of our lives as human beings, as individuals and together.

Sorting Things Out: Liking and Disliking

According to Jung, "feeling is a kind of judgment, different from intellectual judgment in that its aim is not to establish conceptual relations but to set up a subjective criterion of acceptance or rejection…T]hinking organizes things under concepts, while Feeling arranges them according to their value." [2] The "workaday" Feeling process is "liking" and "disliking." Feeling types experience this all day long.

Akin to liking s preferring, a feeling that helps us make choices based on a feeling, rather than on logic and analysis of options. Liking and preferring are vital to the creative process.

Often set aside as irrelevant, the feeling of liking or disliking are not taken seriously, yet they provide crucial human information. In the fullness of Feeling processing, one arrives at choices by personally evaluating all the options according to one's feelings about them, such as: "I love this. I like that. That is okay. I hate that." Feeling discriminates by subjectively ranking as to better and worse, more important and less, more appealing and less desirable. No reasons given, no reasons needed.

It is as if our Feeling function is always holding its own popularity contest as to our experience. We use Feeling processing when we are asked to rank or rate products or films, for instance. Do we give a film five stars ("I loved it"), four stars ("I really liked it"), three stars ("I liked it"), two stars ("I didn't like it") one star ("I hated it")? Our Feeling function is capable of evaluating with even more subtle shades of differentiation.

Our Feeling function naturally evaluates, not to criticize, but to choose, accept, reject and prioritize. It knows what—and who—is "better" and "worse" for us, who or what has more value or less value to us. The Feeling function puts everything and everyone in a natural hierarchy of value that helps us trope like a plant toward what is life-enhancing and away from what is not.

If you are a Thinking type, Feeling is your Fourth Function, a rather exotic if puzzling way of processing life both in people you encounter and in yourself. If you are an Intuitive type, you have Feeling processing as a close Second or as a handy Third Function. If you are a Sensation type, you have Feeling as either your most familiar processing function, liking or disliking your Sensation perceptions; or, if you process using Thinking, Feeling is your Third Function, which you can use especially when relating with people.

Feeling Facts

The minute we try to use logic and analysis, Feeling processing withdraws into the background. "Nothing is more injurious to feeling than thinking," Jung wrote. [3] The Feeling process must be experienced, or "felt." Thinking by its nature interferes with that process.

While Thinking seeks proof, expert opinion, research and analysis in order to know if something is real or true, Feeling knows it directly. A Feeling processor may be fascinated by a particular fact or two, but won't pour forth a long list of them about a subject. What matters is how they are feeling about the topic or the discussion.

The Feeling function feels with the certainty of fact—one's own empirical "feeling facts." The Feeling function says, "I like that," or, "I don't like that," or feels uncomfortable. It knows if something or someone "feels right" or "doesn't feel right" or is or is not reliable. It feels, "That is true!" or "That's not true!" How does it know? It feels it.

These "feeling facts" are just as real and true especially to a Feeling processor, as the date, time, headline or someone's name and title are to a Thinking processor.

Born to Feel

Feeling is our earliest processing function in life, and it starts out strong. We are born into relationship, and our psychological growth continues in relationships throughout our lives. We develop and refine our Feeing function while processing our interactions with our parents, siblings and other caretakers, our pets and toys. We "like" this stuffed toy, while another leaves us indifferent. One activity feels good, not another. We relate to this aunt or uncle readily and not to that aunt or uncle. We learn how to "read" the reactions of others and do what pleases them and ourselves. We learn to value, trust, love and appreciate special people around us, just as we are deeply nourished by being valued and appreciated by them. Expressing what we like and don't like guides our care-takers. We sympathize with others and are healed by their sympathy for us. In adolescence, we again experience a special intensity of Feeling processing as we bond with friends, fall in love and feel passionate enthusiasms that often spark lifetime interests.

Parents know Feeling processing well, perhaps without recognizing it. As human nature in the raw, small children express their feelings without inhibition, using their eyes, faces, voices and whole bodies. Sensitive grownups learn to interpret and dialogue with this eloquent early self-expression as information about the child's experience. When parents see their child's Feeling function reacting, their own Feeling functions "feel" it, and, if it's something "wrong," they want to help their child get back to a state of wellbeing, and are even guided by Feeling as to how to do it. Thus the child learns the art of Feeling, and parents often expand their Feeling repertoire.

Our Feeling Education

Though our Feeling function is a powerful on-going source of human intelligence, in the course of a modern life we can all too easily lose touch with it. As cognitive abilities expand, children are often encouraged to "outgrow" Feeling processing. Along with their toilet training, children are urged to be more reasonable and to "think for themselves" as focus moves to their increasing verbal ability and intellectual understanding. What we like and don't like no longer matters quite as much. A child's Feeling responses to what happens may be cut short by such comments as, "Oh, that's enough now, you're too old for that," rather than allowing learning to continue through empathy and the allowing of time for the Feeling process to resolve, understand, heal and move on.

By school age, Feeling processing tends to recede further into the background as children are guided to perform and be competent, independent little decision-makers. Schools rarely test and track for Feeling ability as they may for Thinking. What a child likes or doesn't like becomes less relevant or incidental. Empathy training is entering the classroom, and schools are trying to create sensitivity to diversity. Day to day, however, developing the Feeling function is made rather difficult amidst the pressures of having to "get the right answer" and perform other Thinking tasks, especially with a deadline. A natural psychological inclination to process experience with the Feeling function, which requires time to "feel things through," may even be misinterpreted or "diagnosed" as a malady and the Feeling function as a "dys-function." When classrooms are focused on educating the Thinking function and teaching for test scores, even the most gifted Feeling processors can be seen as having a so-called learning disability, despite evident ability in understanding situations and attracting friends.

With the Feeling function put in the corner, so to speak, Feeling processors can baffle even the best educators, who know that "gets along well with others" does not necessarily get someone into the college of his or her choice. As a high school teacher wrote on a Feeling processor's paper: "You threw yourself into this with your characteristic zest, but the piece doesn't hang together as well as it might, but I brush that aside in admiration for the work you put into this, and the plums you extracted. Call it A minus."

An important role for the Feeling function is to guide our attention toward activities we "like," in order to develop and express ourselves through our natural personal affinities and preferences. "What's your favorite subject?" is an important question for the Feeling function. Many students do better in classes and courses they feel passionate about and with teachers or professors they like and admire. They write a better paper and enjoy doing it more when they care about the subject matter and organize it according to the aspects they are excited about and value.

Just as important, our Feeling function wants to attend to the feeling states of others, share what is fun, help someone who is suffering and create harmony where there is discord. Our Feeling function seeks a sense of belonging. In Feeling processing, interrelatedness is more than just a concept, it is actually felt as a natural human experience. Practicing to let such feelings be our guides through whatever we encounter in the world—that is truly educating the Feeling function.

A Well-Kept Secret

This special kind of intelligence, the wisdom of our feeling responses to life, is of a power and refinement many of us may glimpse only rarely, despite having it within us. Though Jung identified the Feeling function a century ago as a fundamental part of human psychology, Feeling may be the least familiar psychological function, as it must so often be "switched off" in a rational, objective, efficiency-oriented culture. This is especially true in most modern workplaces, but Feeling processing is also missing in our relationships where it wants to help us thrive. On the other hand, if one travels to certain places in the world, for instance Italy or India, Feeling is evident in the very fabric of life and is experienced in personal encounters throughout the day.

Not that Feeling has disappeared from our lives, far from it. The Feeling function is often trying in its personal way to get our attention. Many people are beset by a deep loneliness, despite an active social life. Others experience a painful feeling of being un-met in their relationships. Some suffer from physical symptoms that defy rational diagnosis. Our Feeling functions long for us to feel passionate about life, to engage with pleasure and vitality and to live and work according to our most fundamental values, but find these are somehow elusive. Some yearn for a sense of their soul. Many suffer persistent doubts about their self-worth and can barely take in a genuine compliment. These are symptoms of what psychoanalyst and author Robert A. Johnson in *The Fisher King and The Handless Maiden* calls our "wounded Feeling function." Superficial sentiment often passes for feeling, and genuine feelings may be considered irrelevant, disruptive, or self-indulgent. The result is that nearly everyone's feelings are hurt many times a day.

Neuroscientists studying empathy have identified at least ten different regions of the brain dedicated to creating feelings of relatedness with other human beings. They have found that childhood environments lacking empathy cause this innate capacity to deteriorate. The same could be said about the dangers to the human Feeling function itself in so many contemporary environments where Thinking processing is necessary and where quantifiable results are rewarded. Multitasking relegates Feeling processing to a few moments on the sidelines. Our increasing attention-energy focused on and into digital devises, along with the pace of daily life directed by the ticking of an inner clock, simply add to the challenges our Feeling function faces every day, especially for Feeling processors.

The Feeling function may be modern psychology's best-kept secret, and thus one of its most important opportunities. As we get to know more about the Feeling function, our life experience and our relationships become richer and more genuine and life itself takes on new value.

Recognizing Feeling

Affection, sympathy, enjoyment, tenderness, respect, gratitude, contentment, appreciation—these are qualities considered to be of great value. How often during the day do we actually *feel* one of them? Whenever we do, we are experiencing our Feeling function.

Most of us have been moved to tears while watching a movie or reading a book or have experienced saying or doing something because we "felt like it" or felt "moved" to say or do it. The Feeling function "moves" us, according to what feels real, true and right for us. What we experience doesn't need to be proved and cannot be contested—we *feel* it.

We often experience Feeling processing as we listen to music. When we really *care* about someone or something, a place, a pet, the Earth, even an idea, we are experiencing Feeling processing. In grief, Thinking is naturally set aside and we find ourselves in Feeling's healing realm. Even being delivered from a dangerous situation or realizing the generosity of a parent or the bravery of a friend can inspire a profound Feeling response.

Beauty triggers our Feeling function. It is the home of our aesthetic sense. Looking at a sunset over the ocean or a vista of distant mountains or a city skyline at night, we stand affected and awestruck. Our mind stops and we just take it in, feeling something exquisite and indescribable. Standing before a painting, seeing a face in a crowd, reading a perfect phrase—in all our aesthetic responses, we are moved, rapt, "sent." Feelings themselves can be beautiful. Feeling processing at this level fills us with pleasure that is both physical and somehow transcendent, as if touching our heart, soul and spirit together.

In describing this subjective way of understanding reality, Jung used the German word "Gefühlsleben," meaning "emotional life" or "to live by one's feelings," though he wrote, "I freely admit that this problem of feeling has been one that has caused me much brain-racking." [4] "Brain-racking," in fact Thinking processing of any kind, has to be suspended for Feeling processing to do its special kind of work.

People Processing

In our Feeling functions, we process a kind of living field of energy between us and our surroundings. Using the Feeling function's intelligence, people take the measure of one another. What is this person's character? What is his or her emotional state? Is he or she being real and straightforward, or hiding by posturing? How safe am I with his person? "Feeling out" the person tells us whether he or she has beneficial intents or will cause trouble. We get a feeling of happy attraction, of "liking," or perhaps of calm safety and wellbeing, or else we feel distrust, alarm, disgust or aversion.

In our Feeling function, we evaluate our surroundings. How do we feel here? Do we feel good being here? Do we like it? Do we feel happy, comfortable and safe, or inhibited and guarded? At any moment, our Feeling function may respond to an intuition, a sensation, even at times to a thought or idea we read or hear. What do we feel about it? Does it feel important? What do we "feel like" doing about it?

There are fragments of Feeling scattered throughout the polite social interactions we take for granted, such as "Thank you" and "Good to see you" when they are truly felt. When we are asked, "How are you feeling?" we assume the person is asking about our health, but our Feeling function might answer, "I'm feeling pretty happy today" or even, "I'm feeling miserable," whatever would be true. In almost every modern environment, the need is great for the least bit of Feeling conveyed. A senior supervising doctor named Barbara making rounds with medical residents in a big city hospital taught them something they did not learn in medical school: when approaching a patient's bedside, *smile*. Sure enough, a simple smile of relatedness invariably transformed the interaction that followed.

Our Feeling function "reads" our organism as it responds to whoever and whatever appears before us. Encountering someone or something we like we may feel pleasure, wonder, caring or delight. When someone is lying, our whole organism may cringe with suspicion and distrust. When a brand new tool breaks in our hands, our Feeling function feels it like a wound.

The Feeling function operates on the fundamental human level of our basic needs and motivations— to protect ourselves and our children, for instance, to bond with people who are attractive and helpful or to act on opportunities for nourishment, safety and well-being. Our Feeling responses of pleasure and affection or fear and mistrust are universal and go on underneath the most sophisticated cultural rules of behavior.

What is more, our feeling states are transmitted to one another, from Feeling function to Feeling function. Feelings are "catching." In short, if someone is happy, stressed, sad or upset, everyone feels it.

The Processing of Life

If the Thinking function says, "I think, therefore I am," the Feeling function says, "I feel, therefore I am *alive*." As long as our heart is beating, our Feeling function is processing the quality of our personal experience, including our relationships, our surroundings, our work and all our activities.

Humanity has survived not only because of our capacity to reason, but also because of our ability to attribute a feeling value to people and circumstances. Informing us with feelings with a positive or negative resonance, Feeling processing helps us understand and act on what our instincts are telling us, thus tapping us into the vast intelligence of human evolution and of nature itself.

We are part of nature, and our Feeling function relates us to nature psychologically. It rejoices before a field of wildflowers or an unobstructed view of the ocean. When we really look at an animal, a flower, a tree, a stone, a sunset, or listen to a bird singing or even taste fresh water, nature communicates to us directly via Feeling's language.

Our Feeling function knows what is natural without reading labels. It knows instinctively what is good for us and for nature and also feels nature's distress. Driving by an orchard, a Feeling-type website designer saw trees planted only three feet apart. The ground had been so covered with herbicide that the earth was a uniform gray-brown. Every tree was wired tightly to a metal stake. He felt horror, even nausea. "They spent so much money, and the trees looked sick and angry," he said. "How can the fruit be any good?"

Made for Love

Feelings of loving connectedness "feel good" to the depths of our Feeling intelligence. The kind of love so many of us hunger for emanates from the Feeling function—to be genuinely valued and appreciated in an open-hearted way that nourishes us to our depths. Even without speaking a word, the look of love in someone's eyes creates a current of feeling that is profoundly encouraging and life-enhancing. This gift of Feeling processing is one of the most beautiful psychological experiences human beings can have.

The rapture of falling in love is so desired in part because it breaks through to Feeling-function territory in us. Defying all reason and escaping the boundaries of the intellect, being in love is a pure experience of valuing and relating. We love our beloved, we love life, we love everyone, we even love ourselves and feel we've never looked so good or felt so happy. The world turns from black and white to color. Every song has meaning; we write poetry and paint paintings; we dance to the musical language of Feeling.

Many seek an experience of Feeling in the ecstasies of romance or other "peak" experiences, but Feeling processing is available in small, exquisite moments. Perhaps we glimpse our dog asleep in the sun or a photograph of Paris. A child makes eye contact on a bus and is curious about us; a friend touches our shoulder or a bright red bird flies by the window—a brief moment of Feeling can hearten us for the rest of the day.

We humans want to feel affinities and to affiliate. The Feeling function is the part of us that experiences affection and that sympathizes with others and is encouraged by their sympathy for us. Feeling related to someone or something makes us feel profoundly happy. Our Feeling function knows what we have in common and starts from there to relate, respond and communicate. Feeling then proceeds to report on the interaction with great subtlety, such as feeling the strength or weakness of a connection.

Refinement of the Feeling function permits many kinds of relationships. While we have one word for "love," we are capable of so many feelings of relatedness and can care about people in many different ways. We can value someone without "loving" him or her. We can love a person without sharing our daily existence. We can care about a person for what he or she has done for us. We may "feel like" keeping in touch with a person without the desire to go further. We can connect intensely for five minutes or for fifty years. These and many other subtle feelings are all valid and vital and animate all the relationships that humanize our world.

The Feeling Function's Best Friend

We can learn a lot about the essence of the Feeling function by observing the behavior of dogs, who are like avatars of pure Feeling. They value their owners completely and devotedly. Their joy is uninhibited, as is their gratitude and protectiveness. They are also deeply knowing. Jung once remarked that his dog, lying in his outer office, somehow felt the psychological condition of a patient before he did; Jung would then know from the noises the dog made.

In our heart of hearts, we have the same soulfulness, strength of passionate instincts and capacity to appreciate and love deeply. We can be completely devoted and can want to protect ourselves, our space and our loved ones. We can have fun, play and enjoy life, and we can want to serve and be useful. In fact, our dogs often teach these Feeling qualities to us.

The Wellbeing Function

Our subtle affinities, attractions and aversions guide us toward the Feeling function's ultimate goal: our wellbeing. As a plant turns toward the sunlight, Feeling tries to direct us toward whatever produces good feelings and a life-enhancing connection. While the Thinking function strives for logic, order and factual certainty, wellbeing is the measuring tool of the Feeling function. Through our body chemistry communicating to the mind, our Feeling function wants to keep our reality in harmony with our deepest personal needs and instincts. Our Feeling function can "feel" how close or far away we are from these. It processes our on-going quality of life, so we can accept what enhances our wellbeing, health, happiness and growth and reject what does not.

To feel good and in harmony may sound simple and self-evident, but significant intelligence goes into recognizing and interpreting feelings as guideposts in one's life. Human feeling is a very subtle instrument. It has little to do with the usual ways we try to "feel good" in our culture, which can seem like blasting our feelings through twenty-foot speakers. Rather, the Feeling function is the playing of our heart-strings, capable of the most exquisite, refined and nuanced tones. In its ineffable way, people's Feeling functions are responsible for the emotional atmosphere or climate of a relationship or of an environment. Simply being aware of our Feeling function, its presence and on-going influence, improves this invisible but palpable aspect of our life.

When something threatens our wellbeing, we get, as a Feeling type put it, "an awful gut visceral feeling that something is wrong." In fact, when we experience a "gut feeling," a "gut reaction" or "gut instinct," it is actually the Feeling function at work processing visceral responses to our current situation. Our gut intelligence—researchers call it our "little brain"—is eloquent, as is our whole organism. We might feel a lightness and clarity, for instance, when we are with the right person or a "good" situation. "Bad" feelings are heavy, tightly constricting or heatedly alarming as they alert us to danger or an incompatible situation.

Feeling good—about ourselves, about a person, about a situation, or for no known reason at all—is one of the precious benefits of tending the Feeling function. Our Feeling function seeks out experiences that nourish and cheer us and that enrich and express our emotional lives. Our varied circumstances are constantly presenting opportunities to feel these personal responses by which our Feeling function can guide us.

Feeling and Emotion

The Feeling function is not the same as our emotions. Technically, emotional experience is in the Sensation realm. We perceive emotions physically as our bodies are affected in various ways. Emotions involve a complex biochemical system. Our Feeling function picks up these biochemical signals and processes them psychologically, so we can understand their messages and act appropriately. This psychological capability within us reads and works intelligently with emotional data the way Thinking does with ideas and facts.

If our Feeling function goes unnoticed, early emotional responses and messages do not get processed adequately. Our Feeling function's subtle sensibilities become intensified like water forced through a narrow pipe to emerge as full-blown emotions. The Feeling function has to work awfully hard to figure out the true meaning of intense emotions, when it can register emotional signals early with the sensitivity of a galvanic skin response. If we do not notice, the Feeling process grows in intensity. "The way a feeling happens is that I feel something, but I can't see it clearly at first," a Feeling type says. "But it wants to be seen, and if I don't acknowledge it, it keeps raising the stakes until I do see it."

We tend to experience Feeling processing at a higher velocity or voltage than necessary; it has to shout, when it is capable of communicating much more subtly. Unfortunately, not knowing that their Feeling functions even exist, many people feel at the mercy of powerful emotions. Even those who feel passionless on the outside can be like walking volcanoes on the inside. Suppressed Feeling processing can seep out as stress and anxiety. Without an opportunity to learn how to deal especially with "bad" or warning feelings, with what they are trying to tell us or where they naturally want to take us, many learn simply to release the pressure by venting, blaming and hurting others or themselves. When our instinctive feeling responses are not accepted, we might push them away out of fear, distaste or habit, but when they get bottled up and erupt, it is often in ways and with results that frighten or repel us all the more. Many people, even Feeling types, come to know the Feeling function only as outbursts, "melt-downs" and regrettable overly passionate exchanges.

If picked up early, taken seriously and truly felt, the Feeling process can respond "intelligently" before one's body chemistry goes into the full swing of intense emotion. Any feeling that arises is a rich source of information. When our Feeling function first signals that something is wrong, we may feel it in any number of ways, in the "pit of the stomach" or a warming of the skin or perhaps in a tensing of our jaw, back or shoulders. Our Feeling function can even process our fight-or-flight reactions early, perhaps allowing us make a more judicious response than just to throw a fist or run away.

The Feeling Function is human; it is part of human nature and is timeless. For our Feeling Function, it isn't the 21st century, it is on DNA's time. It doesn't care that the school bus arrives at 7:05 or that you have five meetings today or that the legal speed limit is 75 MPH. It yearns for more than a quick exchange with a loved one. As the wisdom of our organism, our Feeling Function knows what is beneficial, nurturing and life-enhancing to us as living human beings. It is a fact of modern life that there is a deeply human part of us that just naturally resists and struggles against the break-neck speeds and schedules of a so-called successful way of living. This is especially true after a certain age, which is not very old and nowadays lasts a long time. Ignored, our Feeling responses too often deepen into physical symptoms. Regular awareness of this important part of us and giving it conscious recognition, perhaps even dialogging with it and allowing it to express itself with words, can make the crucial difference between health and illness.

The more often we check in with our Feeling function, the better our relationships work and the better we feel overall. Skill in managing one's feelings not by restriction or control, but by acknowledging them early on, when Feeling responses are fresh and true, creates the delicacy of feeling so often lacking in contemporary life.

The Feeling Process: What A Relief!

While in the Thinking process we think things through, in the Feeling process we move through feeling to feeling toward realization, understanding and resolution. Inner pressure or tension and its release are as familiar to the Feeling process as questions and answers are to the Thinking process. When we feel internal distress or conflict—perhaps things aren't right in a relationship or in a work situation—our Feeling function works with our inner turmoil. If we give it our attention and allow the twistings and turnings of successive feelings, perhaps writing, painting, vocalizing or doing movement about them, the Feeling process leads to resolution and release, a new standpoint, perhaps peace and acceptance, a clearing of the inner atmosphere and what one Feeling type calls, "blessed relief."

Some Feeling responses can bring immediate certainty and resolution. At other times, the Feeling process takes longer as one's understanding grows and changes. As we are often in the habit of turning off the Feeling function, assuming that Thinking is preferable, Feeling processing may be unfamiliar or uncomfortable. Just as research and analysis take time, the Feeling process too takes time and attention. To process life's events and encounters for their emotional and instinctive meaning, the Feeling function needs time between them. Today's tight schedules are guaranteed to bring protests from our Feeling function.

In fact, our Feeling function offers us a whole other sense of time and timing, aside from the "clock time" that tends to dictate the way we conduct our lives. As our organism's prodigious intelligence, Feeling has its own sense of time—natural time. It is tuned in to a natural sequence of events or steps in a procedure that enhance our physical and emotional wellbeing and that work on a human level. It is a visceral yet cognitively perceptible understanding of what to do when. Though it is all too easy to overlook or override, our Feeling function "feels" and knows what is important, its own sense of priorities as we face a task or our day. By listening to our Feeling function, even if simply to reorder tasks for the day, we feel so much better.

As the Feeling function works on a dilemma, it responds to new input that arises; perhaps another interaction with a person occurs, a new insight comes or a new feeling about the situation. Attending carefully to the inner experience of Feeling processing, far from the "selfishness" so distrusted by our culture, brings a succession of feeling understandings that are part of a larger reality and can influence a whole situation. Thus it becomes a personal inner process we can turn to and trust, even as the best thing we can do. When you get it resolved on the inside, the outside situation is often resolved as if all by itself.

The Authenticity Function

One of the Feeling function's most important roles is to tell us what is genuine—the real thing. Using the Feeling function is far from the naïve, undiscerning openness to the world that one might assume or fear, quite the contrary. Our Feeling function knows when people are being sincere or inauthentic. It feels the validity or incorrectness of an idea irrespective of its source. Genuineness and honesty feel good, falsehood feels suspect and potentially dangerous. When the Feeling function feels someone or something doesn't ring true, it sounds an alarm felt subtly or vividly. So-called first impressions contain important Feeling-function intelligence. "This man is a con man," it might tell us, or "I like him and trust him."

Our Feeling function comes installed with our own personal "phony meter." This Feeling-function "phony meter" is related to the human experience of trust and its opposite of distrust, one of the earliest and most fundamental forms of intelligence we get from Feeling processing. Our Feeling-function "phony meter" signals a warning, whether about a person, statement, product or policy. We may learn to rationalize it away or override it with social conditioning ("Go over and give Uncle Charley a big kiss." "Now, be *nice* to your cousin Alice."), but while people may want us to believe certain "facts" are "true," our Feeling function is telling us otherwise.

Our Feeling function wants to bestow on us a sense of integrity that comes from living in an authentic way, rooted in our true selves, by showing us the activities, situations, people and ideas that express and affirm who we are, as well as those that do not.

Quality v. Quantity

Feeling processing inevitably brings quality-mindedness. With today's emphasis on making as many as we can as inexpensively as possible, quality might be advertised, but not delivered. Quality is assumed to be costly. It means expensive personal attention, continual testing and fine-tuning, a higher "reject rate," starting over and doing things again.

Instinctively assessing ineffable values such as quality and the degree of excellence, our Feeling function feels pleasure when we encounter real quality, whether in a person, restaurant, car, song, pair of shoes, work of art or electric drill. Our Feeling function wants to guide us in our work—doing things right feels better. Feeling-function responses inform us of the quality of people who are genuinely committed and naturally good at what they do. We "feel" the inherent quality of real wood, real fabrics such a cotton, linen and wool, even real food not concocted in chemistry labs.

"I've Got Chills!"—The Language of Feeling

Some of the deepest, most powerful human experiences can leave us speechless, but they are certainly felt. When someone's Feeling function is activated, his or her whole being fills with energy that communicates. The Feeling function can be struck by the sheer amazement of things, with no need to know anything "about" them. While Thinking uses words, Feeling expresses itself in punctuation marks, italics and emojis, in sighs, endearments, expletives and other sounds of instinct—"Oh!" "Whoa!" "Meh.." "Yikes!" "Yay!" or simply "Wow!"

Feeling's expressive repertoire includes smiles, frowns, and a host of physical gestures and movements. The body jumps up and dances with Feeling, our arms fly up, hands fly to the heart, punch the air or pat someone's back, voices shout and squeal. A big sigh or taking deep breaths clears and refreshes our feelings. Feeling speaks eloquently through the eyes.

Enthusiasm is an experience of the Feeling function. In the original Greek, enthusiasm meant the experience of being filled with a divine force. When we are genuinely enthused, we feel an impassioned inner energy about someone or something. We want to jump up, dance and sing. Enthusiasm is infectious and communicates from Feeling function to Feeling function.

While the Thinking function seeks to comprehend *what* is being said, the Feeling function hears and responds to *how* it is being said, the tone of voice or the rhythm of the words. The Feeling function reads the meta-language underlying what people are saying. Beneath their words are motivations and feelings. Perhaps they are afraid. Perhaps they don't really believe what they are saying. Perhaps they actually want you to do something for them. Our Feeling function knows.

Creating Atmosphere

The Sensation function works to create the "look" of a place, while the Feeling function is responsible for the emotional atmosphere. Simply being aware of our Feeling function, its presence and on-going messages, can improve this invisible influence wherever we are. The warmth of feeling can be like a spritz of lavender in a room. A dinner table may not be elaborately set, yet still convey a welcoming, happy ambiance for one's guests. A living room decorated with Sensation and Feeling in harmonious colors and patterns feels welcoming, indeed a room where pleasurable living can go on.

Feeling with Intuition can create an inner "feeling" environment that is supportive and harmonious, one in which people can do their best work or have the courage to be themselves and to heal. Wherever Feeling is working with Intuition perceptions, people relate to one another with sincerity and enjoyment and create with inspiration.

The Art of Feeling

"Poetry is the record of the best and happiest moments of the happiest and best minds," wrote Romantic poet Percy Bysshe Shelley. The Feeling function also expresses itself in storytelling, song, dance and other jewel-like encapsulations of Feeling experience and understanding.

Feeling processing comes alive in opera and on stage, as well as on the movie and TV screen. "When you're doing a film, you're trying to get the audience to see, not just with their eyes, but with their gut, to feel those emotions," said Arthur Hiller, director of the feeling-rich classic film *Love Story*, told *Vanity Fair*. (Footnote 5] As we see in the Feeling-rich acting performances of Sean Penn, Kate Winslet, Marlon Brando, Marilyn Monroe, Meryl Streep and James Dean, certain actors launch themselves fearlessly into their acting. "I loved the emotional nakedness, the brutal honesty about what can sometimes happen in a marriage," Feeling type Kate Winslet told the *New York Times* about why she championed the making of the film *Revolution Road*. [6]

Music is particularly expressive of the Feeling function, from blues to Beethoven, from opera and country to salsa and rock—even birds singing to the sunrise. Many singers are Feeling-endowed, such as Mick Jagger, Lady Gaga, Bruce Springsteen, Norah Jones, Frank Sinatra, and many others who sing and perform with their Feeling functions. Our Feeling functions seem to resonate in feeling tones of major and minor. Music and other sounds, from harmonious to raucous, are vibrations that "tune" our feeling state and affect the quality of our Feeling process.

Musicians and composers often speak of the feeling aspects of their art. "Music's potency comes from encoding internal feelings and internal life," cellist Yo Yo Ma said [7] "I can recall sitting in a concert hall as a child and hearing music that created in me feelings of nostalgia for unknown places and times." "For me, inspiration comes from trying to connect with an audience," composer John Adams told a Harvard audience on the performance of *The Wound Dresser,* his setting for a Civil War poem by Walt Whitman. "Music is fundamentally the art of feeling—in this instance my feeling, my take on Whitman's feelings. Whitman was not ashamed of his feelings."

Just as music communicates directly to the Feeling function, so does color, whether in paintings, clothing, design or nature. In the arts and in life, "Colour=Feeling," Jung wrote. [8]

Gifts of Feeling

Our Feeling function loves to share. Gifts of feeling include not only things, but also heartfelt compliments and words of support and encouragement. A potent Feeling gift is genuine listening. It is a powerful and nourishing experience to be listened to and valued by someone using the Feeling function.

Politeness is a refined form of Feeling expression, such as "Excuse me" and "Thank you," full of honoring and appreciation. In fact, the moment you feel grateful, your Feeling function is activated and relating in the most human of ways. Even "Ciao," whether offered in friendly and respectful greeting or in departure, comes from an ancient word meaning "your servant."

The Feeling function holds for us a code, written in our hearts, of kindness, honor and dignity. The Medieval era brought a flowering of the Feeling function in the formalities of chivalry. Even today, human beings naturally recognize the nobility of a sensitive heart. Our Feeling function is like our inner royal court, where the highest human values are recognized and served, and their lack is suffered. Our Feeling function "esteems." It recognizes valuable human qualities such as integrity, dignity, respect, authenticity and genuine sincerity. When we carry ourselves with dignity, from the Latin word for worth and worthiness, it communicates that we value ourselves as human beings. Witnessing dignity is uplifting and allays fear and distrust.

The Healing Function: A Good Word About Feeling Bad

For many people, feeling has become almost synonymous with feeling bad. Suffering is a bad word in our culture. We avoid suffering in as many ways as we can. A range of feelings is grouped together as negativity, which has become another bad word to be banished. As soon we find out that a feeling is unpleasant, we try to ignore or override it or we rationalize it away.

No one wants to hurt emotionally any more than physically. But suffering, at least for a while, is natural and at times essential to the Feeling process. Unfamiliarity makes the prospect of hurting more frightening. Yet just as pain signals us to address and heal our bodies, our Feeling function's discomfort alerts us when something is wrong.

Intrinsic to our Feeling function is not only suffering, but healing from suffering. The Feeling function is where we heal emotionally, a natural and organic process as vital to life as physical healing. In fact, the state of our Feeling function is reflected in how readily we can heal from life's painful experiences.

When encouraged to do its work, the Feeling process attracts wisdom for healing and growth like a magnet, including the right book to read or film to see or the sympathetic friend who appears wanting to help us. From our earliest days, suffering and the healing and caring responses of others help us develop our Feeling intelligence and resiliency. Avoiding or evading our suffering merely denies us access to the very source of the healing we need.

Inevitably, feelings get hurt, but there is deep intelligence in our so-called hurt feelings. If we acknowledge the legitimacy, indeed the normality, of emotional suffering when we are hurt, we can allow the Feeling process to take good care of us. Usually we find that the pain is quite precise and targeted, perhaps addressing a pattern of disrespect or a tender spot in ourselves that calls out for clarification and understanding. Experiencing the hurt and really Feeling-processing it reveals how truly strong we are as human beings and how feeling-wise we are made to be.

The phenomenon of healing, both physically and emotionally, is one of life's least appreciated wonders. Just as our bodies muster a powerful and complex combination of systems to heal a physical wound, our psyches do the same for our emotional wounds. True healing cannot really work through logic alone, though the Thinking

function may help define our inner conflicts and struggles intellectually. The Feeling function does not "reason things out" or simply
decide that "things are all right now." Emotional healing is a naturally
slow process; one's entire organism must recover and heal, with the
deepest understandings often coming in a series of revelations. The
Feeling process can require courage, but the Feeling function itself
provides it.

The Valuing Function

At the heart of the Feeling function is the inner experience of
valuing. Valuing someone or something is a profoundly pleasurable
experience. Though the actual experience of valuing may be hard
to describe, it is heartwarming and often poignant to feel. We may
catch a glimpse of our parents, our child, our dog or cat, and they
feel suddenly dear to us. Standing in the midst of a bustling downtown street, we may feel how much we "just *love* this city." A stranger
offers to lift our heavy suitcase, and we feel how much we appreciate
this person and the gesture of help. We may even be working at our
desk and suddenly feel how worthwhile and rewarding our work is.
We may feel proud of our child, friend or a family member for what
he or she has done. The highest from of valuing offered to us by our
Feeling function is the feeling of the sacred. Every time we value
someone, something or ourselves, we are furthering the Feeling function's life-enhancing capabilities.

Thinking may make our to-do lists, but it is Feeling that sets our
priorities according to what is most important and valuable to us.
Our culture offers many "default" values, such as success, achievement, efficiency, productiveness, prestige or net worth. We may
admire celebrities, desire expensive brands and pursue "the good life."
But our Feeling function knows the value of a person irrespective of

his or her credentials or financial portfolio and feels the worth of an object based on its quality, irrespective of its cost. "Value judgments" use Feeling processing. Feeling values go to the fundamentals of a truly good life as a human being—including quality relationships, nourishing food, an environment we treasure, fulfilling work and activities that further our wellbeing.

By communicating their genuine enthusiasm and valuing, Feeling types and processors can make dynamic leaders, deputizing people, motivating them, making each person feel important and valuable and bringing out the best in their teams or staffs. As a software designer named Kumar recalled admiringly about a Feeling type boss, "He knew I could do it before I did."

The creative influence on others of bestowing one's valuing was recognized by Feeling-gifted film director Anthony Minghella (*The English Patient, Cold Mountain, Truly, Madly, Deeply*). "I think that the job is … just to give as much love as you can to everybody around you," Minghella said while filming *The No. 1 Ladies Detective Agency*, "[to] make them feel good about what they are doing and proud of what they are doing. Because we are doing an amazing thing together."

The power of our valuing can be conveyed to others simply by feeling it. A high school teacher named Cate says that she often takes a moment to look at her students and just value them. "I feel the ways in which they are special," she says. At an end of the year convocation, when she got up to make a speech, the whole school rose up and applauded for ten minutes. It is a "feeling fact" that the inner experience of valuing, whether expressed or not, can make a profound contribution to the overall situation wherever we may be.

Valuing Ourselves

The Feeling function is crucial to our own sense of worthiness and self-worth, and here its woundedness is keenly felt. In fact, the health and strength of our Feeling function is reflected in how well we care for and honor ourselves, both alone and in the midst of our relationships with others. Our Feeling function is where we love, like, respect, enjoy, are kind to and otherwise value ourselves, whatever others' reactions and opinions might be. It is where we feel and monitor the quality of our lives, work and relationships, giving us our sense of self-esteem, self-acceptance and integrity.

We are often hardest on ourselves, for our Feeling relationship with ourselves can be the least well tended. While trying to conform to the values of our family or our culture brings certain rewards, real self-esteem comes from appreciating and respecting our true selves and making choices accordingly. Betraying ourselves doesn't feel good in our Feeling function, which tells us when we are expressing our real feelings, strengths and qualities—who we really are—and floods our being with strength and wellbeing when we are living in authentic alignment with them.

As to Women and Men

Historically, women have been believed to be particularly endowed in the feeling realm, and Jung tended to agree in that relationships, he observed, often rank high among women's personal priorities. [9] But psychologically, everyone has a Feeling function, and many Feeling types and processors are men.

Everyone feels. Everyone "likes" and "values" certain people, places and activities. Everyone needs and thrives on the emotional nourishment of true relatedness. These are the gifts of Feeling function in everyone.

Feeling Too Little, Feeling Too Much

Monitoring and becoming versatile and resilient in our Feeling function is an important psychological skill today. The predominance of the Thinking function in modern life is considered normal, but to think so much, we experience our personal, instinctive responses to people and events only rarely or only in extreme situations. These responses—the responses of our Feeling function—are crucial to knowing who we are.

Yet with media communications constantly offering the afflictions of humankind and highly charged emotional opinions, our Feeling functions can suffer overload, so much so that we become ill, even dangerously so. Just as the Thinking function can take over and become mechanical or compulsive thinking, so the Feeling function can engulf us with feelings of helplessness, anxiety and grief.

It is important to remember the Feeling function's close relationship to our physical organism and its internal biochemistry. Working creatively with our Feeling function is crucial to our heath, physical as well as emotional. Feeling gratitude for specific aspects of our life, for instance, is well known to assuage upsetting feelings of fear and anxiety. Sending blessings feels good because it calms agitated or alarmed internal biochemistry, affecting the environment in ineffable ways. Affirmations and mantras are intended to move attention energy out of negativity into more neutral, creative or healing internal feeling states. Kindness, to someone else or to ourselves, is an intimate feeling that is creative and heartening and pulls us out of suffering that may have become en-mired and hopeless. With such awareness, we can change our inner feeling biochemistry in subtle but very real ways.

Science of emotion expert Barbara Frederickson at the University of North Carolina has found that, as positive emotions infuse mind and body, they expand our outlook and we become more creative, wise and resourceful. According to scientists at the HeartMath Institute, "heart intelligence" underlies cellular organization and guides and evolves organisms toward increased order, awareness and coherence of their bodies' systems. In other words, working creatively with our Feeling function is crucial to our personal wellbeing. Moreover, because our organisms communicate to other people, Feeling function to Feeling function, taking responsibility for the state of our Feeling function is one of the most valuable contributions we can make to our world.

Feeling Types: Virtuosos of Feeling

"I am happiest when I make the people I love feel good."

— A Feeling type

Feeling types are humanity's experts in personal and interpersonal emotional life. People with Feeling first in their psychological hierarchy feel everything with special intensity and sensitivity, and yet they have a special kind of psychological strength to do the Feeling processing that is their first priority. Most important for them, and for the people around them, they want to feel good, and they want everyone else to feel good, too.

For Feeling types, their feelings lead. Feeling processing is their primary navigational system, their immediate experience and their way of getting direction in their life. Their Feeling functions provide wisdom for them to live by and to share. For Feeling types, processing the nuances and depths of human relationships and monitoring their own inner feeling responses and state of wellbeing are their form of genius, even their *raison d'être*.

Like having a good ear for music, the Feeling function of Feeling types and processors "hear" both harmony and discord in the surrounding environment. Interpreting their body's instinctive responses, their Feeling function feels good when they get along with people and when people get along together, which they know is safe and pleasant. They do not like feeling conflict and hostility and try to resolve them.

Ask a Feeling type a question or bring up a topic and he or she will respond not with a quick-witted retort or list of facts, but with his or her feelings about the subject. Feeling processors tend to rely on their personal responses and instinctive common sense, a pragmatic psychological process combining accumulated life experience with feelings in the moment. Whatever is said will be Feeling-toned. Jung observed that Feeling types are always in the process of subjective "valuations." All day long, a Feeling type experiences, "I like this, I don't like that," or they are evaluating by comparing and ranking, as in, "This is better (or worse) than that." A Feeling type is constantly discriminating among events and people by experiencing his or her feelings about them, processing in subtle gradations of connectedness and inner movements *toward* what feels right and *away* from what does not. Brain researchers Antonio and Hannah Damasio at the University of Southern California have identified this kind of Feeling-intelligence activity in the insula, or insular cortex, of the brain. Feeling types and processors may someday be found to be particularly insula-endowed.

To take in information to process, they have access to both Sensation and Intuition perception, while using one perceiving function more often.

FEELING	SENSATION	INTUITION	THINKING
First	Second	Third	Fourth

or

FEELING	INTUITION	SENSATION	THINKING
First	Second	Third	Fourth

Already A Feeling Type

A little Feeling type can reveal himself or herself early on. On her way home every day, a high school teacher named Cate picked up her daughter Olivia at daycare. Strapped in her car seat in the back seat, facing the rear of the car as dictated by law, little Olivia cried and whimpered in sadness and frustration all the way home, obviously deeply forlorn. The daily drive from daycare was nearly unbearable for her mother until one day, Cate reached her arm back toward Olivia and the child tenderly took her hand. Now connected with her mother after a day of separation, all crying stopped. From then on, awkward as the position was for Cate, they made the drive home holding hands.

People Matter

Feeling types learn a lot about themselves and about the world in context of relationship. While many people are able to use their extraversion skills socially, relating with Feeling adds a whole other dimension. Feeling types' relationships are very individual and very important and intense, however long they may last. Being loved and valued by a Feeling type, whether he or she is a parent, child, friend, sibling or mate, is like experiencing a corner of heaven. No one cares for you like a Feeling type. You are appreciated, supported, served and nourished on many levels.

Feeling types and processors bring warmth and life to any encounter. You feel comfortable and accompanied; you are liked and valued. You are being attended to as *you*. Your feelings about what you are saying, even if unexpressed, are being heard. You find yourself saying things you would never say to anyone else. You leave them with the feeling you have been well *met*.

Feeling types go straight to basic human truths of a situation that are often overlooked or discounted by others; they discern nuances and subtle cues that others miss. "I go through all the different feelings in the room," a Feeling-type business consultant named Rich says, "my own and the other people's, until I get to what feels to me like the real situation of what's going on here." Focusing on that, he knows how to influence what happens in his own unique, sensitive and savvy way. Walking into a party, restaurant or meeting, a Feeling type immediately gets a visceral sense of the scene; to borrow a term from film making, they pick up the "room tones." The Feeling function says, "I feel good here. I feel safe and welcome." Other rooms feel "dead," like a house whose occupants have checked out.

In no time, their whole organisms pick up others' emotional states, happy or unhappy, angry or peaceful, approachable or hostile. "I know if they are not themselves," a Feeling type named Sean says. "I know if someone has been thrown for a loop or has been hurt by something or carried away by an event in their life. This is what interests me." He can then do what Feeling types are made to do—to relate on a human level.

Connection Energy

As one Feeling type put it, "I fall in love many times a day." Whether it is with a person they meet, a landscape they come upon, a passage they are reading, a food they are eating or a project they are working on, Feeling types affiliate whole-heartedly, body and soul. They interact with people and their environment the way a cell meets up with another; it opens its membrane and shares of its substance. The extraverts tell you how they feel about what you have said or what they have experienced. The introverts are feeling similar responses, though deep within, manifesting in their eyes or the corners of their mouths.

Feeling types are attractive to others on the most instinctive human level. People *like* them, because they like and are in tune with people. "I go into a room full of strangers feeling good, open-hearted and caring about people in general," an extraverted Feeling-type theater producer named Alexa says. "I move about the world in a permanent "yes" mode. I feel surges of generosity and well-wishing that say to everyone in the world, 'Go forth and prosper!'"

Walking down the street with a Feeling type, one is amazed by the greetings and smiles, the automatic ease with which other people relate to him or her. Even introverted Feeling types are accessible, because their relationship channel is always open, and people know it. The extraverts welcome others as if with open arms. Even the introverts, awkward as they might seem, make a palpable connection with the real you.

Generous to a Fault

By its very nature, the Feeling function empathizes and "feels the same way." Boundaries, limits or a sense of isolating self-protection are foreign to the Feeling function and must be learned in the Feeling way—from painful experience. "Everything I like, I automatically think of someone I can share it with," a Feeling-processor says.

Witnessing another's need or distress, Feeling types give of themselves often totally "without thinking." Indeed, they will give of themselves nearly unconditionally—their time, attention, sympathy, money, talents and enthusiastic support, and they are never happier. A little Feeling type on a school bus saw a boy drop his lollypop and gave him hers. Inheriting $10,000, a grownup Feeling type gave most of it to a friend who was having a hard time.

Feeling types can even take on the mission of everyone's happiness in a group of friends or in a family. Other people instinctively feel and often come to depend on this generosity of heart. As one Feeling processor commented, "I did the feeling for my mother, because she was too busy and overburdened to feel for herself."

Feeling types and processors may learn the hard way to be "selfish" enough to remember to consider their own vital needs. One chill January day in Chicago, a young Feeling processor named Arnelle, on her first day on the job as a social worker, went to visit a family on her case list. During the assessment interview, she was appalled to learn that the mother of this large family did not have a winter coat. In a wave of Feeling, Arnelle took off her own coat and gave it to the woman, who seemed overwhelmed and confused. It wasn't until Arnelle was out on the frigid Chicago street again that she realized that she herself now had no winter coat.

The Agony and the Ecstasy

A grandmother called her little Feeling granddaughter "Sunshine and Shadows." The emotional "set-point" of a Feeling type is always changing. A day may bring a range of feelings from joyful happiness and pleasurable wellbeing to the very depths of sadness, touching on several feelings in between. Indeed, Feeling types are made for an intensity of feeling that would blow the fuses of any Thinking processor. While Thinking types may have the ability to compartmentalize their attention and to separate off unwanted emotions or feelings— to "not think about that right now," for Feeling types the feelings or emotions that arise command their awareness. Whether pleasant or unpleasant, they will be felt.

Living or working in close proximity with a Feeling type, little or big, can be enlivening, to say the least, as they respond to life so richly and deeply. Every experience is heart-felt, and their heart-strings, whether expressed or heard inwardly, are virtuosic. Feeling types can slump in misery or simmer in alienation, then return to their irresistibly warm, responsive selves when the inner sun comes out again.

They are sometimes thought to be "moody" or temperamental in personality. The Feeling function indeed responds to conditions, possibly even dimensions, which even the most aware Feeling type is not able to identify. Like human barometers, Feeling types experience an on-going sensitivity to how people are treating one another; when something is wrong, or when all goes well; when human values are being honored, and when they are not. When this Feeling intelligence is ignored or discounted by significant others, it can create stormier psychic weather for them and for the people around them. Such storms, however, are often the only way Feeling values can come to the fore and ideally to be included.

The Feeling type cannot avoid the Feeling function's special relationship to suffering. The ancient Greeks knew about it, and Greek theater often portrayed this Feeling truth. Greek drama featured a catharsis, in which a character in crisis was cleansed and released from a powerful emotional conflict. The Feeling type must endure a similar build-up of tension, crisis and release. Many of us may fear the intensity of such an experience, but a Feeling type is made to "go there." Going through a particularly intense working-out of a problem or dilemma, a Feeling type may struggle and suffer for hours or even days. But Feeling types are made to suffer *intelligently*. At last, the Feeling type reaches a feeling of resolution, an outlook or action that feels right, a sense of "blessed relief" and inner freedom. The catharsis has come, they have arrived at their inner truth, and the Feeling type is happy again.

Made for Real Life

For Feeling types, sincerity is all-important. The Feeling function implicitly demands: "Be yourself. Be genuine. Relate straight." They work hard to create and maintain genuine harmony and good feelings. They want to know if they have hurt you. They suffer when they are being hurt. Feeling types and processors appreciate honest, mutually respectful and sympathetic, non-accusatory discussions of what is going on for you and in the relationship.

They want true-to-life reality; even gritty is good if it's real. Police investigators may require a lie detector, but Feeling types don't need one. Their built-in "phony meter" sounds an alarm in the face of inauthenticity. "When I pick up that someone is fake, I immediately disengage," a Feeling-type entrepreneur named Eleanor says. "I know when whatever they are saying is nonsense or boring, which means to me it is irrelevant." A Feeling-type art dealer named Eric gets a feeling of anger or physical disgust when he sees a fake signature or colors in a painting or print that an artist would never have used.

A good phony meter can make a Feeling type a trusted advisor. "They pay me to tell them what is really going on in the enterprise," a Feeling-endowed corporate financial officer named David said. The Feeling function gives Feeling types a clear and penetrating view of reality that cuts through surface appearances and any attempts to cover up or obfuscate. Eleanor, the Feeling-type entrepreneur, says that meetings can put her in a bad mood as she picks up the absurdity of some of the participants' theoretical musings. "It annoys me, or I get so bored," she says. "They don't seem to know how far afield they are. I get frustrated with all their tangents. It's like, 'How many ways do you have to say the same thing?'" The Feeling function can bring a breath of fresh air into a group with this no-bullshit factor, though it can also be discredited or discounted. Eleanor says that her sense of the real can make her less than welcome in some environments, but she can quickly discern a Feeling-friendly situation.

Working with Feeling

Whatever their official job description, Feeling types and processors often have someone sitting by their desk telling them their troubles. When a Feeling type feels another's unhappiness or discomfort, he or she wants to make the person feel better, and very often they succeed. It is said that Feeling types want to nourish, heal and teach. In fact, they have to do enough of all these things, or they themselves will suffer. They want to nourish others by feeding them good food and real wisdom or by just caring and listening. They want to teach in a generous sharing of what they know to be true about life and love and how reality works. Relationships are their milieu and they accumulate a treasure house of wisdom about them.

Learning how to trust what they feel and to integrate their feelings into an effective and viable mode of interacting with the modern world shows how much EQ Feeling types really have. Troubled by the disharmonies and meanness often created by competition, Feeling types and processors seek a win-win situation in which the activity, however intense, encourages everyone's wellbeing and enhancement and aims toward a valuable goal. To relate as they must, Feeling types and processors become ingenious at interpersonal "work-arounds." One Feeling processor's work in an international aid agency involves frequent gatherings with Thinking processors. "After listening to a lot of facts, I keep trying to get to the *person*," she says. "I smile, I tease them to get them to laugh, or at least see some sparkle in their eyes."

Mentors, role models and other influential relationships figure prominently in the careers of most Feeling types and processors, who themselves can be very supportive as mentors and net-workers. Frequently led by their enthusiasms and relationships, neither of which they can hide or lie about, Feeling types often experience unconventional career paths. Making choices based on what "feels right at the time," they may follow a meandering series of serendipitous opportunities, as well as situations they must suffer through, learn from and get themselves out of. Feeling types sometimes must learn how to negotiate the realities of business with awareness and using Feeling's own special tools. "More engagement with people and less analysis," a Feeling-type organizational consultant named Mike says about his job requirements. "Work for me is always a labor of love."

A Special Fate

Being a Feeling type in a Thinking-intense society can bring out a certain brand of heroism. Feeling processors have to do battle with requirements to be different from who they are. If they cannot "explain themselves" with precision, present factual information quickly in an orderly manner or "prove their point" on demand, they may not be taken seriously, or they suffer derision for being "inconsistent" or illogical. Too many Feeling types and processors don't think they are smart or learn to feel defensive or habitually to retreat. The heroes and heroines of Feeling must keep returning to their feelings as their main points of reference regardless of messages from their environment, and not give over to others their powers of knowing what is real and true.

Savvy Feeling types know that reasoning is important to others; they hear it going on all around them. They know it is required in school and in most professions, and they work out a way to approximate it or otherwise do what is required of them. But Feeling types do not believe that reasoning is a method of arriving at truth, at least not for them. Feeling types often "just know" the right answer. Observing others trying to reason their way through important life situations, they are puzzled by such struggles. "Even as a child, I'd listen to grownups and I always knew when they weren't right," a Feeling type says. "I could hear it in their voices. Their faces didn't match what they were saying."

Feeling types often have to make a special effort to accommodate to the "clock time" that runs so much of Western culture. Feeling processing responds in the moment and does not work on a schedule or deadline; judging the amount of time a task will take is not in the realm of the Feeling function. As ever, however, if being or producing on time is important to the relationship, they will gladly make the effort.

Though Feeling types encounter incomprehension or dismissal of their feelings by some, other people yearn for their passion and vitality and their warmth of deep relatedness and seek them out for their Feeling intelligence and wisdom. Feeling types are admired for their expressiveness and creativity in Feeling-rich realms like poetry, drama, storytelling, music, even cuisine. In fact, Feeling types offer naturally and without effort what is needed by people as much as anything: real relatedness. Feeling types and processors have great gifts to dispense in the realm of heartening and healing others simply by being and expressing who they are. When they are true to themselves and to their Feeling process, they will say and do the right thing in nearly every circumstance.

Extraverted Feeling Types: Joie de Vivre

Quickly establishing rapport with people wherever they are, extraverted Feeling types are naturally the life of the party. Social occasions are their favorite milieu as they "work the room," making everyone feel good about themselves, about the event and just about being there. Exuding warmth and charisma, they instinctively know where to direct their attention to include and connect.

Extraverted Feeling wants to know everyone. When preparing to enter high school, an extraverted Feeling type named Charles studied his class roster and learned the names and faces of every student in his class, all 600 of them. Now a corporate manager, Charles makes the rounds of his floor every morning, finding out how everyone is and their latest news and ascertaining the feeling tone of the day. He considers it part of his job, as well as his main source of satisfaction and pleasure, to relate to people, appreciate them and spread encouragement and good feelings.

Actors Drew Barrymore, Kate Winslet, Jason Segel and Juliette Binoche bring extraverted Feeling to the movie screen, but all extraverted Feeling types are gifted artists when it comes to sincere communication and self-expression. Their natural emotional range is broad and nuanced and they respond with their whole organisms to the feeling potential in a situation and try to bring this reality to the fore.

Passionate expression is part of extraverted Feeling. What a gorgeous day! Isn't this rain *wonderful?* This is such a *great* product! They are doing their best to have everyone join in. A daughter affectionately describes her extraverted Feeling-type father as "'CAPS LOCK ON." In fact, people with extraverted Feeling can burst with such spontaneous and genuine feeling that at times they incur curmudgeonly distrust and not a little envy. They often learn to stifle themselves in a culture in which cool is cool.

Nevertheless, people with extraverted Feeling are almost always approachable. They prefer to communicate with others in person, in order to see their expressions and feel the interpersonal chemistry. In social interactions, extraverted Feeling types make it understood that they are totally engaged with you and with what is going on, and this genuine personal engagement is infectious and effective. While renting a house in France with his family for two weeks, an extraverted Feeling type named Simon made daily rounds of town shops and market stalls buying food for the evening meal. With his instinct for quality, he quickly found the best vendors and was given the shopkeepers' best fare, without his knowing more French than "Bonjour!" By the end of the visit, he had made friends throughout the town—*"Ah, voilà notre ami Americain!"*

When they keep themselves "tethered" to their Feeling function, their internal "phony meter" guides them. Extraverted Feeling wants important interpersonal information out in the open. According to Jungian psychoanalyst Marie-Louise von Franz, extraverted Feeling types "have very few illusions about people, but will be capable of evaluating their positive and negative sides appropriately." [10] Any feeling, truly felt, is welcome.

Introverted Feeling Types: Still Waters Run Deep

Introverted Feeling types have the same range of feeling experiences, but privately. Their Feeling process is less obvious or audible, though their eyes may communicate that they are feeling something. If introverted Feeling types seem to be in their own worlds, they are, but their Feeling functions are seismically sensitive to how you are feeling, too, as well as to the Feeling aspects of what is going on. From their inner world, they empathize deeply and see others' true selves. Little escapes them. They have a constant readiness for peaceful and harmonious coexistence, although they may give strangers no hint of their amiability until it is earned.

While Feeling extraverts tend to all the world's needs, introverted Feeling types tend to individuals, as well as to the richness of their inner life. In *The Pregnant Virgin,* writer Marion Woodman tells of an experience while she was very ill in India. After several days in her hotel room, she finally had the strength to go down to the lobby to sit on a couch. Before long an Indian woman appeared and sat quietly next to her. The next day it was the same, and the next. After several days of the woman's gentle presence, Woodman felt well enough to venture outside the hotel. As she was leaving, an Indian man, who spoke English, approached. "You had the aloneness of the dying," he said, "I sent my wife to sit with you." Gifts of introverted Feeling are often shared in silence. [11]

Introverted Feeling types live more happily in the realm of Being than in the realm of Doing. But, as Jung's colleague Marie-Louise von Franz pointed out, "they have a very strong hidden influence on the surrounding society, for they have secret ways of establishing values....[They] simply behave as though {they] thought one thing was valuable and another not," This deep inner Feeling quality sets standards. Introverted Feeling types "very often form the ethical backbone of a group," von Franz continued. "[W]ithout irritating the others by preaching moral or ethical precepts, they themselves have such correct standards of ethical values that they secretly emanate a positive influence on those around them...[that] forces one to be decent if they are present." [12] She adds: "One often finds the introverted feeling type in the background where important and valuable events are taking place, as if their introverted feeling had told them, 'that is the real thing.'" [13]

Whatever they choose to do will be from a deep motivation. "I'm shy," explains Grammy Award-winning singer/songwriter India Arie. "The only reason I started performing is [that] I believed in my songs." Though she plays several instruments, her favorite is acoustic guitar. "It's an instrument where the sound resonates from the inside," she says. "My songs are very introspective, and I sing from my heart." [14]

Surrounded by a boisterous extraverted world that feels so foreign to them, introverted Feeling types can suffer from loneliness, but come to accept it. "I knew early on I was made for solitude," an introverted Feeling-type painter named Kurt says. "When I realized so much happens for me and for my painting, I came to respect that. It's what I'm here for." Meanwhile, trusted family and friends "check in" on him in his studio during the day and welcome him when he emerges. "He knows more than anyone," an admiring friend says.

In an extraverted culture, with its can-do confidence and sturdy toughness that can rough-ride over anyone's sensibilities, introverted

Feeling can manifest with an instinctive, brooding, fiercely authentic energy—as in performances by James Dean and Sean Penn and in smoldering heroes like Heathcliff in *Wuthering Heights*. Many teenagers go through a period in which their introverted Feeling is activated as they process the complexities of their social environment. They see life's realities truly and insist, sometimes ferociously, that people be absolutely genuine and authentic. Their sensibility is poetic and romantic, but when unheard and confused or outraged, some introverted Feeling types or processors may resort to expressing their deep feelings eruptively. If they feel heard and safe, however, they can be as tender and loving as a human being can be and can develop their own special kind of strength and wisdom in a mean-streets world.

Feeling Types' Fourth Function: Thinking

The Thinking function resides in the remote fourth place in a Feeling type's hierarchy. Even for the most intelligent and savvy Feeling types, the logical, orderly, analytical processes of thinking do not normally occur to them, nor are they of much interest. But from out of the Feeling type's Fourth Function, thoughts and ideas can appear that are real "mind-blowers."

Feeling types do think, though not like anyone else. "They think very well, and very often have deep, good and genuine thoughts, unconventional thoughts," Marie-Louise von Franz writes in *Jung's Typology*, but their thoughts "come and go as they like." Feeling types' intelligence is even questioned, she adds, because "they cannot produce thinking at will." [15]

Given the emphasis on Thinking throughout modern life, the inaccessibility and undependability of Fourth-Function Thinking can cause Feeling types considerable consternation and stress. As they

attempt to communicate what they know, having Thinking processing in their illusive Fourth Function can be a source of frustration as
well as annoyance and deep self-doubt. Yet thinking is also a fountain
of wonderment and even enlightenment. A book or lecture can be
mesmerizing. Whenever a Feeling type says, "Wow," he or she has
just had a thought, seen a concept or heard a well-chosen word—a
"visitation" from out of their Fourth Function.

The Saving Idea

When a Feeling type is suffering in the midst of a quandary, he
or she cannot "reason things out." But if he or she keeps an inner
window open to the Fourth Function, a concept or idea may come
"out of the blue" that brings resolution, understanding, clarity and
relief. This saving idea may come from a conversation, something
they read or hear, a song lyric; the Fourth Function can use anything.

When thoughts appear, they can come to Feeling types without
the filter or contamination of conventional notions. To their own
amazement most of all, out comes a fresh and unexpected idea, a way
of solving a problem or the essence of a phenomenon. The Feeling
type corporate manager who walked the halls getting the feeling tone
of the day once stayed up all night and wrote a concise memo struc-
turing a business deal that transformed his company's whole way of
thinking. A Feeling type can come up with a word or a phrase so
innovative, so perfectly descriptive, it leaves Thinking types, admir-
ers of verbal mastery, shaking their heads with amazement. Feeling
types often use words in a highly original way, although they may
not remember later what they said. With the power of their Fourth
Function behind their words, Feeling types are some of the world's
greatest storytellers. Their speeches and lectures can deeply motivate
their audience. They can distill concepts to their essence. Making

sense beyond ordinary sense, their words can teach and heal on a deep level.

The Ecstasy of Thought

Their Fourth-Function Thinking carries Feeling types to a glorious abstract realm of seminal ideas and universal concepts. A Feeling type looking up a word in the dictionary is in a state of delight and reverence. One clear, true, explanatory fact or principle will suddenly appear, or they see the proper order or sequence of steps in a project, thrilling them. A new idea or concept can fill a Feeling type with intellectual enthusiasm. Quite single-mindedly, they may dive into thick tomes called *Civilization* or *Reality*, or launch into a surprising new subject of study.

A Feeling-type entrepreneur named Sean, who grows pear trees in a small orchard next to his house, learned from a friend that one can make pear wine. Finding a wealth of information about pears on agricultural university websites, Sean, an extravert, was soon expounding to his family and friends on the details of determining ripeness, storing fruit, processing it, the precise yeast to use to make the best wine from pears, the proper equipment, all the facts reported by expert pomologists. When harvest time came, Sean brought family and friends together for a wine-making weekend, creating memories for everyone and good pear wine as well.

The Fourth-Function Thinking of extraverted Feeling types tends to be introverted and studious. It seeks the crystal clear philosophical thoughts and ideas about life or the nature of reality that come out of their own invisible inner thought process. Theirs is a focused, precise, introverted kind of Thinking that inspires them to study and dig deep for the reasons and concepts that underlie explain what exists.

The Fourth Function of introverted Feeling types tends toward extraverted Thinking, that is, great thoughts and sweeping ideas about outer world realities and events, current or from history. For introverted Feeling types, their deepest thoughts tap into the expansive, global, all-encompassing ideas of extraverted Thinking. An introverted Feeling type might become captivated by the intellectual breakthroughs of the Renaissance or the history of the European Union and revel in every fact and concept he or she can find.

Not For Daily Consumption

As with everyone's Fourth Function, Feeling types must approach a Thinking task slowly and not to try to use Thinking for too long. The Fourth Function tires quickly and cannot be presumed upon all day, every day. If they need to think, Feeling types often approach it with the help of an "entry ritual." Michael, a Feeling-type artist and designer, devotes a few minutes first thing in the morning and last thing at the end of the day to sit and read a thought-provoking book, keeping a pen and notebook by his side. The ideas in the book, or that come to him while reading, provide profound and exciting inspiration and are often just what he needs to know.

Though under the right conditions Fourth-Function Thinking can go to the essentials of a subject, it is not dependable as a daily workhorse. At one point, a Feeling type no longer sees any order in what he or she is studying, and it is no longer inspiring and fun. People with First-Function Feeling are rarely inclined to become attorneys, university professors, tech-support staff members, accountants or other "experts" whose professions require all-day thinking. However, a Feeling type's Fourth Function at its best offers a "living process of contact between thought and fact" [16] that is rare even among many Thinking types.

Dark Thoughts

Every Fourth Function has its "inferior" or "dark side," for instance, when one is tired or rushed. Feeling types suffering from information exhaustion may resort to adopting an idée fixe, or to borrowing conventional ideas and thoughts they've heard about or read, even though such thoughts do not reflect their true knowledge and understanding. Their Thinking function expresses itself in negative ways, it often uses negative words or thoughts. "There is this strong, critical voice in my head telling me how I screwed up, how I made so many bad decisions," a Feeling-type songwriter says. "It doesn't matter that I was following my most cherished dreams or helping people I cared about."

"In such moments when the inferior function wells up and the control of the superior function fails," writes Marie Louise von Franz, a Feeling type can get "over-critical thinking judgments" or "cynical negative thoughts… The thought is that 'I am hopeless, everything about me is wrong.'" [17] Sharp critical judgments can also come out against others, in a radical "un-valuing" that can be shocking and jar the usual harmony desired in their relationships. This can happen when the person is feeling threatened, exhausted or unwell, but also when the Fourth Function may be trying to draw their attention to the need to establish more order and form into their life.

Consulting the Muse

As usual when working with the Fourth Function, a "drop of the opposite" works magic (see Chapter 9). For instance, Feeling types can consult their Fourth Function regularly and on purpose, in effect asking their Thinking function to weigh in and contribute on the important aspects of their work and personal life, such as a reason for doing something or a logical procedure or time schedule. A little bit of structure added to the day or the week or a project helps a Feeling type feel and be more productive. When Fourth-Function Thinking is approached in the right way—"invoked" is an appropriate word—a Feeling type can be like a diver, going deep into the Thinking realm and coming up with a fact, concept, thought or idea, a pearl of great price.

It helps to set up optimal conditions for encouraging their Fourth Function to make an appearance. A Feeling-type digital-book designer named Matt remembers doing very well on tests in school because conditions were right. Tests were given first thing in the morning, prime time for his Fourth-Function Thinking. The testing room was always quiet, with everyone focusing intently and not relating to one another. The tests had a time limit, just the length of time his Fourth Function could work well.

Later, entering business school, Matt started the year feeling intimidated by his smart well-informed classmates, but he unexpectedly made his mark when he and his classmates were given a problem faced by a company. "What did the company do?" the professor challenged. "Everyone was giving answers I felt wouldn't happen in a real-life situation," Matt remembers.

That night alone in his room, in a burst of inspiration, he outlined what would happen if the people in the company acted realistically. The next day in class, after a lengthy logical discussion, Matt raised his hand and said, "I respectfully disagree. Here is what I think happened." He started to cite events from his outline when the professor took some chalk and wrote Matt's points on the blackboard word for word. When they had finished, the professor said, "This is what in fact happened."

Powerful Mediators: Sensation and Intuition

Given the frequent demands for Thinking in modern life, Feeling types must make use of their mediator functions often when they need to be orderly, logical and objective. Feeling-Sensation types can use their Sensation function to help them. They can turn first to the Sensation realm of aesthetics, material objects or hands-on physical activity to connect them with Thinking. To remind himself what to buy at the store, rather than keeping a shopping list, one Feeling-Sensation type using his mediator Sensation function puts empty boxes on a counter by his back door.

Invited by her new boyfriend to a party where she would be meeting a lot of his business associates, a Feeling-Sensation type named Evelyn was worried. "I knew that it would be a social situation requiring mental cleverness in which I feel totally at a loss," she recalled. Turning to her Sensation function, she had a manicure and a pedicure and took a trip to the mall for the right lingerie to wear under her dress. Once confident in the Sensation realm, Evelyn faced the occasion with less anxiety and more confidence. All went well, she got along well with everyone and naturally she looked great.

Feeling types can also approach Thinking via their Intuition function as mediator. In conversation with Thinking processors, a Feeling-Intuitive type may direct a conversation toward recent insights he or she has had or toward a topic that has captured his or her interest. Feeling-Intuitives often read books by visionary thinkers, whose intuitive insights make the connection with thought. A Feeling-Intuitive psychotherapist says, "When I have to think, I get by with Feeling sutured to Intuition." His Intuition function sees patterns in a client's life situation, which he can then articulate to the client.

Feeling-Sensation Types: A Feeling for the Good Life

Combining their Feeling process with Sensation's perceptiveness, Feeling-Sensation types are constantly relating personally to their physical environment and to their bodies' signals. Liking or disliking, feeling attracted or not, feeling happy or troubled or bored, all are experienced both psychologically and physically.

Feeling with Sensation brings a lot of beauty into the world, the kind that warms the heart and uplifts the spirits. As a popular Feeling-Sensation hair stylist in Boston named Jadira says, "I want everyone who gets up out of my chair to feel wonderful about themselves."

Standing in the office of a Feeling-Sensation type, a friend exclaimed, "I could live in a room like that!" Feeling what people need, Feeling-Sensation types design space for living and working. They set a scene. The colors they choose naturally create a happy serenity. Fabrics and woods are natural, chairs comfortable. Feeling-Sensation types create a mood and a place where people want to be. In preparation for a meeting, a Feeling-Sensation type consultant named Juliette was moved to "prepare the room." She created a "centerpiece" on the table with a scarf and vase she brought, which she filled orchids she picked up on her way there. She created an atmosphere in the room that was both aesthetic (Sensation) and cheerful and lively (Feeling). The meeting went well and her clients delivering their presentation appeared relaxed and confident. Halfway through the meeting, one of them leaned over and thanked her enthusiastically for her "contribution," although the client was not able to identify exactly what it was.

The combination of Feeling and Sensation readily exchanges physical affection and comforting. Others around them trust them and even instinctively reach out to touch them.

Especially gifted at interpreting the intelligence of their body's most subtle responses, Feeling-Sensation types have an instinct for healthy food and quality products. Alexa, the Feeling-Sensation type theater producer, wore baseball caps and used suntan lotion on her face as early as the 1970s—"It was less expensive than moisturizer," she says—and the benefits show.

Natural gourmets of life, Feeling-Sensation types, like Sensation-Feeling types, have an innate ability to sense quality and value and to know what looks, feels and tastes good by feeling it in both a sensual and an emotional way. An extraverted Feeling-Sensation type entrepreneur named Brendan often offers to cook for friends, even for business lunches—the more the merrier for him. Equally good as a chef and as a host, he cooks to make other people happy. "I feel that feeding people delicious food nourishes them in such a deep way it is actually healing," he says.

Even in a rapidly changing environment in which products are discontinued, brand names no longer ensure quality and even good businesses suddenly cut costs or change names, Feeling-Sensation types naturally scout around and find today's best quality, whether in food, shops, restaurants, real estate offerings, art works or places to visit or live in, all from Feeling's sure, instinctive sense of furthering wellbeing and happiness.

Feeling-Intuitive Types

Rather than tending to the quality of the outer environment, Feeling-Intuitives want to create a warm, harmonious inner environment, in themselves and in relationship with others. They "feel with" and "see into" what is happening around them and their insightful feelings lead them.

They can live quite well without regular redecorating, so they can concentrate on relating according to their intuitions about people's real needs and natures. With Sensation as their Third Function, the life principle that pleases them is: "Keep it simple." Packing for a trip to a cold climate, for instance, a Feeling-Intuitive writer from California "saw" that if he packed his two flannel shirts, he could wear one on top of the other and be warm enough. It worked.

Feeling with Intuition perception puts out "feelers" and "feels out" the meaning or soul of situations; they perceive by feeling other people's states of mind, needs and motivations. They can "feel-see" how a relationship is faring or how a mood of a group is changing, and they are able to encourage, guide, calm, heal and bring people or factors together and into harmony.

Extraverted Feeling-Intuitives are natural "boosters" and networkers and they can thrive in fields like public relations and promotion and career counseling, especially in their own firms. Spontaneous by nature, they feel first, and think… maybe only after they have learned a painful lesson in necessary boundaries in a predominantly Thinking world. But with their extraverted Feeling, they give other people enthusiastic support, and everyone likes them and takes their phone calls. With their secondary Intuition, they sense what is important and meaningful to others and can see the essential direction in which situations going.

Feeling and Intuition are a relatively rare combination in the Western world, especially when introverted, as such people feel and see too much for comfort in many modern environments. In the right ones, their contributions can be immeasurable. Empathic and insightful, Feeling-Intuitives feel deeply and understand influences and feeling truths that few others even notice. Deeply compassionate and wise about life and relationships, they can be psychological healers of the highest order. Often visionary, they can see the profound movements and influences affecting humanity. They are aware, even at times awash, in their own inner feeling impressions. These can be rapturous or gut-wrenching. Their own inner suffering, which can extend to the whole of the human condition, may at times feel overwhelming. If they are hurt by a friend's rejection or by witnessing or intuiting cruelty, they suffer deeply until Intuition can scan the situation and come up with the insights that explain what happened. Thus their wisdom builds.

Relating to Feeling Types

Get real. Say what you mean and mean what you say. Feeling types are distrustful of posturing and insincerity. With a Feeling type, you don't have to prove yourself or your point. Feeling processors aren't processing facts and reasons, they are processing *you*. The best approach is an honest belief in your subject or product and a sincere respect for them and for yourself. Stick with the essentials. If what you say doesn't ring true for them, no attempts to persuade will really convince them.

Go ahead, get personal. Personal information matters more to them than a lot of facts. You can approach someone's Feeling function by relating how you became interested in a topic. Feeling types want your feelings, experience and point of view, not to pry or be indiscreet, but because personal reactions and responses are their natural realm. With Feeling processors, it's okay to say, "I loved it" or "It turned me off."

Ask, then listen. Feeling types are rarely invited to verbalize what they are feeling or given the time to do so. "Tell me" are golden words to hear. Sincere questions work, such as, "What are your feelings about that?" or "What is your phony meter telling you?" Listening is an art with few practicing artists, and almost no one listens to Feeling types, who tend to express themselves with passion, if not precision. It's part of their charm. In the pure gush of their feelings, they may not "make sense," thus bringing out the inner squelcher or critic in their listeners. What Feeling types and processors may lack in proof or logic, they make up for with a kind of visceral gut sense of the real underlying Truth. Their strong feelings show that they believe they are onto something important, and they probably are.

Don't meet Feeling processing with Thinking. Witnessing an intense Feeling-function crisis requires understanding and delicacy. However uncomfortable or impatient you may be with a person's Feeing process, insisting that he or she "be reasonable," "get over it," or "snap out of it" merely increases the emotional load on their processing function. Criticizing someone's feeling state or telling them "not to feel that way" will only complicate matters further. Also, interjecting facts and arguments derails their "train of feeling." Especially when painful feelings are being expressed, a listener, in discomfort and concern, may want to jump in to analyze, advise or fix the situation. "Offering solutions throws me off," a Feeling type says. "I can solve my own problems, if someone will just listen to me."

Be there for them, don't go there with them. Feeling processing can take someone into an intense and unhappy period for a while. You may need to step away, even quite far away, from a Feeling crisis or mood. It needs time to do its work; a person's whole biochemistry must change. They may want you to "make the bad feelings go away," or even blame you for them, sometimes vehemently, but these are often an evasion. They can and must process what they are going through and come to clarity, resolution and a way to communicate what they need. Empathize sincerely, be clear for your own part, but don't automatically take it personally. A Feeling type can go through total misery and come through it not only safely, but with a complete resolution of their inner conflict or dilemma, especially if they have a caring, compassionate, "disinterested" witness.

Offer the right kind of support. Even if they cannot express what they are feeling, acknowledge *that* they are feeling. Offer a comment of recognition like, "That's wonderful, I'm so happy for you," "I can see how upset you are," or "You really like (or don't like) that," or "I'm so sorry you are feeling that way" or just "That's awful." Feeling types and processors, when struggling, appreciate sincere expressions of reassurance, such as, "You'll be all right," "We're going to be fine," or "You'll (or we'll) work this out." Genuinely asking, "How can I help?" also demonstrates your concern, relatedness and support.

Value them. A powerful antidote to the negativity of a Feeling type's unhappiness or his or her "un-valuing" of you, should it come out, is *valuing*. Wordlessly value them, value yourself. Focus on the valuable qualities in them and in your relationship. Appreciate the things they do or have done that you have enjoyed and admired. When the Feeling function itself is respected, when we relate to someone in an honoring way, it has power, even at a distance or in silence. The quality and content of our own Feeling state communicates and can help others navigate their own Feeling process.

The Fourth Function Phenomenon

"What takes place in the depths of one's being, in the unconscious, can neither be called forth nor prevented by the conscious mind."

— *The I Ching*

IN CONSIDERING the Fourth Function, placed farthest away from our competent First Function and its familiar, dependable ways, we encounter one of the most challenging and mysterious influences in all of psychology. As the function "opposite" our First, this "other" way of perceiving or processing life experience tends to be held at a distance from our normal awareness. But from its remote position, whatever our psychological hierarchy may be, the Fourth Function affects our life in significant ways, influencing our behavior, attitudes and self-concept, as well as our relationships with others.

Which realm of your life do you try to avoid or seems to cause you the most anxiety or stress? What function tires you when you try to use it? Are there some people who seem particularly hard for you to understand and get along with? Where do you come upon unexpected moments of amazement, even transcendence? These questions touch on the powerful Fourth Function phenomenon.

Akin to the "like" poles of two magnets, the First and Fourth Functions cannot meet, as if there were a force field holding them apart. That force field is our strong, healthy ego-consciousness working hard to perform well in our First Function. Jung wrote that our First Function is the function with which we are "best equipped by nature" to interact with our life circumstances. [1] Yet deep within us, our remote Fourth Function carries a special charge of its own and plays a role in our lives every day. When recognized in ourselves and in other people, the faraway Fourth represents a world of wonders inspiring fascination, attraction and out-of the-ordinary experiences.

Part of Human Nature

The Fourth Function phenomenon, with all that it means, is a universal human experience with profound implications. Everyone has a Fourth Function— presidents and prime ministers, teachers, corporate executives, kings and queens, generals and soldiers, bankers, priests, the young and the old, our parents, siblings, friends, lovers, ourselves—*everyone*.

Whether our Fourth Function is Thinking, Feeling, Sensation or Intuition, this function can seem like having to visit unfamiliar territory. A Feeling-type entrepreneur named Sam thrives in his relationships with suppliers and customers, but he gripes and struggles when he has to analyze cost-to-revenue ratios for investors, do his taxes or other tasks requiring him to do his Fourth Function of Thinking. "I am like a kid having to do his homework," he says. Meanwhile, a

Sensation-type engineer named Rob lies sleepless the night before an off-site seminar on five-year planning for his division, which triggers fears of having to use his Fourth Function of Intuition to look at the future and envision promising possibilities. As Rob puts it, "I get stumped." Being "stumped" is not a failure on Rob's part. Everyone who runs head-on into his or her Fourth Function can feel stumped.

"Switched off" psychologically so we can use our primary function, our Fourth is a realm of life that we may forget about; it can seem elusive, remaining just out of sight. When confronted with using this function, we instinctively feel apprehensive, inadequate or at a loss. Our Fourth Function takes a certain effort to approach. Often to our exasperation, we can't master Fourth Function activities, or we feel vulnerable and exposed doing them. For our protection, we tend to avoid them or may leave them to others.

As strong and proficient as we may be in our first two functions, in our Fourth Function we just don't feel at home. Our hardy self-confidence and sense of competence do not extend to our Fourth Function. We cannot charge forth with the usual ambitious goals and enjoyable competitiveness. On the contrary, when we have to use our Fourth Function, we often feel awkward, inept, impatient, unsure of ourselves. A Thinking type approaching a Feeling-intense relationship encounter, a Feeling type having to organize complex logistics using Thinking, an Intuitive type with a suitcase to pack requiring Sensation, a Sensation type having to intuit the import of someone's strange behavior—each is confronted with a Fourth Function situation.

Will this confrontation be a struggle or an opportunity to use psychological knowledge with wisdom and skill? Identifying and relating to our Fourth Function with a respectful understanding of its nature and purpose can change our experience, deepen our empathy for ourselves and others and bring out its considerable creative energies.

The Fourth Function Phenomenon

When we refer to the Fourth Function, we include the entire function that is opposite the First Function. For a Sensation type, the Fourth Function is Intuition, the entire immaterial dimension of possibilities, meaning and significance perceived by Intuition. For an Intuitive, it is the Sensation function, his or her sensory and physical experience and the material realm covered by Sensation perception. For a Thinking type, the Fourth Function is the Feeling function with its processing of interpersonal relatedness, his or her state of emotional wellbeing and deep personal values. For a Feeling type, the Fourth Function is Thinking and the intellectual realm of ideas, concepts and logical reasoning.

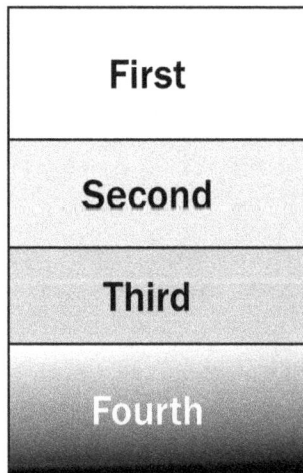

| First |
| Second |
| Third |
| Fourth |

Moreover, the Fourth Function also includes the opposite of our usual predominantly outward or inward orientation of extraversion and introversion. If we are extraverted, our Fourth Function tends toward its introverted aspects. If we are introverted, our Fourth Function tends to be extraverted. For instance, if someone is an extraverted Thinking type, his or her Fourth Function is Feeling, but at its most potent and mysterious, it is an introverted kind of Feeling, a valuing process felt wordlessly deep within. If someone is an introverted Intuitive type, his or her Fourth Function tends toward an extraverted kind of Sensation, the experience of outer-world phenomena on a grand scale.

Perplexing Limitations

Jung referred to the Fourth Function as the "inferior function," referring not only to the Fourth Function as the "lowest" function in our psychological hierarchy, but also to the way it seems to perform when we must use it. There is a certain awkward, uncomfortable, sometimes annoying quality to using the Fourth Function. It just does not feel natural. As the most remote function from our ego, we cannot successfully exercise the same degree of control, will power or discernment. When we are tired or rushed, our Fourth Function is often the first to register protest by "acting up." With effort, we may be able to "handle" Fourth Function experiences; we may blunder through, using other functions or conventionally acceptable ways of doing things. But often when we encounter a Fourth-Function situation, we pull back psychologically, as our hand does from a hot stove.

It is not that we don't like this "other" realm, often quite the contrary. Finding oneself there can be exciting, startling, even thrilling. But a little experience in our opposite realm has a big impact. Enough becomes too much pretty quickly.

An important factor with our Fourth Function is our inherent resistance to it. In our Fourth Function realm, we don't want change or to encounter anything unfamiliar. As our Fourth Function does not respond readily to our bidding, we tend to procrastinate or try to evade tasks or activities that require using it. A Feeling type facing a legal agreement to go through or an Intuitive looking at a sink full of pots and pans— the resistance response rises up and says, "Uh, oh, do I have to?"

A surprisingly intense reaction, in ourselves or someone else, often signals a Fourth Function situation. People often feel uncertain and overly sensitive there, especially if they are approached too suddenly or in the wrong way. "As soon as you get into this realm people easily become emotional," Jung's colleague Marie-Louise von Franz warned. [2]. "Most people, when their inferior function is in any way touched upon, become terribly childish. They can't stand the slightest criticism and always feel attacked." [3] One can be very critical or annoyed at oneself, as well, for not performing up to par.

Even if we manage to respond gracefully, our Fourth Function is not our strong suit, and we know it. In our Fourth Function, we can lack our usual ability to discriminate; we "bite off more than we can chew" or we suddenly find ourselves "over our head." It evokes our anxieties and feelings of incompetence, or loss of control. If we have "inferior" Thinking, for instance, we may have difficulty presenting an argument logically and objectively on demand, and we feel anxious if we have to. If the Feeling function is our Fourth or "inferior" function, emotions can seem frustratingly incomprehensible; we cannot seem to be able to respond in a way that soothes an upset relationship situation. An Intuitive with "inferior" Sensation may be at a loss confronting a attic to clear out or upon entering a big grocery or department store, where a Sensation type easily shops every day of the week. Meanwhile, a Sensation type with "inferior" Intuition may not foresee the next steps to take in a project or imagine what's happening several hours from now, the way an Intuitive does with ease.

None of us likes to see ourselves as limited or inferior in anything, but it is a fact of psychological life that to be good at our First
Function, the opposite function must get much less of our psychic
energy and attention. No human being is made any differently. Even
whole societies have their Fourth Functions. Fourth-Function-re-
lated limitations are normal and inevitable for everyone, but they
need not trouble us when we understand our Fourth Function and
know some helpful ways of approaching it. The Fourth Function
is not the competent workhorse that the First Function is, nor is it
meant to be. But therein is a mystery. This inner opposite function is
meant to play a very different role in our life.

An All-Important Relationship

Even if we cannot develop our Fourth Function to the same
degree as our other functions, we can build a good relationship with
it. As in all relationships, our attitude greatly influences the quality of
the interaction. We may direct our other functions to varying degrees
toward accomplishing our goals, but the Fourth Function has a mys-
tifying way of evading or thwarting us; we come to distrust or fear it,
as we might a stranger. If our attitude toward our Fourth Function is
negative, if we are impatient, antagonistic or dismissive, our experience with it will inevitably be one of struggle. When we work wisely
with its limits and treat it as the special realm and dynamic force it is,
the Fourth Function shows us its very positive aspects.

We often feel a lack of control in our Fourth Function—we
are "stumped." But in the midst of a Fourth Function situation, we
can act in partnership with it. What we can do, as Woody Allen has
observed about creative success, is "show up." Rather than "do it,"
we can simply present ourselves to our Fourth Function with our
needs in mind. At first, facing a Fourth Function task may feel like
looking—or leaping—into a void. But if we show up, without any

expectations as to what is "supposed to" happen or how it "should" be done, our open-mindedness is rewarded. Inspiration enters.

Working with one's Fourth Function is a creative process. As master woodcarver David Esterly says, "At that messy halfway point, in mid-course, the work will tell you what needs to be done next, if you're open to it. The work will tell you where it wants to go." [Footnote 4]

Unexpected Genius

Jung observed that the Fourth Function is where the forces of the unconscious come through to us more readily, bypassing the vigilant control of our ego. The Fourth Function, Jung wrote, is "partly conscious, partly unconscious." [5] It offers that "gap" in the encompassing circle of our personality. We can "do" in our Fourth Function, but through the gap, the Unknown, some would say the transcendent, seems to have fairly free access to us to do some significant doing.

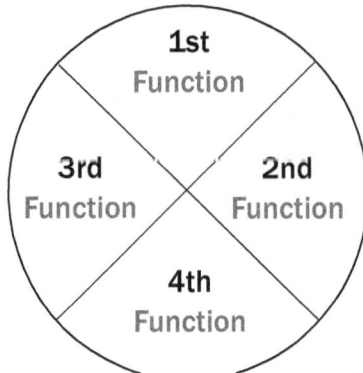

It is said that we do not use our Fourth Function, it uses us. Whether our Fourth Function is Feeling, Thinking, Sensation or Intuition, it presents situations with a foreign or "out of the blue"

character. We say, "I did not see that coming," or "Where did that come from?" "Out of the blue" come moments of consternation, but also of genius. These tend to be so unexpected and unpredictable that we can scarcely take credit for them. As we have seen, an Intuitive can unexpectedly make a memorably nourishing and delicious soup, a Sensation type can come out with an insight that stuns his or her listeners, a Thinking type can make a gesture of valuing that brings a friend to tears and a Feeling type writes the memo that explains a financial deal with such clarity that everyone now understands it and knows what to do. From out of the Fourth Function come startling results. We experience them as gifts.

Originality

When we do use our Fourth Function, these results are different from those of someone who has that function in first position and has studied and accumulated years of experience and know-how. Often, Fourth Function expression is quite spontaneous or comes in unexpected inspired "binges" that amaze. What emerges can be uncharacteristic of our "normal" selves or it can come through our normal activities in sublime and unexpected ways.

An extraverted Thinking type artist named Pamela, whose Fourth Function is introverted Feeling, did a portrait of a friend who had just had a child. In the portrait, the nuance of expression somehow perfectly captured the new mother's interior feeling state of peace and happiness. Pamela's Fourth Function felt it and conveyed it in the act of painting.

A Feeling type named Eliot, with Fourth-Function Thinking, had the idea of building an atom smasher for his high school senior physics project. In books in the library, he studied the principles on which atom smashers worked and compiled actual construction diagrams (he had Sensation as his Second Function). He persuaded companies throughout his city to donate parts, and he built his atom smasher. When it didn't actually smash atoms in the end, he hypothesized as to why it didn't work, as in the best tradition of scientific reporting and analysis—all with his fourth-placed Thinking function.

One autumn, an Intuitive named Beth, with Fourth-Function Sensation, experienced an image that suddenly came into her mind of a large, soft, colorful and warm afghan lying on her couch. She had never thought of herself as dexterous and had no experience in the realm of crafts, but she asked around and found a well-respected knitting shop and told them what she wanted to do. Suddenly she was surrounded by talented and knowledgeable Sensation perceivers telling her which needles to buy, offering her patterns to follow, showing her yarns. She didn't put herself on a time schedule, but kept her image in mind as she knitted. A year later, the afghan was lying on her couch. It was always the first thing people commented on when they walked into the living room.

In the Fourth Function, success must be defined differently. Though it can inspire prodigious effort, its inspiration cannot be predicted or counted on for practical day-in-day-out purposes. What results is a marvel in and of itself that stands as a tribute to an astounding part of ourselves.

A Little Corner of Heaven

Even in small doses, our Fourth Function can provide special experiences, even moments of real bliss. An extraverted Intuitive-type market research analyst named Caitlin experiences her Fourth Function of introverted Sensation when she swims laps in a lane by herself at her local pool. An extraverted Feeling-type website designer named Richard loves to sit first thing in the morning and study philosophy, communing with his Fourth Function of introverted Thinking.

An introverted Thinking-type writer enjoys taking his dog out to the park, where he joins other dog owners and their dogs for a happy experience of his Fourth Function of extraverted Feeling. In the park nearby, an introverted Intuitive therapist neighbor named Anne, whose Fourth Function is extraverted Sensation, takes a tai chi class for an exhilarating and restorative session of outdoor physical activity, thus nourishing her Fourth Function through extraverting in the Sensation realm in a mindful, ritual way.

Given its mysterious gap in the encompassing circle of our psychology, our Fourth Function can seem rather overwhelming. It is not possible to ignore or resist its realm altogether in life, though. We need it. Plus which, it won't let us; it will get our attention one way or another. (Fanaticism usually involves an ignored Fourth Function.) But if we can approach it with a kind of devotion or mindfulness, this attitude honors it and keeps us safe.

Enraptured

When we fall in love, we are often in Fourth Function territory. Thinking types with Feeling types, Sensation types with Intuitive types—we can be charmed by the functions that often lie dormant in our own workaday psychological life. We admire facility in a function we see prominent in others, and we want to affiliate with it for a closer look. The person seems to hold a mystery. When we find ourselves captivated by someone, or even by a place, a work of art or an animal, they have likely "activated" our Fourth Function. In their presence, our experience of life seems to grow exponentially with a surge of Fourth Function energy. At times, our Fourth Function comes to the fore with such force that it wholly takes us over, temporarily eclipsing our usual ability to choose or discriminate.

A person who is our typological opposite frequently brings up a reaction in us that is one of fascination and attraction, but not always. The person might annoy us or seem a little scary or frustratingly incomprehensible, or seem to see or do things the "wrong" way. We might feel an uncomfortable twinge of envy. Or we may note that the person is having one of these reactions to us.

A "visitation" from the Fourth Function in the materialized appearance of our opposite typologically often measures high on our personal Richter scale, shaking us out of our habitual mindset. It can also be serious psychological business. Meeting our Fourth Function "out there" feels like an inner destiny. Maybe the love of our life has come to us at last. Or could he or she be something else as well, a messenger or a Muse for something new and important that wants to be known, to grow us, or to made real in some creative way? Either way, Fourth Function breakthroughs "out of the blue" can be extremely inspiring, even life-changing.

The Iceberg Effect

Though it is tempting to berate ourselves for what we seem not to be "good at" or to chase after what we feel we lack, we are not meant to "have" our Fourth Function available like a handy tool in our toolbox. Yet when we focus on experiencing and expressing our natural primary-function endowment, this unpredictable, perplexing, at times wondrous part of our psychology does work through us in unexpected ways. There is a creative arc between our First and Fourth Functions. When we concentrate our efforts on using our primary functions, doing our best at playing the hand we are dealt, so to speak, we allow our Fourth Function to come through in its own way.

This is what Sensation-type Earnest Hemingway did as to his Fourth Function of Intuition. Early on in his career as a writer, Hemingway identified what he called his "iceberg theory" of writing, in which the underlying meaning is hinted at, rather than explicitly stated. As Hemingway explained in *Death in the Afternoon*, the writer "may omit things that he knows and the reader, if the writer is writing truly enough, will have a feeling [i.e., an intuition] of those things as strongly as though the writer had stated them." [6] While being true to his typology and focusing on the Sensation facts of his characters' situations and interactions, Hemingway understood that he was showing only the tip of the iceberg of truth. He intuitively trusted that his Fourth Function would do the rest in his writing, and it still does.

A Drop of the Opposite

Painters say that, when mixing a color on their palette, if they add a small touch of the opposite color on the color wheel, it brings the color vividly to life. When using a color in a painting, a dab of that color in the opposite corner or side of the painting mysteriously creates compositional balance and harmony in the mind of the beholder. In the same way, while we are using our primary functions with ease and competence, keeping a small amount of our Fourth Function in mind seems to revitalize our experience and create a potent sense of wholeness in the results, as well as in our life. [7]

When our Fourth Function with its realm is ignored, avoided or forgotten, it can erupt like a genie bursting out of the bottle. It becomes a "problem," even takes over our life to the exclusion of any-thing else, like the Intuitive who can't find a file in all the piles or the overworked Thinking type whose neglected partner protests—loudly. It is important not to be a closed system banishing the Fourth Func-tion altogether, nor delegating its tasks entirely to others. Just as the yin and yang symbol portrays a drop of the opposite in the middle of each, if we keep doing what we do best with our First and Second Functions, yet keep a mental window open to the Fourth Function, including it, consulting it, it will add its magic and enhance the qual-ity of our daily life.

A Sensation-type corporate executive, for instance, takes ten minutes every Monday morning with his Intuition function to envi-sion his week ahead. An Intuitive teacher uses her Sensation function to do Crockpot cooking; before school in the morning, she fills it, turns it on, and thus creates healthy, delicious dinners for her family. A Thinking-type technology department head writes one paragraph a day in a journal to stay in touch with his Feeling function's indica-tions of what is now most important to him in his life. A Feeling-type novelist keeps university course lectures by her bedside to invite cre-ative ideas from out of her fourth-placed Thinking function. It may take a certain discipline, even courage to turn voluntarily in its direc-tion, but making even the smallest or simplest effort to bring in the Fourth Function is of great value to our work, enriches our life and sparks the imagination.

Down to Basics

While we develop our primary functions to meet the complex demands of life, our Fourth Function is not meant to be so sophisti-cated. We don't usually take a degree in it, apprentice with a mentor or other common learning methods. Yet for this reason, our Fourth Function remains quite unadulterated, uncontaminated by convention and connected directly to the very fundamentals of life in its realm. These it is able to take care of—no more, but also no less.

According to Jung's colleague Marie-Louise von Franz, "The inferior function is actually the connection with one's deepest instincts, with one's inner roots, and is, so to speak, that which connects us with the whole past of mankind." [8] our Fourth Function grounds us in the simple, elemental human realities so often lost in our overly complicated daily lives.

Ordinarily, our life can be as complex as we are able to handle, but this cannot be true in our Fourth Function or its realm. It is not designed to keep us up with the newest fashions and fads, nor to adhere dutifully to family or cultural traditions. Here we experience ourselves and our life in a unique way that is simple, genuine and timelessly, universally human. There are many Thinking types, for example, who because of the power and purity of their Fourth-Function Feeling can relate to animals in a remarkably direct, heartfelt and instinctive way that humans have always had and animals respond. A Sensation type with Fourth-Function Intuition may not spend months pondering the possibilities of a relationship, but he or she can get a vivid inkling of its potential and jump right into the right marriage. For an Intuitive, a single flower or a bird singing in the backyard can suddenly provide a moment of intense Fourth-Function Sensation's physical aliveness. For a Feeling type, his or her Fourth-Function Thinking can go straight to the back-to-basics fundamentals of how things work, from a motor to software to precepts of philosophy, history or mathematics. Thus our Fourth Function reminds us of who we really are as human beings.

The Mediator Function

Dealing with Fourth Function situations, great or small, there arises a universally human challenge. Our normal everyday ego-consciousness from which we live our life can use our first two functions with confidence and ease. But when we face situations, or even the prospect of situations, requiring that we use our remote Fourth function, our normally competent egos often balk. (This is true as to using our Third function as well, though to a lesser degree; often just giving ourselves time there is all that is required.) These hidden inner dynamics can cause stress, from temporary frustration to intense anxiety.

Fortunately, as we have seen in Chapter 4 on our four-function hierarchy, built into our psychology is a function that helps us connect with our elusive Fourth Function—our Second or Mediator Function. Easy to approach and use, our Second is our "function in the middle," so to speak. With its mediating help, we can allay resistances to facing tasks that we might otherwise want to avoid. Our Second Function does not compete "functionally" with our Fourth, but complements it. If our First and Fourth Functions are perceiving functions, our Second Function is a processing function, and vice versa. This crucial difference allows our stalwart Second to serve as a mediating bridge to our Fourth Function and to enlist it as its helpful and competent liaison and partner. (Our Third Function, which also does not compete, can be used as Mediator, if less stalwartly.)

Using and relying on our Mediator function purposefully is an invaluable psychological skill. A Feeling-Sensation-type entrepreneur named Jered, for instance, uses his second-place Sensation function to mediate with his Fourth Function of Thinking. "In order to be able to work at my desk, I have to make my office space Zen-like and unencumbered," he says. "If a pile of papers is out of order visually, that becomes all that I see, all that I can concentrate on." Serving as Mediator, his second-place Sensation function creates visual order and cleanliness to connect him to the rational order and clarity of Thinking processing. As another example, a Sensation-Feeling type sales and marketing representative named Aiden makes ample use of his second-place Feeling function as Mediator with his Fourth Function of Intuition. When he needs to strategize with customers or for his career path, he enjoys a close relationship with his head of sales, whom he likes, admires, learns from and trusts for guidance. In the Feeling aspects of this important relationship, Aiden is able to connect with his Fourth Function Intuition's realm of planning for the future. An Intuitive-Thinking type can use Thinking to approach a Fourth Function Sensation task; a Sensation-Thinking type can also use Thinking to approach Intuition; a Feeling-Intuitive can use Intuition to approach Fourth Function Thinking; a Thinking-Intuitive can use Intuition to approach an intense Fourth Function Feeling situation, and so forth.

Our Mediator function is our own completely natural way to reach over and psychologically grasp hands with our Fourth Function. Whenever we need to do a Fourth-Function task or enter its realm, we can turn to our Mediator for competent assistance, at least for long enough to get the job done.

How to Approach the Fourth Function: With Care

Even with our Mediator function handy, Fourth Function activities require particular attention and awareness. Our Fourth Function is always special territory; it is not business as usual, psychologically. If we launch ourselves into a task with the same ambition to accomplish and succeed that we can when using our first two functions, the results will likely be exasperating or even harmful. However, as our Fourth Function is "partly conscious," that is, accessible to our conscious will to a limited extent, we can operate within it, so long as we respect its rules, cooperate with its way of working and honor its natural limitations. Here are some guidelines to keep in mind when relating to the Fourth Function:

Approach it slowly. Ease into the task. The Fourth Function is a "zone." To enter, it is helpful to perform some kind of preliminary activity, perhaps using the Mediator function, such as cleaning our desk or fixing tea (using Sensation), making a list or an agenda (using Thinking) or discerning what is most important or valuable (using Feeling), imagining our options using Intuition. Our Fourth Function likes to be "invited" by setting up the right conditions for it.

Waste time for a change. We need to keep a much slower pace in our Fourth Function, so that we can be attentive. Like nature, our Fourth Function will not be rushed. When we have to do something in our Fourth Function, the tendency is to do it as fast as possible, to "get it over with." Experience in our Fourth Function can be intense. "It does not help to get impatient," Jung's colleague Marie-Louise von Franz advises. "And naturally that is what is so discouraging about getting up the inferior function: one has not the time for it... One should rather accept the fact that in this realm one has to waste time. That is just the value of it, because that gives the unconscious a chance to come in." [9]

Don't do it for very long. Because our psychic energy is limited in our Fourth Function, tasks can take effort and careful attention. We tend to wear out unusually quickly or lose focus or interest. Our psychological circuits can easily become overloaded. It is unwise to try to use our Fourth Function when we are tired or hungry. To overtax our Fourth Function merely encourages frustration, self-doubt, even failure. Know when it's time to stop or take a break. Do small portions of the task at a time. Step back and acknowledge what you have achieved or what has occurred.

Keep it simple. Simplicity is the watchword in the Fourth Function. We benefit from simplifying whenever we can in the realm of life it is meant to cover, or when we are under its influence, and picking our battles, as it were. Everyone's Fourth Function is capable of providing the basic essentials in its realm, but not according to the higher standards of what you may see around you. Keep your Fourth Function activities uncomplicated. If you are an Intuitive doing the cooking, for instance, you might plan two courses, not seven. If you are a Thinking type and must to talk with an employee about performance problems, focus on one or two key aspects, speak slowly, and keep the interview clear, uncomplicated and brief. This principle goes for our expectations and requirements of others when approaching their Fourth Functions, as well. It is wise to keep them limited to what is simple and most important.

Suspend judgments. As to Fourth Function activities, dispense with the usual assumptions. Set aside self-criticism, perfectionism or sense of competition. Don't compare yourself with anyone, though you might observe and learn from someone who does it well. The Fourth Function is not meant to earn us a top salary in a life-long career. We have our first two strong and dependable functions for these things if we want them. It might even be a relief that there is a realm of life in which we don't have to achieve ultimate mastery and expertise. In fact, it's not fair to ourselves to aspire or push toward rigorous "performance goals" in our Fourth Function, as it does not work in that way. Instead, approach the Fourth Function with an open mind and a sense of childlike exploration and discovery, as artists do. The Fourth Function often has "beginner's luck."

Perseverance furthers. If we add the pressure of having to "perform" with it, the Fourth Function feels very strenuous and stressful, and also probably won't work very well. But as with "the little engine that could" in Watty Piper's classic children's story, perseverance in doing life's necessary Fourth Function tasks in the right way, slowly and attentively, really does win in the end.

Don't take the job. Many people are unhappy in their jobs without realizing that the work is requiring too much of their Fourth Function. In general, neither our Fourth nor our Third Function is made to perform the all-day, all-week demands of a job. Workarounds may be possible temporarily. But work that routinely demands too much of our Third or Fourth Function is the wrong use of our psychological gifts and abilities. On the contrary, it leaves us weakened and vulnerable, just as a plant growing in an inhospitable environment fails to thrive.

The Fountain of Youth

The Fourth Function has a childlike quality——easily frustrated, discouraged and tired and short of attention span, but also imaginative and resourceful and capable of more than we give it credit for. We may not want to make a professional career out of our Fourth Function, but pure creativity does come through, as well as the adventure of something new. In our Fourth Function, we have access to the spontaneous quality of a child at play. Approaching Fourth Function tasks with guileless, childlike earnestness and curiosity, we can see what is there afresh, try out new things in the moment and explore. In this way, being in our Fourth Function can be inspiring and inspired.

Jung pointed out that our Fourth Function isn't very "civilized" or "refined" by the "conscious learning" we can apply to developing our primary functions. [10] Thus in our Fourth Function we never get jaded, as it were. We can recover our natural humility and sense of humor. We can face a task or situation with a Fourth Function state of mind; one might call it intelligent innocence. If we devote our attention to a Fourth Function activity with the open-mindedness of a child, the Fourth Function itself guides us. We may feel unsure or unprepared, our methods might seem unusual, the results may be unconventional, but just as likely, they have a touch of pure creativity that even a trained expert rarely accesses.

When experienced without presumptions or judgments and setting aside our usual expectations for performance, our Fourth Function can be like magical territory beyond the mirror. When we no longer bother about being able to "do it well" or in some conventionally acceptable way, when we just "show up" with good intentions, there can be an open fresh-air quality to our Fourth Function, where we can enjoy new and surprising aspects of its realm with a sense of discovery. Something new and exceptional can come through that gap in our personality's accustomed circle of experience.

Growth Opportunity

As we develop our first three functions, we grow in competence and understanding. Jung saw this path of development as our "individuation" process, the irrepressible growth process built into our nature toward awareness of our whole selves. We also experience increasingly the meaning of our encounters with the Fourth Function. As we attain mastery in our primary functions, we tend to want to keep to the familiar, but the natural energy of growth is inevitably toward the unknown, including our lesser-known functions.

The Fourth Function works on this growth-edge of our lives. Our Fourth Function is persistently trying to "grow" us. As we become more familiar with our other functions, our Fourth seems to present more opportunities, including alluring ones, for exploration both of ourselves and of this "new" area of life. It may take hindsight to recognize, but our Fourth Function often brings an answer or solution, a crucial correction, or it precipitates a turning point into a fertile new direction.

According to Jung, in our Fourth Function we are related more directly to the unconscious, "the matrix of our unborn future." [11] Our typology, though inherent, is far from static. It is dynamic and creative and constantly fuels our experience and self-development. Growth can be unsettling and therefore resisted. For this reason growth experiences may need to come through our forgotten Fourth Function, which then holds the key to fulfilling the ground plan of our life. We can try to refuse that growth or hold it off, but there is no stopping nature.

Everyone who is continuing to grow as a person faces the challenge of his or her Fourth Function, an innate aspect of ourselves out of which a whole new dimension of life is revealed. It takes a certain bravery and inner strength to present oneself to the Unknown and to hold the tension of unknowing. But when we face a Fourth Function task or situation, if we slow down and direct our attention to it respectfully, a partnership arises and the task gets done. It is as if, rather than "doing" your Fourth Function, it will "do it" through you. In our Fourth Function, we encounter a natural wisdom and intelligence that will be unique. Be ready for surprises, delights, possibly even a revelation.

Knowing the limits of our Fourth Function, while also being alert to the special experiences that can come through it, is one of the most remarkable opportunities offered by our typology's inner dynamics. The Fourth Function brings a healing dose of realism that we are human. We are made to be unique and complete human beings, not the perfectly accomplished performers in every realm of life we believed we had to be. Yet our Fourth Function also serves as an internal reminder of our innate and adventurous potential for exploring new life experiences. It is said that we spend the first part of our psychological development trying to avoid our Fourth Function, and the rest fascinated with it. We yearn naturally for this sense of life's vast richness, as when we see our Fourth Function glorified in someone else and feel its attractions.

The more we acknowledge the Fourth Function's intentions to "grow us," the more we can cooperate—and the less the Fourth Function needs to up its amperage, as it were, to get our attention. Rather than resisting or fearing the unfamiliar and unknown, our experience with our Fourth Function can be transforming. Its realm can offer adventure and wonder and be a source of regeneration. The more we appreciate the small, regular, "ordinary" Fourth Function experiences for what they are, the more our Fourth Function can show us its mystery. We can be compassionate toward others' Fourth Function challenges, and we can enjoy coming to know this unknown realm in ourselves and in the world around us.

— $\boxed{10}$ —

Getting Along With Others

OUR DAYS ARE filled with relationships, at home, at work, and long after work. Some are intimate, others are chance encounters, but whatever else is going on we can be sure that typology is involved. When it comes to relationships, ignorance is rarely bliss. Fortunately, we always have typological aspects to guide us. The fundamentals are always there: each person is using a specific function to perceive and another function to process the current circumstances.

We can almost take for granted that a person we encounter will either perceive or process using a different function from the one we usually use. Some of these differences are helpful or pleasantly disconcerting and fascinating. Others are annoying or exasperating. When, on the other hand, we meet up with a person who is typologically a kindred spirit to us, we immediately relax and feel at ease as if we've known the person forever.

Similar typologies create bonds between parents and children and between siblings. We are drawn to certain aunts, uncles, cousins and grandparents and not to others. Differing typologies may clash causing long-standing tensions, frustrations and conflicts. As for our friendships, work, social and community relationships, we know that some instantly "click" and thrive, while others suffer from discomfort and stress, depending on the common or different functions being used.

Typology is an important factor in love, from blazing attractions to the subtle affinities that contribute to life-long relationships. In marriages and intimate partnerships, our shared or differing functions constantly create dynamics and spark passions that are useful to know about and to work with—or around—with understanding.

Given all these factors going on around and within us, typological awareness can easily become an on-going "practice." Our relationship experiences vary widely, but they need not be a complete mystery.

Growing Up with Typology

Often our first reflections on the influence of typology in our relationships have to do with our childhood and the people we spent so much time with in those influential years. As we contemplate our parents, bothers or sisters, and reflect on the special, close affinities, as well as the persistent frustrations and conflicts or hurts, we may see, for example, that our mother was a Thinking processor while we use Feeling, or that our brother was also a Feeling processor, or that our favorite cousin shared Intuition perception with us. When we look at who these important people were, or still are, typologically, our relationships with them begin to make more sense.

We might think about our important romantic relationships, our friends, that boss we didn't get along with or the mentors with whom we did so naturally. These observations and insights may bring us into a better understanding of the people we relate to in our current life. In this way, our knowledge comes to our aid now with our mates, our children, our work colleagues or in brief encounters, enlightening all our interactions and making them go more authentically and smoothly.

Looking back, we may wonder, "Why doesn't (or didn't) my mother understand me as well as my father?" "Why do my sister and I get along so well, but my brother and I always seem to be fighting over something?" "Why do I like visiting Aunt Frances so much more than Aunt Helena?" Looking at our family typologically, we are sure to find that there are family members who are natural fits for us, and others who are different enough to require special awareness for the relationship to go smoothly.

Having a primary function in common with a family member, that is, sharing a way of perceiving or processing, is a joy, a boon and frequently a welcome refuge. You may disagree over details, but you will always have that function as a common bond. When an Intuitive daughter realized her mother was also an Intuitive, she guided their weekly telephone conversations, formerly constrained, into experiences of Intuitive's Delight, free-ranging explorations of what was pressing on their minds that week. Their relationship thrived.

Family relationships often flow along the line of least typological resistance. A brother or sister who share their Sensation functions, for instance, may notice the same things, share interests and enjoy many of the same activities. A parent who processes with his or her Thinking function just the way we do may make more sense to us than the other parent who does not, and with whom we may experience friction or frustrating misunderstandings. If we are a Feeling processor, we may feel closer to a parent who also processes with Feeling, even if we love the other parent deeply.

Once we are aware of them, even very different typologies can find common ground. Perhaps there is shared extraversion or introversion. For an introverted Intuitive daughter, common ground was in the basement workshop of her otherwise "opposite" introverted Sensation father. "When I wanted to be with my dad," she said, "I could always go to his workshop and sit there with him as he worked on some electronics project. Every so often, he'd hand me a tool and say, 'Here hold this,' so I felt I was helping." These times of sharing their introversion created valuable memories. Gearing our interaction towards the typological aspects we share, and keeping this sharing in mind, can cause a family relationship to flourish.

At Home with the Four Functions

In most families, past and present, there is, or can be, a natural division of labor. Sensation perceivers may want to plant and tend a garden together or wash the car; they will enjoy and take pride in the activity because of how good they are making it all look. A Sensation-Feeling and Feeling-Sensation type, for instance, may enjoy sharing their Sensation perception by preparing a three-course dinner together just for the fun of shopping, cooking and eating it and, sharing Feeling together, enjoy the feeling of nourishing others. Intuitive perceivers may enjoy planning holiday get-togethers and, at the dinner table, they may keep everyone informed about the significance of news events. Thinking processors in a family may naturally take to organizing the household, from the schedule for the day to helping their siblings with homework. Feeling processors may do the delicate work of maintaining family harmony, smoothing over tiffs and trouble spots, and doing little helpful things for people.

A family that knows and encourages everyone's primary two functions, that is, each person's main perceiving and processing function, is a wonder to behold and to be a part of. Allowing everyone in a family to be who he or she really is, to use the functions they were born to use, makes for a happier family and one that works very well as a whole. We often refine our primary functions from relating with our parents or older siblings who share them, but we also learn valuable tips and techniques for using our inferior functions from family members who are naturally good at them.

Significant Differences

Relationships in all areas of our life encounter typological issues every day. Two writers named Elle and Kate, for instance, who lived across the country from one another, decided to spend two weeks together at Elle's house working on a book idea. The first day, they installed themselves at Elle's dining room table, which was soon strewn with notes, two versions of a chapter, a laptop, printouts of emails, their phones, tea mugs on napkins.

At the end of the day, Elle's husband Burt walked in from work. They greeted him and returned to their work, but became aware Burt was extremely agitated and tense, walking back and forth behind them across the dining room and into the kitchen and pressing the women about when exactly he should fire up the grill. The two women regarded him with questioning looks. "It's an hour before dinner, and we're still working here," Elle said, "I guess I'm not ready to think about grilling just yet..." Burt left the room, clearly upset.

The next day, as they met again to work, the two women realized that typology had contributed to the uncomfortable situation. Elle's husband Burt was a Sensation type with a very refined Sensation function aware of every item in a room. To come in from a day in his high-pressure office and pass through chaos in the dining room, usually so serene and uncluttered, startled and disturbed him greatly.

This evening when Burt came home, Elle greeted him with, "We apologize to you for the visual assault. We beg your indulgence for another few minutes. We're almost done here." He looked around, rolled his eyes, laughed and took refuge in the bedroom to read. The women soon finished, cleaned up their papers and laptops, and called, "All clear!" Crisis averted by honoring the typology of another person.

With awareness of the typological influences in life situations that arise, we can adjust our attitudes and find solutions. Everyone can work creatively with his or her own typological needs and interests, and with those of the people nearby. While his children were little and a fair amount of natural chaos reigns at home, a Sensation type like Burt might make a project of finding ways to organize playthings that are attractive to him. A Sensation-type woman who thrives on creating an artful body image may have to give herself some leeway during pregnancy and then enjoy exercising to recover her prenatal physique. An Intuitive perceiver, who might not even notice a dirty dish, may realize how important a neater kitchen is to her Sensation-perceiver roommate. Despite a busy family schedule, a Feeling-type child may especially benefit from one-on-one time with each parent.

Respecting a person's typology is the essence of caring and a way to show kindness. Common psychological ground can almost always be found, even if it is based on an open-minded attitude of "*Vive la différence!*"

Accentuating the Positive

Relationships flower when typological commonalities, whenever encountered, are noticed and encouraged. Sharing orientations, extraverts can go out and take on the world together without any of the introvert's inner hesitation; introverts can enjoy an evening "in," reading or studying or sitting at their computers. Furthermore, when we share a function, we immediately recognize someone who resonates well with us. Relating feels quite natural. Communicating and decision-making are done with ease, and we pursue interests and activities together with little effort.

Two Sensation perceivers, for instance, may enjoy a long hike into the mountains taking note of all the plants, trees, water levels in streams and other details of nature they see. Meanwhile, Intuitive perceivers taking a walk together may pay only fleeting attention to the beautiful landscape, but their conversation will roam and come up with possible solutions to all the problems of their world. At a family gathering, two Thinking processors might fall quickly into discussing a news event and exchanging information picked up from various sources. Meanwhile, two Feeling processors have gravitated toward one another to explore their feeling "takes" on a family member's current situation and to share support.

What about the sister and brother across the room, who use opposite processing functions and are bickering, as they have all their lives? A revolution can occur in our relationships when we know what is going on typologically. We can manage our expectations according to another person's natural ways, abilities, limits and comfort zones, as well as our own. Almost any exchange can go better when we know how to adapt our way of relating. At the very least, we are offered the chance to witness how someone else sees and does things.

First Impressions: Extravert or Introvert?

The first insight we often get about someone is how extraverted or introverted they are. Where do they stand along the extraversion-introversion continuum? This information can orient us almost immediately. We can smile, step forward and shake an extravert's hand and know our gesture will be well received. If the person seems introverted, we can step back, put our chin down, as if in a subtle Western version of bowing. In this way, we allow the introvert a buffering moment to become comfortable with us.

As we saw in Chapter 1, extraverts and introverts often fall in love as if nature desires complementary partnerships. In *Psychological Types*, Jung wrote that most people marry someone of the opposite orientation, and that "such marriages are very valuable as psychological symbioses." [1] In their fascination, they serve one another with their respective strengths; they protect one another's weaknesses and broaden the other's experience of life. When extravert Diane and introvert Michael, both chefs, opened a new restaurant together in Manhattan, they discovered the extent of their typological synergy. Introverted Michael works quietly in the kitchen during mealtimes, as well as doing the prep lists and ordering ingredients. Extraverted Diane trains much of the staff, takes care of the phone calls and runs the front of the house. "Now, we are actually able to see projects to completion," Diane said enthusiastically. "We're not necessarily working less, but we are getting more done," Michael added.

Creating a typological balance may require imagination. An extravert may love lively social scenes, while the introvert's preference is for tête-à-têtes. Meeting halfway often involves finding social activities they both can enjoy. This is one reason for the popularity of going to the movies or to a restaurant or of taking a run together, a hike or bike ride, which are ways of having one-on-one time, yet out in public.

After she moved to Chicago, an extravert named Jessica met and married Geoff, who was quite introverted. Jessica's big family all lived in Minneapolis, and she loved to visit them on weekends, going over to her relatives' houses for meals and out at night with her sister, brother and cousins. Geoff enjoyed spending the weekend in their apartment in Chicago, reading, working at the computer, seeing a friend or two for dinner, maybe going out to hear some jazz.

By midweek, they began to struggle over their weekend plans. Once they understood that Jessica was an extravert and Geoff was an introvert, they agreed that the other was not "wrong" in wanting to spend the weekend in the way that was most fun and fulfilling. They loved each other and realized they most of all wanted to be together, whether in Minneapolis or at home in Chicago. Weighing her enjoyment of seeing her large, close family in Minneapolis and her desire to be with her husband, Jessica decided she would go to see her family every month or so, alone if not with Geoff, and the rest of the time she would stay in Chicago. Meanwhile, liking her family as individuals and knowing they were important to her, Geoff agreed that on special occasions, he would go with her to Minneapolis. Interestingly, Jessica's siblings and cousins began making individual trips to Chicago, where they could get to know the city and Geoff could enjoy them one by one. By consciously balancing their extroversion and introversion, Jessica and Geoff began to benefit not only themselves and their relationship, but also everyone in the family.

How are They Perceiving and Processing?

Along with the extent of their introversion or extraversion, we can often discern a person's main perceiving or processing function.

Knowing how a person is perceiving what is going on, or how he or she is processing or coming to understand it, can help you find the right approach and add sensitivity, nuance and skill to your interaction.

What are they looking at? Are they perceiving visual details, what people are wearing, the décor of the room, or are they wondering what is going on in the room or going on with you? With someone with a prominent Sensation perceiving function, you can get specific about physical details. You can ask about a particular tool or chair, watch or pen or jacket. You may ask about their favorite stores or designers. They are likely doing some kind of athletic activity, so you can ask how they're keeping fit these days. An Intuition perceiver is approachable via his or her visionary side; Intuitives are always seeing more in something than anyone else. "What do you see going on ..." in a movie, a news event, a meeting you've just attended, in someone's head? you may ask. Ask an Intuition perceiver about a person's motivation, as in, "Why do you think they said (or did) that?" You can ask them what they see coming up for a work project or next semester or a vacation.

As for the processing function a person is using, Thinking or Feeling may become obvious. Notice what are they talking about and how are they responding to what you are saying. How much of it is in words —that is, using Thinking function—and how much in physical gestures and exclamations expressing Feeling? Are they using objective facts and thoughts about the situation, using Thinking, or relating to you personally as if you matter more than the subject you are discussing—that is, using the Feeling Function?

With a Thinking type or processor, you might ask what they are reading, what projects they are working on or what interests them these days. You may ask where something "fits in," as the Thinking function is always organizing what we perceive. You can ask their "analysis" of a situation; they will think it through for you out loud.

With a Feeling type or processor, you can encourage their enthusiasms. They will love being asked their Feeling evaluations of an event, a movie or a restaurant. Ask them their personal opinion of something, or what their "favorite" is. Tell them what is really on your mind. Your sincerity will be appreciated, and lack of it will be picked up by their "phony meter."

Meeting our Opposites

Encountering people who are our opposites typologically is a common experience, indeed inevitable. Some opposite types avoid one another, feeling awkward around someone with different ways and priorities. Others rarely meet, as they often live in different realms professionally and personally. An extraverted Thinking type, who thrives running community events, might never encounter her introverted Feeling-type psychologist neighbor, and when she does by chance, she is likely to be a bit disconcerted and at a loss, though also fascinated, and vice versa.

You may not always feel close or completely at ease with someone very different from you typologically. You may feel you have to "watch yourself" or hold back; something in you can't quite relax as well as you can with people sharing your primary functions. But opposite typologies can feel real affection and admiration, beholding one another with awe and amazement for their respective skills and abilities, even though their daily activities may diverge greatly.

People with very different typologies, whether family members, friends, roommates, neighbors or work colleagues, can lend one another a hand. They show us aspects of the world that would otherwise remain unfamiliar. People who do not share perceiving functions or processing functions may have to work harder at understanding one another, but with awareness their complementarity can work very well in running an organization or business, for instance, or in childcare. Some of the best dinner parties turn out to be those where the people around the table cover all four typological bases.

Finding Common Ground

Encountering a "type clash" of different perceiving or processing functions, we can deflect or diffuse disagreements and misunderstandings by moving to common typological ground. We can change psychological gears, so to speak, thereby restoring harmony.

Type clash is quite common between Thinking and Feeling processors, for example, but they can take refuge in a perceiving function. Is the other person a Sensation perceiver? An Intuition perceiver? The role of the perceiving functions is to notice and provide information, a generally neutral activity. If two people can stop processing and start focusing on information of mutual interest, all goes well again. "Sorry to interrupt, but I have to ask you a question," another Sensation perceiver might be asked. "Do you notice the spice in the potatoes? What is that, do you think?" Another Intuitive perceiver might be asked, "What was your take on the president's speech? I'd really like to know what you see in it. What do you think will happen next?"

As for type clash between a Sensation perceiver and an Intuition perceiver, they are often noticing completely different aspects of a situation or environment; they may not understand or even care very much about what the other is talking about with such interest. Communication falls flat. But turning to a processing function can help them connect. Two Thinking processors, for instance, can switch gears from their differing perceptions into an objective analysis of an intellectual subject or a set of facts. Two Feeling processors may not relate to the perceptions the other is trying convey, but they can relate to his or her feelings of interest and enthusiasm. "It's amazing that you see that!" "You are so good at that!" They can listen and relate using the Feeling way of liking and valuing of the person. In the strength of this caring and appreciation, Feeling processors can learn from one another's different observations.

Not Joining the Firm: Evaluating Others' Expectations

Our family or society often initially defines us, but an early self-image may not be true to our natural typology. We may grow up trying to meet our parents' or family's or culture's expectations, assumptions or ambitions irrespective of our psychological make-up, so that we set goals for ourselves that we were not made to aim for. We might struggle and reach a goal by using an inferior function, certainly a well-deserved triumph and often an asset, but then find it difficult to stick with the activity or career. Obstacles arise, perhaps excuses and evasions, because our inner energies want to flow in another direction.

Who we really are wants to be expressed in what we do. As soon as we become aware of our built-in psychological gifts, we can distinguish our natural ways from our family's or society's values and directives. It may take some courage, but when we start to use the functions we are intended to use, we often find our way with fresh energy and success. Those who really love us will be glad, perhaps even inspired.

Kindness to Inferiors

Just as important as encouraging everyone in their primary functions is being sensitive and aware of their so-called inferior functions. People's Third and Fourth Functions are members of the family, too, as they are in any organization or group. Rather than being annoyed and frustrated when someone tries to use a Third or Fourth function, we can ease up, be sensitive, gently help out or cheer him or her on, remembering that we may need their encouragement and help in our own "inferior" realms.

An introverted Intuitive named Emily needing to face her inferior Sensation realm says, "I will only go shopping with my sister Hannah. She's a godsend. I just tell her what I'm looking for and follow her into a store that to me is like a maze." Emily's sister Hannah is an extraverted Thinking-Sensation type. With her extraverted confidence in crowds and her practical, thoughtful hands-on Thinking-Sensation approach to finding things in a store or mall, Hannah enjoys taking Emily under her wing. Her Sensation function helps find what Emily is looking for and also inspects it to see if there is anything wrong with it. With her Thinking function, Hannah points out important facts that help Emily narrow down choices—an Intuitive's dream in a shopping companion.

In another family, a brother and sister have formed a useful typological partnership at parties. Brother Eric, an introverted Thinking-type, feels apprehensive about being with people unless a subject of mutual interest can be found. He can often be seen at the elbow of his extraverted Feeling-processor sister Mariel, as she addresses everyone by name, eases introductions and seamlessly brings her brother into groups and conversations. Eric depends on Mariel to get their friends together on weekends, and Mariel enjoys having her smart, strong-minded little brother along. "He impresses people," she says. "He keeps things from getting out of hand."

The "Wow" Factor

One of the most vivid experiences of our typology in action, as we have seen, is when we fall in love or even experience a moment's intense infatuation. We think we fall in love mysteriously or at random, but it is not completely so. Among the myriad ingredients stirred into the caldron of love and sexuality, it is always worthwhile looking at typology, its dynamics and its natural attractions.

Nature tends to draw opposites together as if it were good for the overall enhancement and enrichment of life. Excitable people and calm people, take-action types and idea people, even blonds and brunettes, can be fascinated by their differences. This goes also for extraverts and introverts, Thinking and Feeling types, Sensation and Intuitive types. Meeting someone of your same typology gives you a glow of affirmation and affinity, while encountering your typological opposite can feel like a blast of gamma rays. Our hearts seem to beat faster for someone whose typological strengths, though different from our own, combine with ours to make a well-functioning whole.

Any time we feel sexual attraction we may be encountering a living example of our typological opposite. Our opposites impress us with how brilliantly they feature a function we "lack." Face to face with our opposite incarnate, we can have a ravishing, exhilarating feeling of being totally completed by that person. Being apart may be painful, because we so much want to feel whole once again. When the moon starts to rhyme with swoon, your opposite could be near.

Relationships with our typological opposites—extraverts with introverts, Sensation perceivers with Intuition perceivers, Thinking processors and Feelings processors — can be very exciting as we register an arc of psychic electricity. Witnessing our opposite "in person", we cannot take our eyes off him or her, or can't get his or her image out of our minds, as if we are meant to get a good look at these mysterious, compelling qualities, so we can learn all about them from a natural. There is "chemistry," an invisible attraction that you can't explain by looks alone. Other people just as good-looking don't attract us in the same way.

There may be another factor involved when we feel that positive chemistry, whether with a love interest or even a potential friend. We often greatly admire someone who has our second function as his or her first. We look up to the person who excels at our second function, much the way of a younger brother or sister looks up to an older sibling. A Thinking-Sensation type often admires a Sensation type, for example, or an Intuitive-Thinking type is attracted to a Thinking type. Our own version of the function seems so much less capable, yet understands and appreciates what the other person can do. Likewise, our own first function often attracts the admiration of people for whom it is their second function. A Thinking-Intuitive or Feeling-Intuitive often admires an Intuitive type. This charming typological phenomenon between primary functions sparks and enriches many good relationships and helps them truly endure. We have to make sure, however, that we are not overly worshipful or unduly influenced. The admiration may be well deserved, but we need to make sure we are using our own sturdy and capable second function for ourselves.

Meeting at the Intersection

Though nearly all typologies can and do work in romantic and other partnerships, people in long-term intimate relationships almost always share either their processing function or their perceiving function. Sharing either a first or second function with someone is a channel of communication, an intersection where you can always come together. It can provide the very basis for a successful relationship. "I can't tell you what a delight it is to share enough of the same typology to have domestic life go smoothly!" a newly married writer said, after years in an unhappy relationship with a man with whom she shared neither her perceiving nor her processing function. A shared function helps two people be on the same wavelength. They communicate easily, sympathize and share interests and priorities, understandings and points of view. When they share a perceiving function, either Sensation or Intuition, people notice similar types of things. Conversation is often about what each person is noticing and they can make similar choices. If they share a processing function, as do two Thinking processors or two Feeling processors, they respond to their circumstances and experiences in a similar way.

Common interests and activities, similar ways of seeing things, sharing what is most important personally—these can keep a relationship going for the long run, even give a relationship it's *raison d'être*. One New York couple, Celine and Harry, both share Sensation perceiving. The esthetics of their home, cooking together in the evening, dressing with great style, as well as doing all the lovingly hands-on tasks of taking care of their two children, all the Sensation-rich aspects of life, provide them with great enjoyment and nourishment. That Harry processes with his Thinking function and Celine with her Feeling function may cause minor instances of type clash to arise — Harry may take a long time to make a decision, while Celine's instinctive Feeling responses have already made her choice and she is ready to move on. But overall, the Sensation realm matters most and they appreciate the contributions made by his well-researched and thought-out logical approach and her potent instincts to their very successful life partnership.

Another couple, Cate and Frank, are both Thinking processors. They use different perceiving functions and notice different aspects of their environment. But it is more important to them to share one another's way of making decisions in a rational manner and of understanding and organizing life in a way that is reasoned, deliberate and logical. They both seek facts and rely on them and maintain an overall objective tenor in their relationship and home life. As for using their different perceiving functions, the division of labor works well for them. "I use my Intuition function to plan the trip, and he uses his Sensation function to pack up the car," Cate says. With her Intuition, Cate sees into trouble spots in Frank's job and "assembles" interesting meals from the organic, gourmet take-out counter. Using his Sensation function, Frank often cooks and he created and maintains a garden in the summer and also built a deck outside their back door as another "room" of the house. Once again, a good relationship is nourished by sharing one function, while their opposite functions enhance life together in complementary ways.

For Jung, from his decades of observation of couples, there was one caveat in the typological dynamics of love, one combination that he reportedly felt should not be tried. This was a combination so opposite in their basic natures that there could not be enough mutuality for a successful marriage. This combination was extraverted Sensation-Thinking and Introverted Intuitive-Feeling. People of these typologies can be very attracted to one another, and they can be loyal and admiring friends and synergistic work partners, but there is not enough real understanding of each other's needs and character for the details and rigors of a day-to-day personal mated life together. With no intersection of functions to help them, the twain cannot meet.

"When is He/She Going to Change?"

As advice columnist Carolyn Hax once wrote: "Cruel Life Joke

No. 12: Differences heighten attraction, but they chip away slowly at love." Or they might just be typological. If one is unhappy in a relationship or it doesn't seem to be working, it may be a question of typological dynamics that with awareness and communication can be addressed. Is the other person using a different function from yours to perceive or to process whatever is going on? We often hear that "people don't change," but seeing a person in a new way may make a significant improvement.

However much they care for you, though people can grow in understanding, they cannot change their typology. If they try, there arises a painful artificiality or distortion of themselves, just as a blue-eyed person can try to wear brown contacts but will still have blue eyes. Our psychological fundamentals are givens and not meant to be "fixable." No one, however differently they do things, is typologically "wrong." A Thinking type will always naturally process experience logically and objectively, and a Feeling type will always "feel" his or her truth personally via visceral instinctive responses. Intuitives will naturally, automatically, want to see larger contexts and pictures and meaningful connections that will be obvious and apparent to them, but will not necessarily see your new jacket or curtains. A Sensation type will immediately relate to the physical aspects of what is there, without "wondering" very much about why they are there or what they might mean. If someone tries to restrict these natural domains and ways of functioning, a person becomes crippled, as though their feet were bound. However, when these differences are really seen and appreciated, magic can happen.

Take the opposites of Sensation and Intuition perceivers. As people who live or work with an Intuitive know, for instance, it is hard for him or her to throw anything away. The things they keep around them have meaning or personal significance, though perhaps not practical uses or esthetic qualities. While they accumulate things that capture their interest, they are less inclined to clear them out, as they "might need them sometime." Many Intuition perceivers are able to ignore clutter or a haphazard décor, while Sensation perceivers are not. With real honesty about their needs, compromise is possible on both sides, perhaps setting aside a time to work together on a certain pile or cluttered corner or designating a "halfway out" place in the attic. This is part of the relating aspect of relationship.

As for a Sensation type, for whom Intuition is the Fourth Function, he or she may be so wholly focused on the experience of the moment that an important plan is completely forgotten. If you are working with or relating to a Sensation type, leave a note or call ahead and confirm an appointment, and do not take it personally if you hear, "I'm glad you called. I'd completely forgotten about it." In fact, with a Sensation type, you can try spontaneity. While it would be considered an insult to many, calling a Sensation type on Saturday morning for a Saturday night get-together might delight them.

Thinking and Feeling processors especially bare a unique psychological burden when relating to one another. Feeling-rich conversations outside a partnership, for instance, can be seen as threatening to a Thinking processor. A Feeling processor may find a Thinking processor to be cool and disinterested, when he or she is really not; their Feeling function is at work, deep inside.

Good relationships provide lots of opportunities to be creative together and cooperate with each person's typology. No one is wrong when the relationship is right, and ways can be found that work for both people. Awareness of what is going on typologically is the first step. Removing criticism and judgmental attitudes is a close second, moving on into understanding, cooperation, and a sense of humor about the very human situation you find yourselves in, that of four functions times two trying to make life whole and fulfilling.

Function Not Found

Even though two people share a particular function and work well together in that realm of life, there will still be functions left hanging, and this can become all-important. A Sensation-Feeling-type marketing manager named Martha was in a passionate new relationship with a Thinking-Intuitive journalist, whom she considered brilliant. After a while, however, Sensation issues arose. "He uses my toothbrush, my towel!" she complained to a friend. "He tried to make me breakfast and couldn't even follow the recipe for pancakes. He's had his new apartment for two weeks and hasn't even bought a bed yet! I know these are small things, but..." With her Sensation function "left hanging," her Feeling function was feeling increasingly disturbed and dubious about the relationship. Despite their passionate connection, Martha realized she needed more mutual attention to the Sensation aspects of life that he barely noticed.

The Danger Zone: The Fourth Function

Many sore points, annoyances and frustrations in a relationship involve somebody's Fourth Function. If there is something a person does, or doesn't do, that drives us crazy, it's likely to be in Fourth Function territory, theirs or ours. If our First Function is their Fourth, our loved one, friend or colleague will not respond with the same intensity, adeptness, depth or focused enthusiasm in that realm that we do. If someone else's First Function is our Fourth, we will tire long before they will in an activity they do with ease.

Each person has a Fourth Function, and it is a highly sensitive area. Approaching activities involving someone's Fourth Function causes instant discomfort. Defenses go up, unexpected emotion arises, objections or excuses are made. As we described in Chapter 9, our Fourth Function gives us extremely pleasurable experiences—a little has a big impact—but also unpleasant "inferior" ones, causing reluctance. We are just "not ourselves" in our Fourth Function realm. Indeed, kindness toward another's Fourth Function is a wise practice. People get "touchy," Marie-Louise von Franz warns. "One should never make depreciative or hurtful remarks if people come out with their inferior function." [2]

It can be disconcerting when a partner, friend or colleague, usually so smart and competent and such good company, suddenly becomes petulant or negative or even mean because his or her Fourth Function has been touched. People's efforts in trying to "use" their Fourth Function can be clumsy or childlike; fuses can be short. Nor is it easy to admit what is hard or very uncomfortable for us to do.

One married couple, both with successful and demanding careers, had an apartment in town and a weekend house in the country. The wife, a Thinking-Sensation type writer named Emily, felt that her husband Franco, an Intuitive-type artist, wasn't helping enough with the many aspects of running a house, especially part-time, and she requested that he do certain chores on weekends. Knowing instinctively that he needed to conserve as much of his limited Fourth Function Sensation energy as possible for his painting, Franco balked and tension ensued. Franco told Emily he was not able to do all that she asked of him, but he would be glad pay for her to hire someone to do his share.

Typical of a good marriage, Emily and Franco did some self-examination and met partway. Emily decided she wanted to manage the house herself according to her Sensation standards, but lowered her expectations as to what she by herself could get accomplished. She realized that she actually could use someone's help in the garden, and she found a capable person to come on Saturday mornings, with

Franco picking up the tab. Meanwhile, Franco got her point about sharing some of the responsibilities of the country house and agreed to take on certain tasks he personally found enjoyable, like bringing in wood for the fire and going to the town recycling center where neighbors met and caught up with one another on Saturday mornings.

Friends Indeed

Not confined to families and romantic relationships, typology is an important factor in friendship. Sharing the channel of a typological function make for great friendships that are mutually supportive, validating and inspiring. It invites friendly shorthand of understanding and communication.

Sharing a function or two allows real friendships to develop between men and women and between people of different generations and cultures. Sharing the Thinking function, for instance, allows networks of academics, legal experts or discussion groups that are global in scale. People sharing the Intuition function exchange their insights and discoveries, visions of trends and new possibilities over long distances.

We become friends with people who like doing the same things we do, who share our interests, and with whom we feel at ease. When friends get together, they usually spend the most time in their shared typological realm. A friendship can thrive on sharing a common perceiving function, for instance. People's main perceiving function is what they notice, what catches their interest. Two Intuitive friends named Catherine and Sherine live across the country from each other and rarely meet face to face, but they enjoy long phone conversations sharing insights and observations about their lives and what they see happening in the world. Their Intuition functions can go on long journeys together without leaving their own apartments. Meanwhile, a Feeling-Sensation type named Sam has been good friends since college with a Thinking-Sensation type named Joe; they share Sensation perception. When they get together, they focus in on a home repair project, trading information about where to find the best fixtures at the best prices. Within minutes, they have set to doing a hands-on task together, and at dinnertime, they work the grill together cooking for their families.

When friends share a processing function, either Thinking or Feeling, they experience an inherently easy, natural way of understanding. With two Thinking processors, topics of conversation are organized and follow in a logical sequence. Ideas and subjects are discussed sharing facts and references and with a comfortable objectivity. They feel confident that information will be exchanged or a situation dealt with in a reasoned way and that personal issues, if mentioned at all, will be treated discretely.

Meanwhile, Feeling processors together can sense a comfortable ease and warmth of connection, often before anything is said. Feeling-processor friends easily sympathize, understand or relate to one another, and respond to the feeling tone of situations and people. When with another Feeling processor, they know they are not going to have to make rational arguments to support what they are trying to say or to supply precise sources and expert opinions. They can simply be and express themselves, their likes and dislikes, impressions and enthusiasms, without having to prove their views.

The Feeling Function—a Special Role

Among the things that turn a relationship from black and white to color is being valued by the other person. This valuing—of what one is and what one does—is a part of the Feeling function. Really feeling the value of someone is else powerful. So much the better if it is spoken.

Each of us has within us a kind of psychological genius in the relationship realm: our Feeling function. When a relationship is not going well, our Feeling function lets us know. If we do not acknowledge its subtle responses and cues, it communicates more and more forcefully, which is why an unhappy relationship can dominate our life. As Feeling processing is deeply connected to our physical being, messages gone unnoticed or overridden as unimportant, inconvenient or childish create stress that builds up until emotions erupt or express themselves in physical symptoms or in behavior that can shock us into awareness that "something's wrong." Our Feeling function has probably been telling us this for quite a while, if we only knew how to listen.

The Feeling function is unique in that it is the function that develops and thrives specifically in relationship, from our earliest days on earth. Our Feeling intelligence grows person to person and provides us with essential psychological information for living with and relating to others. The Feeling function is always trying to "make a connection," a point of commonality or communion, and it can usually find one.

Feeling immediately understands Feeling, just as logic communicates automatically between Thinking types. Two Feeling processors can enter a paradise of relatedness. "It's such a blessing to be in deep conversation with someone processing with the Feeling function," a Feeling-type songwriter named Jesse says. "There's a safety, deep sense of comprehension, of feeling 'You get me.' Suggestions are from their personal experience and feelings; there are no 'you shoulds' based on abstract rules."

Natural instinctive Feeling responses may at times be misinterpreted. "I'm married to someone who's married to everyone!" Ira exclaims in the film *Ira and Abby*. "It's always been hard for me to believe that she loves me in particular." Abby is an extraverted Feeling type, who processes life by relating in a personal way to everyone she meets. At times, she may seem to be falling in love with every person she encounters, but she is just being Abby, her extraverted Feeling self. Valuing people is part of her way of processing life, as natural for her as breathing. Ever alert to the feeling atmosphere of their relationships, Feeling types and processors frequently learn to moderate their self-expression given its effect on others. Though for their special loved ones, as Ira learns, no one loves you like a Feeling type, who shares her or his genius for valuing so freely.

Not all relationships require an elaborate Feeling connection, such as those based on Thinking processing at work or in community activities, or in playing sports (beyond the occasional supportive "Good point!" or "Good shot!"). But in our closer relationships, everyone's Feeling function is present and processing, recognized or not, and the quality and feeling tone of our relatedness improves greatly if we acknowledge this and allow it to inform us. The Feeling function's valuing makes its appearance in numerous moments of genuinely appreciating someone's knowledge, skills, abilities, or acts of kindness or courage. These are vital nourishment for anyone.

Our Feeling function is in us to tell us how we are feeling, so we can communicate and behave in our relationships in ways that feel good and right, that feature harmony, mutual valuing, supportiveness, natural comfort and ease. In relationships, Feeling is our inner guide, our heart speaking. Most importantly, our Feeling function is in us for our relationship with ourselves, to value, respect and honor our very existence and our on-going experience, by letting us know about our wellbeing—that is, how well is our Being.

Becoming More Whole

It is fact of psychological life—and of human life—that we are naturally gifted in areas that others approach only remotely or want to avoid altogether. We often can do things for one another, thanks to our various typological endowments, and sincere gratitude for another's good help is always a relationship enhancer. Yet it is also important to remember that each of us is ultimately meant to be a full-functioning—that is to say, four-functioning—individual. We are intended to have the right relationship with each of our four functions within us, so that it works the best way it can for us. We are then able to interact in wise partnerships with others, in interdependency, not dependency.

There is an art to allowing another person to express his or her superior functions, as well as their inferior ones. It is easy to be impatient with others, or to let others do things for us. But even if our companions are geniuses, it behooves us not to lose sight of developing our own psychological totality and its potential.

In every relationship that works well, individuals come together and also "individuate." While our basic natures and typologies do not change, we do grow and explore our psychological capabilities as we mature. We explore, so to speak, our untried selves, which another person may have carried for us for years. As Jung pointed out in *Psychological Types*, as a relationship matures, there is a certain coming to terms. "In favourable circumstances this phase enters automatically into the lives of both types, for the reason that each type is an example of one-sided development," Jung wrote of marriage between extraverts and introverts. "The one develops only external relationships and neglects the inner; the other develops inwardly but remains outwardly at a standstill. In time the need arises for the individual to develop what has been neglected." [3] Meanwhile, he warns, "real courage is needed to risk a rupture of the marital peace." Yet the on-going exploration and development of our functions and personalities are part of the adventure of relationship.

"Know Thyself" and Others

People relate so much better to one another when they know, accept and respect both the other person's typology and their own. When we recognize how people use different functions to perceive and to process life's circumstances, many otherwise inexplicable aspects of our relationships become clearer. We understand better the behavior of the people around us, and knowing what we need typologically helps us guide others in relating to us.

Of utmost importance is to realize that there is nothing *wrong*, not with us, nor with them. On the contrary, when we are all using our functions as we are meant to do, everyone is right. When we let another person use his or her natural psychological gifts and talents, we will see a true wonder -- a well-functioning human being. It may not be the way we would do things, but we have all functions in us somewhere and therefore can understand their way, appreciate it and learn from it.

Every function concerns a vital aspect of life. Our way is valuable; another's way is also valuable. None of us can do it all ourselves, nor are we meant to. By allowing others to do psychologically what they do naturally and encouraging them to express what they see and understand, we get not only a better relationship with each person, but also a more accurate and comprehensive picture of reality.

Ultimately, the most valuable contribution we can make to all our relationships is to be our own genuine selves. We must allow ourselves to be who we are. With the reference point of our natural psychological endowment, we can be true to ourselves wherever we are and whenever we encounter someone else. We relate confidently, artfully, with sensitivity and without apology for who and how we are. We honor our real needs for extraverting and introverting; we allow ourselves to use the functions we use naturally to perceive and process our world. When we allow everyone else to do the same, our relationships become genuine and authentic and take their invaluable places in our lives.

Acknowledgments

I want to express my deep gratitude to the special friends, family and associates without whom this book could not have been written, including Robert A. Johnson, Sean J. McCarthy, Patricia Carlton, Mary Keil, Jane Keil Yoder, Megan, Joe and Julia Sanzio, Sara, Jeremy, Ruby and Eve Kennedy, Sean M. McCarthy, Anne Tinker, Valerie Andrews, Laurie Lisle, Tom Hill, Swift Barnes, Victoria Barr, Michael and Ariane Batterberry, Bettina Walton, Harry Bowers, Dot Barad, Therese Balagna, Paul Bloom, Eric Francis, everyone who has shared his and her experiences, and, of course, my inspiration, Dr. Carl Gustav Jung.

Notes

CHAPTER 1: YOU AND THE WORLD:
EXTRAVERTS AND INTROVERTS

1. See Jerome Kagan, *Galen's Prophecy: Temperament in Human Nature*, Westview Press, 1997.
2. C.G. Jung, *Psychological Types*, Princeton University Press, 1991, p. 332.
3. Knight-Ridder News Service, March 8, 2003.
4. Jung, p. 549.
5. Jung, p. 334.
6. *People*, September 19, 2011, p.101.
7. *The New York Times,* the *Arts & Leisure* section, September 20, 2002, p. 32.
8. Jung, p. 150.
9. Jung, p. 550.
10. *More*, September 2004, p. 38.
11. *The New York Times,* the *Arts &Leisure* section, June 2, 2002, p. 25.
12. *The New York Times Magazine*, June 24, 2001, p. 12.
13. Marie-Louise von Franz, *Lectures on Jung's Typology*, Spring Publications, 1971, pp. 20-21.
14. Knight-Ridder News Service, April 15, 2001.

CHAPTER 3: THE PSYCHOLOGICAL BASICS: PERCEIVING AND PROCESSING

1. C.G. Jung, *Psychological Types*, Princeton University Press, 1991, p. 539.
2. Jung, p. 406.
3. Jung, p. 435.
4. *Harvard Business Review*, May-June 1990, pp. 103-4
5. *Harvard Business Review*, May-June 1990, pp. 103-4

CHAPTER 4: OUR FUNCTION ORDER HIERARCHY

1. C.G. Jung, *Psychological Types*, Princeton University Press, 1991, p. 520.
2. Jung, p. 346.
3. Jung, p. 553.
4. Marie-Louise von Franz, *Lectures on Jung's Typology*, Spring Publications, 1971, p. 15.
5. Jung, p. 405.

CHAPTER 5: THE SENSATION FUNCTION

1. C.G. Jung, *Psychological Types*, Princeton University Press, 1991, p. 461.
2. Jung, p. 554.
3. Author Interview.
4. *More*, April 2002, p. 71.
5. Marie-Louise von Franz, *Lectures on Jung's Typology*, Spring Publications, 1971, p. 22.
6. Jung, p. 363.
7. Jung, p. 539.
8. von Franz, p. 23.
9. von Franz, p. 30.
10. *In Style*, February 2000, p. 108.
11. *AARP*, Sept.& Oct. 2003, "King of the Grill,'" by Frank Gannon, p. 90.

CHAPTER 6: THE INTUITION FUNCTION

1. Marie-Louise von Franz, *Lectures on Jung's Typology*, Spring Publications, 1971, p. 25.
2. C.G. Jung, *Psychological Types*, Princeton University Press, 1991, p. 366.
3. C.G. Jung, *Synchronicity*, Princeton University Press, 1973, pp. 30-31.
4. Jung, *Psychological Types*, p. 553.
5. Jung, *Psychological Types*, p. 554.
6. Jung, *Psychological Types*, p. 454.
7. Jung, *Psychological Types*, p. 539.
8. Jung, *Psychological Types*, p. 365.
9. Jung, *Psychological Types*, p. 367.
10. Jung, *Psychological Types*, p. 368.
11. *Newsweek*, February 8, 2001, p. 48.
12. Jung, *Psychological Types*, p. 519.
13. Jung, *Psychological Types*, p. 365.
14. Jung, *Psychological Types*, p. 454.
15. Jung, *Psychological Types*, p. 369.
16. Jung, *Psychological Types*, p. 406.
17. von Franz, p. 33.
18. Jung, *Psychological Types*, p. 366.
19. *Vassar*, Summer, 2007, p. 64.
20. *Newsweek*, February 4, 2002, pp. 46-47.
21. Malcolm Gladwell, *The Tipping Point: How Little Things Can Make A Big Difference*, Little, Brown & Co., 2000, p. 54.
22. Robert A. Heinlein, *Stranger in a Strange Land*, G. P. Putnam's Sons, New York, 1961, p. 204.

CHAPTER 7: THE THINKING FUNCTION

1. *Newsweek*, January 11,1999, p. 59.
2. C.G. Jung, *Psychological Types*, Princeton University Press, 1991, p. 346.
3. *More,* September 2007, p. 163.
4. Marie-Louise von Franz, *Lectures on Jung's Typology*, Spring Publications, 1971, p. 41.

5. von Franz, p. 42.
6. Jung, p. 406.
7. Jung, p. 520.
8. von Franz, p. 8.
9. von Franz, p. 6.
10. *The New York Times Magazine*, June 2, 2002, p.14.
11. *The New Yorker*, March 13, 2017, p.47]

CHAPTER 8: THE FEELING FUNCTION

1. C.G. Jung, *Psychological Types*, Princeton University Press, 1991, p. 538.
2. Jung, p. 435.
3. Jung, p. 520.
4. Jung, p. 538.
5. *Vanity Fair*, March, 2010.
6. *The New York Times*, December 12, 2008, *The Arts*.
7. *USA Weekend*, October 11-3, 2002, p. 8.
8. *The Spirit in Man, Art, and Literature,* Collected Works Vol. 15, Princeton University Press, p. 140.
9. Jung, p. 356.
10. Marie-Louise von Franz, *Lectures on Jung's Typology*, Spring Publications, 1971, p. 43.
11. Marion Woodman, *The Pregnant Virgin*, Inner City Books, 1985, p. 179.
12. von Franz, p. 39-40.
13. von Franz, p. 48.
14. *USA Weekend*, Sept 20-22, 2002.
15. von Franz, p. 12.
16. von Franz, p. 49.
17. von Franz, p. 46.
18. von Franz, p. 45.

CHAPTER 9: THE FOURTH FUNCTION PHENOMENON

1. C.G. Jung, *Psychological Types*, Princeton University Press, 1991, p. 450.
2. Marie-Louise von Franz, *Lectures on Jung's Typology*, Spring

Publications, 1971, p. 15.

3. von Franz, p. 21.

4. *Harvard Magazine*, July-August 2013, p. 35.

5. Jung, p. 450.

6. Ernest Hemingway, *Death in the Afternoon*, Charles Scribner's
     Sons, 1960, p. 192.

7. I am indebted to Jungian psychoanalyst Robert A. Johnson for this
insightful and practical psychological technique.

8. von Franz, p. 58.

9. von Franz, p. 12.

10. C.G. Jung, *The Undiscovered Self*, Princeton University Press,
     1990, pp. 44-45.

11. C.G. Jung, *Psychological Types*, p. 407.

CHAPTER 10: GETTING ALONG WITH OTHERS

1. C.G. Jung, *Psychological Types*, Princeton University Press,
     1991, p. 517.

2. Marie-Louise von Franz, *Lectures on Jung's Typology*, Spring
     Publications, 1971, p. 26.

3. Jung, pp. 517-518.

www.ingramcontent.com/pod-product-compliance
Lightning Source LLC
Chambersburg PA
CBHW022329280326
41934CB00006B/576